CHRISTIAN MORALITY

CHRISTIAN MORALITY

NATURAL, DEVELOPING, FINAL

Being the
GIFFORD LECTURES
1935–1936

BY

HERBERT HENSLEY HENSON
BISHOP OF DURHAM

OXFORD
AT THE CLARENDON PRESS
1936

OXFORD UNIVERSITY PRESS
AMEN HOUSE, E.C. 4
London Edinburgh Glasgow New York
Toronto Melbourne Capetown Bombay
Calcutta Madras
HUMPHREY MILFORD
PUBLISHER TO THE UNIVERSITY

PRINTED IN GREAT BRITAIN AT THE UNIVERSITY PRESS, OXFORD
BY JOHN JOHNSON, PRINTER TO THE UNIVERSITY

that Socrates was not the first who endeavoured to draw men
off from labouring after, and laying stress upon other knowledge,
in comparison of that which related to morals. Our province
is virtue and religion, life and manners; the science of im-
proving the temper, and making the heart better.'[1]

No religious or ecclesiastical qualification is required
in Gifford lecturers. They may, or may not, themselves be Christians, but they must discuss their subject
in a scientific spirit. This condition I have tried ever
to keep in mind, and, of course, it has determined my
modes of expression in no slight measure. If, therefore,
in referring to the Founder of Christianity, I have
seemed to speak with something less than the profound
religious homage which is usual and, indeed, inevitable,
among Christians, the reader will remember that he is
confronted by a Gifford lecturer, not by a Christian
bishop. While, however, I invoke the protection of an
equitable consideration, I do not think anything that
I have said really conflicts with what I, in common with
my fellow Christians, personally believe.

It remains that I should make some acknowledge-
ments. First, I desire to express my heartfelt thanks
to the University of St. Andrews for the kindness with
which I was received; next, to my dear friends, the
Principal and Lady Irvine, for their more than generous
hospitality; finally, to my friend and chaplain, the Rev.
C. K. Pattinson, for much help in the preparation of these
lectures, particularly for his pains in providing an Index;
and to Miss Fearne Booker for correcting the proofs.

HERBERT DUNELM

AUCKLAND CASTLE.
15 *February* 1936.

[1] *v.* Sermon xv: 'Upon the Ignorance of Man'.

CONTENTS

Tertullian and Bishop Butler agree in affirming the naturalness of Christianity. General Smuts in his Rectorial Address made the same assumption, identifying human with Christian. Civilization is not merely mechanical; it is also moral; and only as such can it command universal acceptance. The moral presuppositions of Western civilization are historically Christian. The affinities of morality are with religion, and only with theology in so far as it expresses religion. Yet theology always presupposes religion. Natural theology is coextensive with human theology. Human nature is not static, but developing. The term 'natural theology' examined. As contrasted with revealed religion, it belongs to an obsolete mode of thinking, and draws its origin from religious controversy. 'Revealed' religions are revolts of morality against degenerate religion. The Gifford lecturer concerned with facts, not with their interpretations. For him revealed religion is only a specific phase of natural religion.

All religion is both natural and revealed. The notion of an Age of Innocence, in which natural religion flourished, has been welcome to controversy-vexed generations, and has suggested the notion of recovering the lost treasure. History differently conceived now. Savage religion is no more 'natural' than Buddhism or Christianity, only more rudimentary. Christianity is confessedly that version of natural religion which is the most highly developed. Paley's declaration in A.D. 1794 remains without effective challenge in A.D. 1935: 'the question lies between this religion or none'. Recapitulation. 'I am proposing a new method. Instead of arguing from philosophy to theology, and from theology to morality, I suggest that the process may serviceably be reversed, and we may argue back from morality to the theology which inspires and determines it, and from the theology to the philosophy which properly it supposes.'

Student of Christian Morality bound first to satisfy himself as to the quality of his material. Critical questions can no longer be decided by ecclesiastical authority. An official teacher of Christianity, albeit an amateur, must judge the experts when they differ. Critical experts invite the judgement of an amateur public. The new method, 'Form-Criticism', considered. Dibelius. Lightfoot's *Bampton Lectures*. Historical character of the Gospels, a vital concern for the student of Christian ethics. John Stuart Mill's *Three Essays*. No subapostolic Christians capable of fabricating the New Testament. Textual changes trivial in character. An illustration of critical method. 'Form-Criticism', as advocated by its thoroughgoing exponents, destructive of Christianity. Klausner's testimony to the historicity of the Synoptics.

The dominant factor in the development of Christian Morality has been the bequest of Judaism. Morality of the Jews in the time of Jesus

CONTENTS

New Testament as a supplemental canon of Scripture. Apostolic Tradition accepted without discrimination. The Jewish colouring of Christian Morality not wholly advantageous, e.g. the undue influence of St. Paul's Rabbinic notions about women.

(2) From the first, Christianity has developed under pressure of actual situations. The Christian notion of duty is ever relative to the actual situation. St. Paul's attitude towards slavery morally obsolete. The ethical development of mankind gives freer expression to the principles of Christianity; it invalidates the principles of other religions. Development of Christian Morality distinguishable from temporary accommodations, e.g. acquiescence in the Slave Trade. Whitfield's casuistry. Butler's uneasy conscience. Erastianism not the result of development, but of an illegitimate accommodation.

(3) Christianity as the Religion of Humanity welcomes and assimilates all truth, and stimulates the human faculties. The paradox of Christendom. Influence of the Resurrection in stimulating human faculty. It is no accident that science has developed within Christendom. The Greek heritage could only be appreciated and utilized in a Christian atmosphere. Cf. the withering of civilization under Mohammedanism. Strangeness of the Christian paradox. Ecclesiastical history an armoury for the assailants of Christianity. But the genius of the religion steadily operates.

Christian view often misconceived as irrationally ascetic. Asceticism true and false. Jewish religion not ascetic. Jesus, though non-ascetical, suggested ascetic ways of life. Situation of early Christians stimulated ascetic tendency. Sexual depravity of ancient world uncontrolled by philosophy. Christianity in sharpest collision with non-Christian society, ancient and modern, in sexual morality. Feminist Movement mingled. Its rapid advance due to its revolt against the ascetic principle in traditional morality. How far have new factors entered into problems of sex? How far do these affect Christian Morality? Teaching of Jesus respecting sexual relations impressively original. Monogamy among the Jews. Jesus did not legislate on divorce. Varying understanding of His words in the Church. Modern view of the equality of the sexes a new factor. Polygamy the citadel of female inferiority. Christian view of the family. Facile divorce no guarantee of sexual equality. Sexes equal, but different in function and aptitude. Political status of women a matter of practical expediency respecting which Christianity is wholly indifferent. Christian marriage normally implies the family. Purposes of marriage reappear as motives for marriage. Ethical interest of mankind concerned with parenthood. Christianity marked a new epoch in civilized domestic life. Exaltation of childhood by Jesus. Christian treatment of children in sharp contrast with the habit of pagan society. The modern situation. Professor Carr-Saunders on 'Voluntary Parenthood'. The phrase examined. How far can such 'Voluntary Parenthood' consist with Christian Morality? Resolution of the Lambeth Conference. New knowledge brings enhanced responsibility. Effect on marriage. Rightful use of contraceptives conditioned by Christian asceticism. Modern degradation of sexual life. Discipline the condition of moral liberty.

CONTENTS

I
INTRODUCTION

WHEN I received the distinguished and unexpected honour of an invitation to deliver a course of Gifford Lectures, I had to consider very carefully whether I could discover a subject which would not only be fairly brought within the large limits of the Gifford Trust, but also would not lie too patently outside the narrow limits of my own capacity. I examined very closely the language of Lord Gifford's Will, and noted the plainly expressed design that the general subject, *Natural Theology*, should be liberally understood, and then I sought to discover how in fact the long succession of Gifford Lecturers had actually understood it. I found that the courses of Gifford Lectures had been remarkably diverse in type, treatment, and temper, that they had covered a wide range, and that, taken in their totality, they constituted an examination from many points of view of the entire subject of religion, its philosophical presuppositions, its primitive expressions, its historical development, its ethical consequences. I concluded, therefore, that I had a fairly free hand, and I decided to limit myself to a single aspect of the vast theme, and that an aspect which had long exercised my mind, and which, for many cogent reasons, has within recent years acquired a notable and even menacing prominence. The subject of my Lectures is *Christian Morality*, which I shall maintain to be natural, developing, and properly final.

In this preliminary Lecture I propose to take a general

4261   B

view of the scheme outlined in Lord Gifford's Will, and to indicate both the process of thought by which I have been led to my choice of subject, and the method of treatment which I shall adopt in the following Lectures of the course.

Two familiar and pregnant sayings, the one from an apologist of Christianity in the third century, and the other from an apologist of Christianity in the eighteenth, may well serve to indicate my point of view. Tertullian, in the Treatise *De Testimonio Animae*, which has been described, not excessively, as the most original and acute of his works, claimed for Christianity that it expressed the beliefs and aspirations of the human spirit itself. It was, in fact, natural religion *par excellence*. Thus he apostrophizes the human soul:

'Stand forth in the midst of us, O soul! I appeal to thee; yet not as wise with a wisdom formed in the schools, trained in libraries, or nourished in Attic academies and porticoes; but as simple and rough, without polish or culture, such as thou art to those who have thee only, such as thou art in the crossroad, the highway, and the dockyard. I seek of thee that which thou bringest with thee into man, that which thou hast thyself learnt to think, or hast been taught by thy Creator, Whoever He may be. Thou art not, so far as I know, Christian. The soul is not born Christian, but becomes Christian. Yet Christians beg now for a testimony from thee, as from one outside them; a testimony against thine own that the heathen may blush for their hatred and mockery of us.'[1]

Tertullian, arguing against the pagans, claimed that the human spirit is naturally Christian. Fifteen hundred years later Butler, arguing against the Deists, who were neo-Pagans in their attitude towards Christianity, main-

[1] v. *De Testimonio Animae*, cap. i.

tained that Christianity is but the 'republication' of natural religion.[1] That is the assumption on which I propose to ground the argument, that the morality which Christ's religion properly requires is precisely that which the conscience and reason of modernly civilized men approve.

This morality, we shall maintain, has developed wonderfully in the course of time, yet throughout that development has ever borne the character of an increasingly adequate expression of the principles expressed at the first in the life and teaching of Jesus. We shall conclude that Christian morality is, in unique and plenary sense, natural, the expression of natural theology.

Thus we shall affirm the view which Bishop Butler expressed in the terms of eighteenth-century thought, viz. that it is only in Christianity that natural religion receives fair and full expression:

'Christianity is a republication of natural Religion. It instructs mankind in the moral system of the world: that it is the work of an infinitely perfect Being, and under His government; that virtue is His law; and that He will finally judge mankind in righteousness, and render to all according to their works, in a future state. And, which is very material, it teaches natural Religion in its genuine simplicity; free from those superstitions with which it was totally corrupted, and under which it was in a manner lost.'[2]

To Tertullian and Bishop Butler I will add a more recent witness. General Smuts, in his memorable Rectorial Address, the echoes of which will not soon

[1] v. *Analogy*, part ii, c. i.
[2] v. *The Analogy of Religion*, part ii, c. i.

die away in St. Andrews, made 'human' the equivalent of 'Christian'. He spoke of 'the great *human* principles on which our Western civilization rests', and then of 'the principles on which the comity of our *Christian* civilization had been laboriously built up'. It is precisely this equation of human and Christian which is the underlying assumption of my Lectures.

Christian civilization is unique in being thus identified as a matter of course with civilization itself. No one would dream of suggesting any such identification in the case of Mohammedan, or Buddhist, or Brahmanical, or Confucianist civilization. Every one of these is distinctive, anciently rooted, and widely accepted; but the distinctive features are in every case precisely those which are most offensive to the reason and conscience of modernly educated men; the ancient roots are withering in the unfriendly soil of the modern world; the wide acceptance is confined within the limits of race and locality. They have not the potency of universality, nor do they carry the secret of immortality. Natural they were at certain phases of human development, but they cease to be so when those phases have been traversed. One religion, and only one, has been able to inspire a morality which is never obsolete, and thus to vindicate a right to be regarded as, in unique and plenary sense, natural.

A notable passage in Lecky's *History of Rationalism* emphasizes this impressive uniqueness of Christianity:

'There is but one example of a religion which is not necessarily subverted by civilization, and that example is Christianity. In all other cases the decay of dogmatic conceptions is tantamount to a complete annihilation of the religion, for although there may be imperishable elements of moral truth mingled with those conceptions, they have nothing distinctive or peculiar. The moral truths coalesce with new systems, the men who uttered them take their place with many others in the great pantheon of history, and the religion having discharged its functions is spent and withered. But the great characteristic of Christianity, and the great moral proof of its divinity, is that it has been the main source of the moral development of Europe, and that it has discharged this office not so much by the inculcation of a system of ethics, however pure, as by the assimilating and attractive influence of a perfect ideal. The moral progress of mankind can never cease to be distinctively and intensely Christian as long as it consists of a gradual approximation to the character of the Christian Founder.'[1]

Lecky wrote in 1863, but I do not think that his words need any revision in the light of the succeeding time.

In his luminous and disconcerting volume, *Clashing Tides of Colour*, Mr. Lothrop Stoddard postulates that the 'new master' of humanity is 'Western machine civilization', and visualizes the problem which now confronts mankind as that of its competence to assimilate so novel, prevailing, and quite unavoidable an influence.

'Never before', he says, 'has one civilisation prevailed over the entire earth. All mankind, with its wide distinctions of temperament and tradition, is faced with the necessity of adapting itself to a way of life evolved by a single branch of the human species. Can our distinctively Western civilisation be successfully transplanted and generalised?'[2]

The phrase 'Western machine civilization' is plainly an inadequate description, for it fastens on one only aspect of the subject, viz. the economic, and leaves out

---

[1] v. *Rationalism in Europe*, i. 306, 7.
[2] v. *Clashing Tides of Colour*, p. 407.

other aspects which are both more distinctive and more important. If we go to the roots of this 'Western Civilization', of which the 'machine' is but a single and a recent expression, and inquire why it may properly be identified with civilization itself, and without extravagance conceived of as destined in the final event to secure universal acceptance, we find ourselves faced by its moral presuppositions, and these we perforce perceive to be historically Christian. If mankind is to be civilized on Western lines, it can only be because mankind has embraced that morality apart from which Western civilization is in no legitimate sense civilization at all, without which we may affirm with confidence Western civilization could never have come into existence. The 'machine' is not essential to the civilization, but only to a single phase of it. That phase will pass in its turn, but the civilization with which it has been associated, and with which it has been unwarrantably identified, will not pass with it, for the sources of civilization are not ultimately economic, but moral. 'Her foundations are on the holy hills.'

You will perceive that I am asking you to leave both the high latitudes of philosophy and the low lands of anthropology in which so many Gifford Lecturers have pursued their argument, and to confine yourselves to that limited scene in which, in spite of its limitation, all theories of faith and morals must finally come to judgement. In these Lectures we shall move strictly within the sphere of recorded history, for the materials of our argument can only be contributed by historic testimony, and the value of our conclusion can have no meaning outside historic conditions.

I can imagine that some would meet me with the objection that in speaking of 'Christian Morality' I am making use of an expression which has no clear and accepted significance. What are we to understand by Christian morality? Is it to be found in the official decisions of the Christian Society? But the Christian Society no longer speaks with a single voice, and the official pronouncements of the various churches in which it is now distributed vary disconcertingly. Is it to be deduced from the canonical Scripture which all Christians regard as authoritative? But the interpretations of the sacred texts are many and conflicting, and there is no agreed rule by which they may be securely judged. May we appeal from Church and Bible to Christian history? We shall find that moral standards vary from one generation to another, that there are fashions in morality as in all other human concerns, that in ethics as in doctrine nothing continues in one stay, that the orthodoxy of one age may be the heresy of another. In all these objections there is unquestionable validity, and yet, when due allowance is made for them all, Christian morality exists recognizably among men, and its absence outside the sphere of Christian influence is apparent. In the course of our discussion we shall have to distinguish between principles and their applications, between ideals and the conventions which they shape, between ethical developments and ethical retrogressions. You will not fail to notice that the title which I have given to these Lectures, 'Christian Morality, natural, developing, and final', excludes the notion of something formal and static, determined in advance of experience by external authority, whether ecclesiastical or documentary, and carries the whole inquiry into the region of life as it has actually proceeded in Christendom, and does still proceed, varying, subtly responsive to the myriad and manifold influences of environment, pervasive, protean, and recognizably progressive.

In this initial Lecture I must not only vindicate for my specific subject a place within the large limits of the Gifford Trust, but also I must sketch the course which my argument will take. If I can succeed in making my case good, I shall have contributed, albeit indirectly, a consideration of value to the apology for natural theology, which in their totality the Gifford Lectures are providing.

The Gifford Lecturer, I remind myself, has no concern as such with the unknown and almost unimaginable processes by which, in the course of incalculable periods of time, the instinct-ordered brute grew into the self-conscious, self-directing man. Nor is he properly concerned with the attempt to trace the development of the recognizably human characteristics. He assumes the conclusions of the sciences which deal with the præ-human phases of man's development. His concern is with *homo sapiens*, the outcome of the evolutionary process, whose true significance is unfolding itself on this planet in that tiny fragment of time which is called History. Man, distinctively so called, enters on his career as a religious creature, and therefore also as a theologian. Because he is the one, he must needs become the other, since theology is but rationalized religion. Being intellectual he must perforce cast his religion into an intelligible form, that is, express it in terms of a theology. Being social, he cannot escape the necessity of formulating conditions of intercourse with his fellows. Under the continuing pressures of his circumstances, the innate powers of his nature are disclosed and brought into action. Man at the dawn of history finds himself confronted by a threefold challenge. He has to make his count with his own nature, with the society of which he finds himself a member, and with the physical universe which frames his life. In the effort to respond to this threefold challenge he rises to his full stature, and brings into play all the powers of his nature. Ultimate factors in his manhood compel him to worship, to reflect, to sit in judgement on himself, to form relations with others, to admire the world around him, to remember and register his experiences. And, through all these multiplying activities, he is indivisibly one. He is himself, and not another; a self-directing person in the midst of the bewildering universe, self-judging, self-approving, self-condemning, inexorably free in his apparent and afflicting chains. The paradox utters itself inevitably in terms of religion: 'When I consider thy heavens, the work of thy fingers, the moon and the stars which thou hast ordained: What is man, that thou art mindful of him? And the son of man, that thou visitest him? For thou hast made him but little lower than God, And crownest him with glory and honour.'

The dominating feature of man's record in history is certainly religion. Here he rises to his best, and here he falls to his worst. Throughout the entire course of his march through time—from the crudest superstitions of the savage to the sublimest speculations of the civilized man—he is illumined, darkened, inspired, degraded by

religion. Always and everywhere man has been a wor-
shipper of That which is before, about, and beyond
himself, with which he is inexorably linked. Religion
has necessarily shaped morality. The theologian must
needs become the moralist. Duty grows on the stock
of faith. It is matter of fact that religion has conditioned
social behaviour, and social behaviour has reacted on
religion. Morality has been based on theology, and
theology has reflected morality. The implications of
belief must disclose themselves in practice, and conduct cannot but become the authorized commentary
on creed. There is a reciprocity of influences: belief
shaping behaviour, and behaviour revising creed. But
the belief must be genuine, and the behaviour responsible. There is no shaping moral power in merely
conventional professions of belief, nor has the unthink-
ing parasitism of conventional behaviour any religious
significance. Since, however, creeds are formulated,
and, therefore, in a sense, rigid, and behaviour is responsive to a thousand influences, and never long
remains the same, it may easily fall out that the two
may go widely apart. Creeds may shrivel into the
mummy-cases of departed faith, and their professors
may be the victims of custom, continuing to repeat for-
mularies to which they have ceased to give any intelligible sense. This distressing discord is no infrequent
phenomenon in the history of religion, to which it
contributes its most sombrely scandalous pages.

Especially in periods which are called transitional,
because they constitute an interval between more
settled epochs, this conflict between formulated creed
and current practice is woefully apparent. Theology

has, so to speak, parted company with religion, and, since it is enshrined in fixed forms, continues to represent what it has ceased to express. But the affinities of morality are with religion, and only with theology in so far as it expresses religion. Theology apart from religion is a mere logomachy, which may exercise the intellect but can nowise affect the conscience. Hence the moral obtuseness of theologians, on which the critics and adversaries of religion seize with such manifest satisfaction.

The keenest theological interest, the widest theological knowledge, the most accurate theological opinion may coexist in the same individual with depraved habits and a perverted moral sense. Thus of the most infamous of the Popes of the Renaissance it has been observed that his orthodoxy was above suspicion, and that his contemporaries noted with admiration the unusual concern which he displayed for the regular and splendid performance of the public offices of religion. Alexander VI did but exhibit a familiar phenomenon. It was observed of Henry VIII that he was never so ostentatiously devout as when he was meditating some uncommonly atrocious violation of justice. 'Jupiter' Carlyle relates of the well-known Evangelical leader in the Scottish General Assembly, Webster, that he 'could pass at once from the most unbounded jollity to the most fervent devotion'. It would be easy to multiply examples of this painful contradiction. The non-moral or immoral theologian is indeed a familiar phenomenon, never more familiar than in periods of intense religious excitement. Controversial epochs are particularly rich in examples of this sad paradox. Milton was drawing from life the portrait of his own generation when he pictured the devils in hell as absorbed in theological and philosophical speculation:

> Others apart sat on a hill retired,
> In thoughts more elevate, and reason'd high
> Of providence, foreknowledge, will, and fate;
> Fix'd fate, free will, foreknowledge absolute:
> And found no end, in wandering mazes lost.
> Of good and evil much they argued then,
> Of happiness and final misery,
> Passion and apathy, and glory and shame;
> Vain wisdom all, and false philosophy.

Yet theology always presupposes religion, of which it is the rational explication. Men's reflections on their own intuitions, impulses, and experiences have ever taken shape in theories as to their origin and significance. There can be no intelligent or satisfying religion apart from an adequate theology, no adequate theology which is not rooted in religion. 'Natural theology', in the only sense in which a modern thinker can employ the term, is coextensive with human theology, that is, with the varying theories about that awful power, however conceived, which religion in all its myriad forms postulates.

It would, indeed, be more reasonable to speak of natural theologies than of natural theology, for in the course of history mankind has returned many answers to the questions which exercise the minds of religious thinkers. And all these answers have an equal right to be described as natural. Human nature is not static but developing, an integral part of a developing universe. Accordingly, that which is 'natural' at one phase of its development will be archaic, unmeaning, even apparently false at another. It follows that 'natural theology' is the equivalent of theology itself, a vast and various product of human reason active in the sphere of religion throughout the whole course of human history. Theology is the rationalized expression of religious experience, the formulation of the postulates which interpret and maintain the current versions of faith and morality.

We must examine more closely the content of this word 'natural'.

The subject of the Gifford Lectures is broadly stated to be 'Natural Theology', i.e. the theology which is implicit in natural religion. We must inquire what precisely the words imply. The phrase has been commonly understood to suggest a contrast with another kind of religion which is not really natural, but rather to be described as non-natural or artificial, something grafted on human nature, properly alien and perverting. Thus natural religion has been identified with improvised or unassisted religion, the religion which has no other source than the impulses, intuitions, and reflections of the untaught and unsophisticated individual, and owes nothing to revelation, instruction, or example, reflecting without distortion or restraint the fresh promptings of unspoiled human nature. It is to be noted that such a conception of natural religion belongs to a mode of thinking which was more familiar in the past than in the present. While it is obviously congruous with human vanity, it draws its origin from religious controversy. It suggests that among the many theologies which man has framed for himself in the course of history, there is one, the oldest and simplest of them all, which has a unique and incontestable right to be described as natural. The theology implicit in natural religion, it is maintained, stands towards other theologies as the perfect to the partial, the original picture to the distorting copy, the pure to the corrupted. *They* only possess value in so far as *it* has been included in them. Natural theology presupposes a state of nature in which men's conceptions of faith and duty are sane, simple, and sufficient. History, therefore, is to be regarded as the record of a continuing declension from primitive perfection.

When Bishop Butler, in the passage already quoted, described Christianity as 'a republication of natural religion', he implied that there had already been a publication of the same, and assigned as the reason why a republication was needed the fact that in course of time the 'genuine simplicity' of natural religion had been to all intents and purposes destroyed. The assumption of Original Innocence, of a 'Golden Age', a Saturnian Reign, an 'Age of Blessedness' in which mankind enjoyed in perfection fullness of peace, knowledge, prosperity, and happiness, has been persistent, and perhaps in some form or other universal. It has left a deep impression on literature both ancient and modern, and it cannot be truly said to have been even now everywhere abandoned. For it enshrines a truth which the history of religion has attested with monotonous iteration. There is a tendency towards degeneration which has haunted the whole process of religious development, and at intervals created the paradoxical situation in which morality, normally the creature of religion, becomes its critic and the principle of its reformation. The retrogression to a long-abandoned simplicity has, in the actual circumstances, involved a religious advance. The 'revealed' religions are not unfitly described as revolts of morality against degenerate religion.

We are concerned in these Lectures with the facts, not with their interpretation. That religion is at this point or at that time reinforced by an extraordinary impulse, which lifts it outside and above its normal plane, and originates a fresh and more exalted development, is an assumption which may, or may not, be sound. The Gifford Lecturer is not free to make it. He sees the entire pageant of religion as it is presented on the stage of history, an aspect of human nature at once reflecting its fortunes, and giving the key to its significance.

Whenever society has been more than commonly shadowed and vexed with religious conflict, thoughtful men have rested their minds on the distant spectacle of a simpler age, when unsophisticated mankind was contented with the simple creed of Nature, unadulterated by speculation, unwarped by controversy, unstained by scandal. In the seventeenth and eighteenth centuries the theological tradition was subjected to a rigorous and thorough-going process of rationalization. A contrast was drawn between the elaborated theologies of the time and the simpler beliefs of the primitive age, which rose spontaneously in the human mind, and were so congruous with unspoiled human nature as to command universal acceptance. Natural theology was the theology natural to man before the depraving influences of history had disturbed the balance of his nature, confused his conscience, and darkened his spiritual vision. If but that simple creed of primeval innocence could be recovered, men would find a way of escape from the thousand ills of theological strife, and become again rational, tolerant, and united. Primitive man was credited with every kind of excellence. He was idealized, and the idealization was as anachronistic as it was enthusiastic.

A curious instance of this idealization is provided by the sermon on the creation of man preached in 1662 by the famous pulpit orator of the Restoration, Robert South. In the course of his sermon he sharply rebuked the Socinians for holding that 'as to his understanding' Adam was 'a rude unwritten block', and elaborated his own view, which was undoubtedly shared by his orthodox contemporaries. He pictured the first man as possessing in perfection all the knowledge and wisdom which mankind has slowly and painfully garnered in the course of history. These, he said, were but a faint picture of his natural endowments.

'All those arts, rarities, and inventions, which vulgar minds gaze at, the ingenious pursue, and all admire, are but the reliques of an intellect defaced with sin and time. We admire it now, only as antiquaries do a piece of old coin, for the stamp it once bore, and not for those vanishing lineaments and disappearing draughts that remain upon it at present. And certainly that must needs have been very glorious, the decays of which are so admirable. He that is comely, when old and decrepit, surely was very beautiful when he was young. An Aristotle was but the rubbish of an Adam, and Athens but the rudiments of Paradise.'[1]

[1] v. South's *Sermons*, i. 31, 32.

The greatest Puritan poet of the Restoration was in full agreement with the greatest Anglican preacher. Milton's picture of Adam and Eve in Paradise before the entrance of the Tempter is entirely accordant with South's:

'Two of far nobler shape, erect and tall,
Godlike erect, with native honour clad
In naked majesty, seem'd lords of all,
And worthy seem'd: for in their looks divine
The image of their glorious Maker shone,
Truth, wisdom, sanctitude severe and pure,
Severe, but in true filial freedom placed,
Whence true authority in men.'[1]

Beside these delightful pictures set the description of Primitive Man which is offered by Sir G. Elliot Smith in his Essays on *The Evolution of Man* published in 1924:

'The distinctive features of the Human Family can be provided only by the brain-case and the limb-bones, which underwent the characteristic changes long before the jaws and face and rest of the body lost their simian characters. For in the process of the evolution of Man it was the brain which first acquired what can be called the human status. The earliest members of the Human Family must have been merely Apes with an overgrown brain, and probably the first bodily changes that occurred were the modifications of the legs for the new methods of progression, which were in the main the outcome of this higher development of brain. The simian features of the skin and hair, teeth and face, and the general configuration of the body no doubt persisted for long ages after the changes in the brain and the legs had been established.'[2]

The difference between 'natural religion' as conceived by South and Milton, by the Cambridge Platonists,

---

[1] v. *Paradise Lost*, iv. 288–92.
[2] v. *The Evolution of Man*, p. 61.

D

and by the Deists, who may be called their disciples, and 'natural religion' as ascribed by modern men of science is not less wide. History is conceived differently. The point of view has changed. Not now a steady decline from original perfection, but a gradual ascent from original bestiality is the aspect of human history. The modern conception of progress may be said to have its origin in the Darwinian doctrine of Evolution.

'This theory', observes Dr. Edwyn Bevan, 'seems exactly the reverse of the ancient view which saw human history as a series of lapses from an ideal primitive state of virtue and happiness. The further back we go, according to the Darwinian view, the more man approximates to the beast. Instead of the gracious half-divine figures of the Golden Age, we are shown a breed of hairy gorilla-like creatures huddling and gibbering in caves and tearing each other in the blind struggle for life. Instead of the primeval sages, sources of an immemorial wisdom, whose antiquity is its very title to reverence, we are shown magicians and medicine men overawing savage tribes with practices of crude superstition; for a primitive revelation of divine truth we get a jumble of totems and fetishes and taboos.'[1]

In the opening chapter of his well-known *History of European Morals from Augustus to Charlemagne* Lecky discusses 'the Natural History of Morals', and, in the course of his discussion, points out what he calls 'a very mischievous equivocation in the word Natural':

'The term natural man is sometimes regarded as synonymous with man in his primitive or barbarous condition, and sometimes as expressing all in a civilized man that is due to nature as distinguished from artificial habits or acquirements.'

[1] v. *Hellenism and Christianity*, p. 191.

This equivocation, he tells us, implies

'the notion that the difference between a savage and a civilized
man is simply a difference of acquisition and not at all a difference
of development.'

Substitute 'religion' or 'theology' for 'man', and this
passage will be hardly less true.

The equivocation implies the notion that the difference between savage or primitive and civilized religion
is simply a difference of acquisition, and not at all a
development. In fact a savage is not more *natural* than
Plato or Shakespeare, only less developed; and savage
religion is no more *natural* than Buddhism or Christianity, only more rudimentary. It follows, as we have
already indicated, that the familiar distinction (which
is legitimate and convenient enough in certain connexions) between natural and revealed religion is properly inadmissible when religion itself is in question.
All religion is natural, and all religion is revealed, for
the fact of religion presupposes a religious capacity in
man, apart from which neither the intuitions of his own
spirit, nor the receiving of communications from without, could be possible. Religion itself is the demonstration of man's inherent religiousness at every phase of
his history, savage, barbarous, variously civilized.

'All Religion', writes Rashdall, 'is, always has been, and must
always be essentially metaphysical. The crudest savage "Anim-
ism" is a metaphysical theory as much as the most esoteric
Brahmanism or the most cultured modern Theology.'[1]

It may, indeed, be fairly maintained that the very
phrase 'natural religion' implies revelation, for no

[1] v. *The Theory of Good and Evil*, ii. 252.

religion, however simple or primitive, was ever regarded by those who professed it as merely natural. It was acknowledged contact with the Unseen. Men were only then religious in any sense when they worshipped That which was other than themselves. They were only then theological in any sense when they rationalized this worship of the non-human into a formulated belief. God, however conceived, is the necessary postulate of all religion and of all theology.

If it be objected that Buddhism provides an example of a godless religion, since in its pure and original form it was certainly not theistic, it must suffice to answer that the exception is more apparent than real, for Buddhism has practically become theistic. 'So difficult is the experiment of a non-theistic Religion that Buddhism has had practically to deify its atheistic Founder.' In any case, in so far as Buddhism admits no God, it is plainly not a religion which involves a theology, and, therefore, lies outside our present concern.

'The spirit of man is the candle of the Lord.'

The authority of the conscience was only then acknowledged intelligently when the conscience was held to be the channel through which monitions were conveyed to men from a source external to themselves which they could not but hold to be Divine. When we designate some truths as revealed, and some as natural, we do not deny that both have the same ultimate Source. The distinction is one of method, and of measure, not one of origin. Whether truth be gained through the normal ministry of reason and conscience, or be flashed on the understanding by some abnormal illumination, it must needs come from God, the only ultimate source of all truth. I may adopt the words of a former Gifford Lecturer, Principal Caird:

'The inherent nature and value of ideas which have become a possession of the human mind is a thing wholly independent of the question whether they have been communicated to us in a miraculous or supernatural, or in a purely natural way—on the one hand, by a voice from heaven, from the lips of an inspired prophet, by sacred tradition; or, on the other hand, by the observation of nature, by the study of history, by the teaching and influence of other minds, by the moral and spiritual results of our own experience and reflection.'[1]

Therefore, while we may rightly and usefully distinguish savage religion from civilized, and tribal or national religion from individual or universalist, we cannot so distinguish natural religion from revealed. Religion must combine both descriptions. It is all natural, and it is all revealed.

Lord Gifford was not unaware of the widely ramifying character of the subject he selected, and he has expressed it in very ample terms. His lectureship is for 'promoting, advancing, teaching, and diffusing the study of Natural Theology' in the widest sense of that term:

'The knowledge of God, the Infinite, the All, the First and Only Cause, the One and the Sole Substance, the Sole Being, the Sole Reality, and the Sole Existence, the Knowledge of His Nature and Attributes, the Knowledge of the Relations which men and the whole Universe bear to Him, the knowledge of the Nature and Foundation of Ethics or Morals, and of all Obligations and Duties thence arising.'

[1] v. *Gifford Lectures*, i. 5.

Such knowledge as is here indicated belongs, not to the primitive, but to the most advanced phases of religious development. Savage theology is as offensive to the reason of civilized men as savage morality is to their conscience. Religion only becomes frankly ethical when it is thought of as the witness of God within the spirit of man. Deifications of the forces of Nature cannot be ethical. In point of fact the natural religions specifically so designated have been, and are, non-ethical. It was the supreme service of the Hebrew Prophets to point men in their search for God away from external nature to their own spirit. Of this prophetic witness the classical expression is in the prophecy of Micah: 'He hath showed thee, O man, what is good; and what doth the Lord require of thee, but to do justly, and to love mercy, and to walk humbly with thy God?' When Plutarch in a famous essay declares the superstitious man's conceptions of God to be more dishonouring than the atheist's flat denial of his existence, it is evident that he has moved beyond the magical externalism of contemporary paganism, and sees in morality the very essence of religion. Only in the higher religions can 'the knowledge of God' as Lord Gifford pictures it be reasonably looked for. Only with the guiding light of modern science can 'the knowledge of the relations which men and the whole universe bear to Him' be hopefully sought. The religious development of man has proceeded at an uneven pace, with the result that all phases of the process are found to be coexisting. There have been interruptions, periods of stagnation and of retrogression, interludes of sunshine between the mantling clouds. If we would do justice to the facts, we must include in our view of natural theology the grotesque beliefs of the Australian aborigines, who yet live in the Stone Age, and the developed doctrine of cultivated European Christians. The subject is so vast as to be almost limitless. I must perforce content myself with a single aspect, and invite you to consider that version of natural religion which is confessedly the most highly developed, which has affinities with every other, and which, since it alone appears able to commend itself to the acceptance of modernly civilized men, may fairly be described as *the* natural religion.

Paley's declaration in 1794 remains without effective challenge in 1935:

'I desire that in judging of Christianity it may be remembered that the question lies between this religion and none: for, if the Christian religion be not credible, no one with whom we have to do will support the pretensions of any other.'[1]

I am not concerned with the supernatural claims which Christians may advance for their religion, nor with its distinctive theology, but solely with the practical morality which it has produced in its professors, and which properly its principles require. I shall divide my course into two parts. In the first, I shall discuss the historic constituents of Christian morality, and of these I shall distinguish three—Judaism, the Teaching of Jesus, and the influence of the social environment of nascent Christianity. I shall preface this discussion with a lecture on the Sources for the Life of Jesus, in order that I may make clear the measure of authority which I attach to the documents of the New Testament,

[1] v. *A View of the Evidences of Christianity: Preparatory Considerations.*

and I shall add a lecture on Christian morality as it has been disclosed in history. In the second part of my course, I shall deal with some of the new factors which have emerged in the field of ethics, and consider how far they affect my main contention that Christian morality is a satisfying version of human duty.

Lord Gifford indicated the 'leading principles' which should govern the discretion of the 'patrons' of his lectureship. The lecturers might be of any religious description or of none, so only they were 'able reverent men, true thinkers, sincere lovers of and earnest inquirers after truth':

'I wish the lecturers to treat their subject as a strictly natural science, the greatest of all possible sciences, indeed, in one sense, the only science, that of Infinite Being, without reference to or reliance upon any supposed special exceptional or so-called miraculous revelation. I wish it considered just as astronomy or chemistry is.'

In these words I cannot imagine that Lord Gifford designed to exclude from the discussion of the prescribed subject factors which are indeed essential to it, since of all the forces which have shaped the natural religion of modernly civilized man, none has been so potent as those which the so-called revealed religions have contributed. I apprehend that Lord Gifford designed no more than that his lecturers should not base their conclusions on the authoritative dogmata of revealed religions, but should ever keep to the ground of reason and experience. To that condition I willingly subscribe, and shall not consciously do it violence.

Moreover, while thus indicating the 'general aspect' which he would expect personally the lectures to bear,

Lord Gifford generously insisted that 'the lecturers should be under no restraint whatever in their treatment of their theme',

'for example, they may freely discuss (and it may be well to do so) all questions about man's conceptions of God or the Infinite, their origin, nature, and truth, whether he can have any such conceptions, whether God is under any or what limitations, and so on, as I am persuaded that nothing but good can result from free discussion.'

Finally Lord Gifford designed such a handling of the subject as would make the lecturer intelligible to non-academic hearers:

'The lectures shall be public and popular, that is, open not only to students of the Universities, but to the whole community without matriculation, as I think that the subject should be studied and known by all, whether receiving University instruction or not.'

I shall be acting in accordance with the Founder's wishes when I avoid the use of technical language as far as possible, and seek to express what I have to say as simply and directly as I can. Obscurity of speech has never seemed to me a trustworthy evidence of profundity of thought, nor do I think that lucidity is necessarily inconsistent with thoroughness. For the rest I subscribe to the opinion of Bishop Butler, himself a model of compressed but lucid writing:

'Confusion and perplexity in writing is indeed without excuse, because anyone may, if he please, know whether he understands and sees through what he is about; and it is unpardonable for a man to lay his thoughts before others, when he is conscious that he himself does not know whereabouts he is, or how the matter before him stands. It is coming abroad in disorder, which he ought to be dissatisfied to find himself in at home.'[1]

It is sufficiently obvious that so vast a subject as Lord Gifford has outlined in his Will can nowise be handled effectively by any individual lecturer, and we may fairly assume that in providing for a continuous succession of lectures by different persons, he designed to distribute the subject in such a manner as to secure its effective treatment. 'Here a little, there a little' would the work be achieved, as one man after another brought his distinctive contribution to the common task. The philosopher, the man of science, the moralist, the historian—each one from his own point of view would add something, until in the end, by their various and coordinated efforts, some tolerable version of truth might be framed. The list of the Gifford Lectures discloses a wide variety of plan and purpose in the lecturers. When the honourable office of Gifford Lecturer is imposed on one who is neither a philosopher, nor a man of science, nor even an academic teacher, but a professed exponent of religion, perforce a moralist and by choice a student of history, the limits within which the general subject will be treated are sufficiently apparent. Assuming with Lord Gifford that religion is natural to man, and that it expresses itself in congruous morality, I argue that, since mankind is developing, that religion which is truly natural must match the phases of this development: that, therefore, natural religion is there most truly natural where it is most completely developed.

[1] v. The Preface to *Fifteen Sermons Preached at the Rolls Chapel*, 1729.

Natural religion, of which natural theology is the intellectual formulation, expresses itself necessarily in congruous morality, for men act on motives, and these reflect their beliefs. But morality is ever a composite in which many elements of varying ethical quality are combined. Some of these are ethnical, and some local, and some secular, and such can have no universal character and no perpetual validity. But in every morality, along with such contingent factors, there is that which transcends all limits of race, place, and time, and belongs to humanity itself, answering ever more clearly to the requirements of human nature as men develop from lower to higher planes of life. Religions can be outgrown by morality, that is, they may be so closely bound up with the lower factors of race, time, and place that, when these are outpassed, they have no holding power left. This is in fact a familiar feature of religious history. As men advance from lower to higher phases of development, they leave behind them the religious systems which once determined their practical morality. Their traditional religion no longer provides them with the motives and ideals which are indispensable to their moral health. To this general experience there is one remarkable exception. The morality which Christianity inspires and demands is never left behind by the developing race, but ever moves in front of it like the fabled pillar of Israel's guidance through the wilderness, an ideal and a prophecy. This Christian morality, of which the inspiration and power are drawn from Christianity, finally vindicates its claim to be the true practical expression of natural theology.

It is, indeed, true that Christian morality also has

been a composite, and the constituents of lower ethical quality—ethnical, local, secular—have therein been no less apparent than elsewhere. But there has been this crucial difference, that the advance of mankind, while casting these constituents into obsoleteness and oblivion, has but brought out into more illuminating emphasis the higher ethical content of the religion of Christ. Civilized man finds in the teaching and example of Jesus, and in these alone, the principles of a satisfying morality, and the realized ideal of his spiritual effort. Christian morality, disentangling itself slowly from the errors and scandals which have shadowed its historic development, demonstrates finally its character as the true inference from natural theology.

I am proposing a new method. Instead of arguing from philosophy to theology, and from theology to morality, I suggest that the process may serviceably be reversed, and we may argue back from morality to the theology which inspires and determines it, and from this theology to the philosophy which properly it supposes. For, after all, if there be such a thing as natural theology—and nothing less is the assumption of the Gifford Trust—then there must be an adequate foundation for it in philosophy, and it must of necessity find its true expression in a congruous morality. The last cannot but disclose its origin, and, indirectly but decisively, reveal the theology which alone can rightly be described as natural.

In these lectures I shall not concern myself with the metaphysical presuppositions of ethics, nor discuss the ethical theories which have been built on them. My object is simpler, and, in pursuing it, I shall not move beyond the plane of experience. By morality I mean what is meant in common speech, namely, the behaviour of men in society. For it is precisely such practical morality which provides the test of religion. Not the speculations which engage the philosopher, but the considerations which determine the action of average men are the factors which really matter. For the first can only affect the lives of men in so far as they can become transformed into the last. How does religion find expression in conduct? What is its effect on human intercourse? How does it actually shape and colour civilization? The answers to these questions must finally determine the verdict on religion as formulated in theology. I shall submit that, tried by this test, Christianity is found to be, of all the religions which command men's acceptance, alone competent to inspire a morality which modernly civilized men can accept, and find adequate to their needs. I am concerned, therefore, with Christian morality as the climax or perfected version of natural morality, the norm of ethics which, consciously or unconsciously, men must needs accept as they advance in civilization, the standard by which civilized men will finally judge the religions which claim their acceptance.

In Christian morality, I submit, we have a morality which has shown unique power of development, ever drawing fresh elements from its environment, and ever extending the range of its application, refusing recognition to no scientific truth, and declining the test of no practical problem; yet ever holding firmly to the principles of the teaching of Jesus, and pursuing the moral ideal embodied in His life. I suggest that this morality is thus shown to be not only natural and developing, but in its essential character final.

Let us suppose an impartial and intelligent observer of mankind addressing himself in this year of grace, 1935, to the task of forming an estimate of the probable future of religion and morality on this planet. He would inevitably perceive the deep divisions which race and culture create, and he would ask himself whether it was indeed conceivable that any single system of faith and conduct could ever surmount obstacles so ancient and so deeply rooted. He would examine carefully the existing religions and the moralities which they inspire and direct, and he would inquire whether any one of them showed any superior capacity to endure and to expand. He would distinguish between civilized and uncivilized religions, and he would dismiss the latter from his concern as being plainly unable to survive the crude conditions which they matched. Among civilized religions he would discern varying degrees of racial aptitude and cultural rigidity. He would recognize elasticity and assimilative power as integral to universal appeal. He would examine carefully the reaction of religious and moral systems to the distinctively modern conditions of thought and life. Would not such an observer be forced to the conclusion that while religion in all its forms, and the morality which religion creates, were heavily threatened by the novel situations into which the world has come, there was only one religion, Christianity, and only one morality, that which Christianity requires, which have disclosed any adequate capacity to hold their own? If, therefore, religion and morality are, as all theists must needs maintain, integral to human nature, so that the failure of both in front of the novel conditions under which modern society is being brought would mean nothing less than the destruction of all that is recognizably human, it follows that Christianity carries the fortunes of mankind, and that its failure would mean nothing less calamitous than the spiritual suicide of humanity.

II
AUTHORITY OF THE NEW TESTAMENT
I

WHAT are we to understand by Christian morality? We answer shortly. It is the morality inculcated by Jesus Christ, and illustrated by His example. It is the morality implicit in the Christian discipleship, and properly required by the Christian profession. Finally it is the morality which historically has had its roots in the Christian religion, has been enjoined by the Christian Church, and has given distinctive character to the civilization of Christendom. We have here set out the ideal, the theory, and the achievement of Christian ethics; and in these lectures I shall invite you to consider them all. And first of the ideal, which is bound up with the life and personality of Jesus Christ. What are the sources of our knowledge about Him? They are contained in the New Testament, and therein mainly in the three Synoptic Gospels.

The Fourth Gospel traditionally attributed to St. John is not, in my belief, properly regarded as historical, though it enshrines historical elements, and may be partly based on the testimony of the Apostle John. It offers, less a history of Jesus, than a theological interpretation of His person and mission. We may not, indeed, claim for the Synoptic Gospels that they contain no non-historical elements, but we may fairly maintain that these are relatively unimportant and, so to speak, unintentional. The writers were themselves Christians, and they saw the tradition which formed their material in the light of their faith, but they did not consciously manipulate or colour their material in a dogmatic interest. While, therefore, I do not appeal to the Fourth Gospel as a primary source from which to draw knowledge of Christ's moral teaching, I hold it to be legitimate to draw for this purpose on the records of the Synoptic Evangelists.

The undoubted epistles of St. Paul, which antedate the Synoptic narratives, are, in my view, of decisive weight, and their agreement with the general tenor of the Synoptic picture of Jesus provides confirmatory evidence of the highest quality. It is matter of common knowledge that the value of the Synoptic Gospels has been variously estimated. The very circumstance that the One Life was recorded in four narratives which, as even the simplest reader could not but perceive, did not wholly agree together, provoked questioning even in orthodox minds, while, in minds which were not orthodox, it provided the confirmation of doubt, and the material for hostile criticism.

Very early the method of constructing Harmonies of the Gospels was adopted, a method which cannot even yet be said to be wholly abandoned. Of these Harmonies the most famous was the *Diatessaron* of Tatian, a Syrian bishop of the second century, which was long read in the public services of some Eastern churches. It was not, however, until the modern epoch that the problem of discrepancies and variations in the Gospels was seriously faced, and the canonical records subjected to patient and scientific criticism. It would carry me too far outside the subject of these lectures even to trace in outline the course of this development, but for apparent reasons I cannot altogether ignore the situation to which it has led us.

Before the historical student can base conclusions on the New Testament, he must have satisfied himself as to the evidential value of its constituent documents. The exponent of original Christian morality must first make sure of the quality of his material, and not expose himself to the risk of finding his argument disallowed by a destructive criticism. The time has long passed since the questions raised by the critics of the Scriptures could be satisfactorily answered by the decisions of ecclesiastical authority; and, although it must ever remain true that, for the mass of men, disqualified by lack of training and by the conditions of their lives for intellectual exertion, the proverbial *foi du charbonnier* indicates, not only the easiest, but also the most reasonable procedure, yet such a 'short and easy way' with critical difficulties is not open to thinkers and students. They must acknowledge their limitations, take advantage of such assistances as may be accessible, and then follow the best guidance they can find.

It hardly needs that I should disclaim the character of a critical scholar. No man, engaged as I have been for nearly fifty years in active ministry, could possess the leisure, even if he had the ability and inclination, for such self-dedication to the requisite studies as the character of a critical scholar implies. In common with most Christians I have had to depend on the labours of experts for such acquaintance as I possess with the large and complicated subject of Biblical criticism. Nevertheless, as an official teacher of the Christian religion, I could not possibly be myself indifferent to studies on which the

credibility of the New Testament (which is the necessary and authorized basis of all Christian teaching) so
plainly depends. Moreover, as interested in historical
studies, I have often had to consider the difficult
problem of evidence. What are the conditions under
which human testimony is trustworthy? What dis-
counts must be made when ancient and anonymous
documents are examined? How is the core of historical
fact to be extracted from the husk of myth or legend
or deliberate manipulation? In all historical inquiries
such questions demand answer; but when the history
carries the fate of a religion, and when that religion
is none other than Christianity, it is obvious that no
serious student of history could leave them uncon-
sidered, and no responsible and self-respecting Christian
teacher could leave them unanswered.

In point of fact, these critical studies have ever
interested me deeply, and at the start of our present
inquiry I must needs confess some of the conclusions
which I have reached. The critical experts have been
generous in their revelations. They have made no
secret of their methods. They tell us frankly how they
have come by their theories; and if the latter fail to
secure our acceptance, it is largely because we distrust
the former. We are, indeed, more beholden to them for
the facts which they establish than for the interpretations of the facts which they offer. We must needs
acknowledge an obligation to receive the one, but we can
by no means always find ourselves able to endorse the
other. The amateur, we allow ourselves to think, is not
wholly at a disadvantage by comparison with the expert
in these inquiries, for, if his knowledge be less detailed,

his general view may be truer. His perspectives may well be more accurate, though his foreground be less crowded. In any case he cannot escape the obligation of coming to a decision with respect to questions which, if he be a religious teacher, cut so deeply into the main concerns of his official duty. Moreover, the critical experts by their full and frequent publications must be understood to invite the judgement of a public which obviously is mainly composed of amateurs.

We are, indeed, under heavy obligations to the critical scholars, at home and abroad, who have addressed themselves with astonishing industry and considerable success to the handling of the Synoptic Problem; and those obligations are greatly increased by the frankness and lucidity which have marked their popular expositions of critical method and the results to which it has led them. They do not, like the lawyers condemned in the Gospel, 'take away the key of knowledge', nor do they dispute the competence of the untechnical student to understand the problems to be solved and to appraise the solutions suggested. 'It is one of the great attractions of Biblical study', wrote that bold and brilliant scholar, the late Professor Burkitt, 'that the chief document is in everybody's hands in an available form, so that all the main results and many of the processes of learned critical study can be at once made plain to those who will read the English Bible carefully for themselves.' Nor is the benefit wholly one-sided. Critical scholars stand to gain by coming under the sane and sobering influence of the layman's unsophisticated intelligence. Dogmatism is ever at home in the study, and a pseudo-omniscience often becomes the tradition of the lecture hall. These perilous tempers are best detected and overcome in the less artificial atmosphere of the general life. There is need for caution, even for a measure of salutary scepticism. We must not allow ourselves to be swept from our beliefs by the confident affirmations of critical innovators, nor be overmuch impressed by the large acceptance which destructive speculations may command. The record of New Testament criticism is filled with the obituaries of brilliant and widely accepted critical theories. All critical theories, even the most plausible and the most authoritative, must ever bear a provisional character. To-day they hold the field in an unchallenged security, but to-morrow they may be challenged, reversed, and abandoned. Many questions remain open, and probably will always remain so; yet the fact nowise affects the main lines of the tradition.

The general public has something of the character of a jury in these 'Trials of the Witnesses'. It must not be bullied by the prestige of eminent advocates, or brow-beaten by unexamined assumptions. *Dolus latet in generalibus*, that is, plausible generalizations are the favourite disguises of fallacies. Preciseness and lucidity are the twin guardians of accuracy. We must make sure that we know what precisely we mean. When, for instance, the Bishop of Birmingham, preaching recently to the University of Cambridge,[1] assured his hearers that 'in the Gospels we have the results of popular preaching and popular myth-making': that 'the records are not history in the modern sense, but in part results of meditation and religious enthusiasm,' and when on

[1] v. *The Cambridge Review*, Oct. 19, 1934, where the Bishop's sermon is reported in full.

the basis of these formidable assumptions he proceeded to ask, 'Do we thereby lose much worth keeping?', it is apparent that we are not in a position to answer his question until we know exactly what he intends us to understand. 'Popular preaching and popular myth-making' do not have an impressive sound, and it is important that we should know how much in the Gospels has no better foundation. When, moreover, the evangelical records are said to be 'in part results of imaginative meditation and religious enthusiasm', it is obviously of crucial importance that we should know exactly how much of them is thus to be described. When we are told that the records of the New Testament 'are not history in the modern sense', we can hardly avoid the suspicion that we are intended to regard the 'popular preaching' as largely fictional, and the 'popular myth-making' as no more respectable than most mythical manufactures are commonly found to be. Two observations immediately suggest themselves. In the first place, the Synoptic narratives regarded as a whole are not at all like what 'popular preaching' and 'popular myth-making' would naturally be; and, in the next place, it is quite certain that the compilers of these narratives believed themselves to be writing history. The familiar marks of popular preaching in every age are actuality and exaggeration. Aiming at an immediate effect, the popular preacher is before all things topical in his references and dramatic in his methods. To the congregations in the synagogues of the Dispersion, to which in the first instance the Christian Message was delivered, the Synoptic narratives, even if they had been available, would have been little suited to the preachers' purpose.

To the polytheistic populations of the Graeco-Roman cities they would have made little effective appeal, and, indeed, would have been largely unintelligible.

We are not, however, wholly without knowledge of the original Christian preaching, for we have in the Acts several examples of Apostolic sermons, and we see that they were altogether unlike the Synoptic narratives. The preachers did not concern themselves with the teaching, nor yet with the life of Jesus, but they dwelt on His Messianic character, they affirmed His Resurrection as a fact within their own personal knowledge; they appealed to the prophecies contained in the Scriptures as finding fulfilment in the career of their crucified Master; they confidently announced His imminent return in victory and judgement. In view of these tremendous events in the recent past and in the near future they called men to repentance. They did not, after the manner of the Evangelists, relate the parables of Jesus and rehearse His deeds. The burden of their preaching was something far more urgent and terrifying. Moreover, when St. Paul carried the Gospel beyond the frontiers of Palestine into the larger world of the Empire, his preaching was fairly represented by his address to Felix and Drusilla, when, we are told, 'He reasoned of righteousness and temperance and the judgement to come'. The time soon arrived when the belief in the nearness of the Lord's return ceased to dominate Christian minds, and then discipleship had perforce to be seen in the normal contexts of relatively settled social life. When the Christian Church had definitely severed itself from its association with the Jewish synagogues, and was developing on its own lines, the method of the preachers could not but change. They were henceforth concerned less with offering reasons for believing in Christ's Messiahship, and rousing consciences with the near prospect of His judgement, than with instructing the Christians as to the practical requirements of their new religion. For this purpose the teaching and example of the Saviour were obviously of supreme importance. The Tradition preserved in the Synoptic Gospels became the very manual of the Christian preachers, the inexhaustible source of instruction, the treasury from which the Christian scribes, like the 'householder' in Christ's parable, 'could bring forth things new and old'.

This stage was soon reached. The Epistles of St. Paul presuppose settled Christian communities in which a pastoral ministry was active alongside the prophesying and speaking with tongues. The latter were already causing as much embarrassment as edification, and the great Apostle makes very evident his own preference for the calmer and more normal ministries. While its first founders yet lived, the Church had taken shape as an ordered and permanent institution. The apostles and prophets, who depended on immediate inspiration, were already giving place to presbyters, preachers, and teachers who rested on the Jewish Scriptures and the Tradition of Jesus.

The Tradition, based on first-hand testimony, and everywhere recognized as in the fullest sense authoritative, provided the material on which the Christian preachers worked, and it remains on record in the canonical Gospels in a form which reflects their needs, moods, and hopes. They were themselves believers;

their purpose was to persuade and to edify; they were responsive to the hopes and fears of the communities which they served. But always the value of the Gospels depended on the preacher's assumption that they are records of fact. Only so could they be edifying and authoritative.

The Christian preacher has found his message in the truth of the Gospel history, and devoted his efforts to showing its relevance to men's actual situation. Destroy the historical character of the narratives, and you have emptied the preaching based on them of substance, relevance, and persuasive power. 'History in the modern sense' does not differ in any essential particular from history as the Evangelists understood it. No doubt the modern historian, equipped with exact statistics and an elaborate criticism of sources, familiar with the teachings of modern science, and protected from error by many devices which were inaccessible to the ancients, attains a far higher level of accuracy than the ancient, but he is neither more honest, nor more discerning, nor more intelligent, nor necessarily, in the total effect of his work, more truthful. The ancient historian was not unaware of the distinction between fact and fiction, and he assuredly designed to give a truthful account of events. That this was the case with the evangelists cannot be disputed. Their belief that their work would serve their Master's cause, and lead men to understand more adequately the religion which they professed, did not imply any conscious repudiation of the historian's normal and recognized obligations.

The Evangelists wrote as Christians for Christians, but they were not necessarily on that account the less

G

trustworthy. That, as they frankly confessed, they wrote with a didactic and edifying object may explain their selection and arrangement of the material at their disposal, but certainly does not imply any deliberate falsification of it. The famous Prologue to the Third Synoptic demonstrates as much. Nothing could be clearer or more definite:

'Forasmuch as many have taken in hand to draw up a narrative concerning those matters which have been fulfilled among us, even as they delivered them unto us, which from the beginning were eyewitnesses and ministers of the word, it seemed good to me also, having traced the course of all things accurately from the first, to write unto thee in order, most excellent Theophilus, that thou mightest know the certainty concerning the things wherein thou wast instructed.'

If, in agreement with the tradition of the Christian Church and with the conclusions of many eminent modern critics, we identify the writer of this Prologue with St. Luke, a Greek physician, who was the companion of St. Paul and the author of the Book of the Acts, we are carried into the heart of the Apostolic age, and have irresistible proof that the version of Christ's life and teaching which the New Testament contains was identical with that which Christ's own contemporaries delivered. That version lies behind the Pauline Epistles, and illustrates the occasional references to the Lord's life and character which those compositions contain. The assumption that, because the earliest Church was persuaded that the Parousia was at hand, it therefore took no interest in the tradition of the Redeemer's earthly career, is not only improbable in itself, but is contradicted by the composition of the evangelical narratives. That there were in the Apostolic age some Christians so obsessed with the imminence of the Second Advent as to withdraw themselves from the normal obligations of social life is sufficiently proved by the Second Epistle to the Thessalonians, where St. Paul rebukes them sharply, but the ordinary Christian felt no such logical compulsion to sacrifice his immediate duty to his formal belief.

Human nature changes little, if indeed it changes at all. We may safely assume that our modern experience had its parallel in antiquity. Every generation of Christians, and certainly our own, has been familiar with individuals and groups who are so obsessed with some aspect of the religion they profess as to lose all sense of proportion, and thus to concentrate their interest so completely on that one aspect as to become lop-sided and impracticable. It was with the Apostolic Church as with the Church of later times. The imminence of the Parousia was an unchallenged article of Christian belief, but it coexisted in Christian minds with much else. The nearer and normal interests of life in the world were not, save in the case of eccentric enthusiasts, cancelled by it. I suspect that forgetfulness of this well-authenticated capacity of religious minds to admit conflicting opinions, and ever to chasten impracticable theory by indispensable habit, is at the root of much confident dogmatizing about the thought and action of the Apostolic Christians. Experience continually renewed disallows this confident dogmatizing.

The human mind is found to be curiously patient of contradictions. What in theory is held with even passionate conviction may, and commonly does, go along with a habit of life which seems to conflict with it. The difficult task of the preacher is to waken men to a consciousness of this contradiction between creed and conduct, and to move them to some serious effort to effect a tolerable harmony between the two. For the most part, and always in some measure, convention usurps the throne of conscience, and custom, 'heavy as frost and deep almost as life', is too strong for the moralists. It was not otherwise with those first believers. How significant it is that even in the Apostolic age when the imminence of the Parousia was the assumption of Christian thinking, and when the settled hostility of non-Christian society might well be thought to have stripped the world of attractiveness, the leaders of the Church should yet have deemed it requisite to multiply warnings against 'filthy lucre'! The argument from creed to conduct is never so precarious as when the creed is lofty, exacting, and unpopular.

Much attention has been directed within recent years to the conditions under which the primitive tradition as to the life and teaching of Jesus took shape in the period before the canonical Gospels were compiled. The biographical character of these narratives has been challenged, and not without a large measure of justice. Dr. Vincent Taylor in his valuable and interesting lectures on *The Formation of the Gospel Tradition* raises the question, Had the first Christians a biographical interest? and he answers it thus:

'So far as the Evangelists are concerned, somewhat different answers must be given. None of them aims at producing a biography in the modern sense of the term, although all wish to tell the Story of Jesus . . . . The tentative nature of the efforts of Mark and Luke is eloquent of the conditions as they existed in the earlier oral period. The Evangelists could not succeed because for a generation at least a Christianity had existed which was destitute of the biographical interest; no one thought of recording the life of Christ.'[1]

To 'record the life of Christ' is one thing: to be interested in that life quite another. The belief that the end of the world was imminent may fairly explain the disinclination of the earliest believers to write down what they knew about their Master's life, but it is nowise inconsistent with their keen interest in that life. The absence of such interest would have been both unnatural and improbable.

At this point we may properly introduce some comments on the new method of New Testament criticism associated with the name of Dr. Martin Dibelius, Professor of New Testament in Heidelberg. This new method has been fully explained in the volume, *Die Formgeschichte des Evangeliums*, of which an excellent English translation, prepared by Dr. Bertram Lee Woolf 'in collaboration with the author', has been published under the title *From Tradition to Gospel*, and which is examined with candour, acuteness, and good sense by Dr. Vincent Taylor in the work to which I have already referred.

'Form-criticism' has been explained with lucidity, and advocated with ardour by the latest Bampton Lecturer, Professor Lightfoot, an Oxford scholar of great ability. On the other hand, the late Professor Burkitt must be reckoned among opponents. He rejects the fundamental assumption of the new method, namely,

[1] v. *The Formation of the Gospel Tradition*, p. 143.

that our earliest Gospel is to be regarded not as an historical record but as a production of the Christian community, disclosing its belief about Jesus, and reflecting its hopes and fears. After sketching the Marcan narrative, Professor Burkitt proceeds:

'It is possible so to interpret this Tale, for it to be compatible with St. Paul's Gospel. But as it stands, is it possible for it to have been the intentional, or accidental, invention of a Christian writing about 65 A.D., or later? It does not sound to me like *Gemeindetheologie*, the unconscious secretion of a community of believers. Nothing but a strong element of personal reminiscence could have produced it. And therefore I still hold to the belief that it embodies the private reminiscences of Peter, supplemented for the last week by the reminiscences of the young Mark himself. They were both believers, "Christians", of over thirty years' standing. There is a good deal of idealization, of unhistorical embroidery, in the work, but the outline seems to me to be derived from real memory of real events.'[1]

The new method bids us discard the common estimate of the Synoptic Gospels as biographical narratives, and to regard them as mainly propagandist compositions. It assumes that propagandist value in a narrative is necessarily destructive of its historical character. But this assumption lies open to serious challenge. It is, indeed, notorious that proselytizing lends itself easily to fraud, and that zeal, like charity, though in a far different sense, covers a multitude of sins. It is necessary to distinguish. Propagandism need not involve dishonesty, nor does history always need falsification in order to serve a cause. Professor Guignebert's assumption that the Evangelists wrote

[1] v. *Journal of Theological Studies*, April 1935, p. 188.

hagiography and not history, provides him with a short and easy way of dealing with whatever in the canonical documents conflicts with his argument, but it is none the less both arbitrary and questionable.

An illustration from the *Bampton Lectures* will, perhaps, disclose sufficiently the intrinsic weakness of the new method. Professor Lightfoot is discussing the quotation from the twenty-second psalm which St. Mark attributes to Jesus as He hung on the Cross. You will observe how summarily the normal and natural view of the narrative is brushed aside in deference to the assumption of the theory:

'From the point of view with which we have approached this gospel, we must exclude at once a common supposition: namely that in these words the evangelist, in his faithfulness to historical fact, and in spite of every temptation to the contrary, allows us to listen to a final and despairing utterance of Jesus, forsaken by both God and man in his extremity. Such a view assumes a narrator who, interested primarily in historical fact, reports faithfully for posterity a terrible and inexplicable utterance. But all our inquiry has tended to show that there was no narrator of this sort, and the objectivity of this gospel as a whole, in spite of certain possible exceptions, is evidence against it: the passion narrative was written for the strengthening and edification of the Christian communities, not for their bewilderment. We may, indeed, infer that the evangelist attaches great importance to the utterance, since the bystanders at once misunderstand it, seeing very strangely in the word Eloi a reference to Elijah.'[1]

The Evangelist, we may think, could only have attached great importance to the utterance if he had believed that it proceeded from the Crucified Master, and for us, as for him, on no other supposition have the

[1] v. *Bampton Lectures*, p. 158.

words any importance at all. The suggestion apparently is that, because the Evangelist desired to edify his readers, he must not be thought to have had any care for the truth of what he professed to relate. This suggestion, however, is equally superfluous and improbable.

Dr. Dibelius distinguishes various forms which he designates paradigms, tales, and legends. Behind these are the oldest, unformulated traditions which had their origin in the testimony of eyewitnesses, but are only relatively trustworthy, since their survival was determined in the interest not of history but of faith. From this point of view the Evangelists were not historians concerned with recording facts but missionaries seeking to spread a faith. They were only interested in the traditions about Jesus in so far as these assisted their proselytizing purpose. These traditions, moreover, had already received definite shape such as the requirements of the original preachers had determined.

'The question of historicity is, in the first instance, restricted by us to the Paradigms. In so doing, the statement of the problem changes from what was customary for a long time in scientific criticism. Inquiry into the historicity of the Gospels used to be made dependent upon the solution of the question of authenticity, and so attempted to establish the relation of the authors to the eyewitnesses in order to prove how much the evangelists could have known or learned of the real course of things. These inquiries would have led on to a wrong road, even if they had not been burdened with the old question of uncertain authorship, for the very statement of the question upon which they stand is too much of a literary and personal character. The authors of the Gospels, at least of the synoptics, are not "authors" in the literary sense, but collectors. We are not, therefore, concerned first of all with their knowledge of the subject matters, but with the knowledge of those who gave the tradition its form, and this taking form was not mediated by authors but by preachers.'[1]

What precisely are we to understand? Traditions survive for many other reasons than those suggested by the interest of preachers. Why some facts are remembered and transmitted while others are buried in oblivion is a question which every student of history asks, and which no student of history can satisfactorily answer. Even allowing that only those traditions about Jesus survived which the first preachers of Christianity found most serviceable for their purpose, this circumstance does not necessarily, nor even probably, render them historically doubtful. Nor may the student omit the profoundly suggestive question raised by the fact that the history was admittedly such as to make it worth the preachers' while to proclaim it. Preachers are not necessarily bad witnesses to the facts they affirm, nay it is even arguable, since they may immerse themselves in grave difficulties by affirming such facts, that they are exceptionally good witnesses. When, moreover, as Dr. Dibelius admits, the first preachers delivered their testimony when 'eyewitnesses' were yet living, and contradiction would have been readily forthcoming if falsehoods had been delivered, we cannot be mistaken in holding that statements of fact do not necessarily lose their claim to be such because they assist the Christian preacher's purpose. Preachers do not always, nor indeed if they be honest men do they ever consciously, tamper with the facts which they offer as

[1] v. *From Tradition to Gospel*, p. 59.

H

proofs or illustrations of their message. No doubt they select their facts with a specific object, but they do not fabricate or adulterate them. Nor may it be forgotten that faith may illuminate history as well as distort it; and that prejudice is not a monopoly of Christian believers.

I need not remind you that the Synoptic Gospels do not stand alone. The substantial historicity of their version of the life and teaching of Jesus is powerfully confirmed by the evidence of St. Paul. Dr. Dibelius states the case very fairly:

'Paul was converted within the period 32–5. At that time as a Christian, or somewhat later when he became a missionary, he received the traditions spoken of in 1 Cor. xi and xv, a kerygma, and a record of the Last Supper which had already been shaped. Thus as early as the fourth decade there were already in existence texts in Greek about events from the life of Jesus. At that time or later, hence perhaps in the fifth decade, Paul must have also received collections of the sayings of Jesus of which he made use in 1 Cor. vii and ix. Hence we may assert that the weighty elements of the tradition had become fixed in the first twenty years after Jesus' death. We may assume that all the elements of tradition of which Mark's Gospel consists received their formulation in Greek at latest between A.D. 50 and 70. Thus the weightiest part of the tradition had been developed at a time while eyewitnesses still lived, and when the events were only about a generation old. It is not to be wondered at that this part of the tradition remained relatively unaltered.'[1]

Dr. Vincent Taylor has well emphasized the important part in the shaping of this tradition which must have been taken by the eyewitnesses of the Saviour's ministry:

'However disturbing to the smooth working of theories, the influence of eyewitnesses cannot possibly be ignored. The one

[1] v. *From Tradition to Gospel*, p. 294.

hundred and twenty at Pentecost did not go into permanent retreat; for at least a generation they moved among the young Palestinian communities, and through preaching and fellowship their recollections were at the disposal of those who sought information.'[1]

If all this must be conceded, that is, if the original tradition included the first-hand testimony of numerous contemporaries of Jesus, and took permanent forms in a society in which those contemporaries could not but exercise a powerful corrective influence, we may fairly conclude that, after all, no essential interest is involved in the question which form-criticism raises. The actual shape in which the Tradition of Jesus reached the authors of the canonical Gospels does not appear to be of vital importance so long as we can be assured that the Tradition itself was genuine, and has been honestly handled. Neither point is seriously endangered by form-criticism. When a distinction is made between facts and inferences, the new critical method is less formidable than it looks.

Dr. Major, in a characteristic criticism of 'the latest phase of Gospel Criticism', quotes a saying of 'a distinguished New Testament scholar', at whose feet he had sat, which is worth remembering:

'The critical faculty, when it is once aroused in this kind of work, cannot be repressed. When there is no more wheat to gather, then it collects chaff.'[2]

Is it altogether unreasonable or unfair to suggest that the credulity which in former ages facilitated the growth of superstition, and made possible the careers of numer-

---

[1] v. *Formation of the Gospel Tradition*, p. 42.
[2] v. *The Modern Churchman*, June 1935, p. 118.

ous impostors, has in modern times been largely transferred from the religious sphere to the sphere of anti-
religion? The 'climate of opinion', to adopt Glanvill's
famous phrase, has an almost unlimited influence on
the thinking of individuals who are more curious than
informed, and more receptive of what is novel than
attached to what is familiar. At the present time that
influence is definitely hostile to whatever is established,
traditional, and authoritative. This fact goes far to
explain the ready welcome which all sceptical theories
about the Bible or the Christian religion can securely
count upon. These theories are too often accepted
without examination, repeated as if they were indeed
unquestionable, and then made the bases of argument.
In the wholly unprecedented circumstances of modern
society, when popular education has brought into
existence a vast reading public, curious and credulous
but mentally undisciplined, and destitute of any firm
tradition of social habit, no theory is too extravagant
to secure a welcome, so only it be novel, daring, and
destructive. The greedy receptivity of the multitude is unconditioned by knowledge, unprotected by
authority, and robust enough to survive a thousand
disillusionments.

Thus, to give an extreme but illuminating example.
In 1911 there was in Germany a prolonged controversy
upon the theme, 'Did Jesus ever live?' The mere fact
that so extravagant an hypothesis could be thought
deserving of serious debate and become the occasion
of a considerable literature sufficed to commend it to
the popular mind. It is widely spread among the semi-
educated, and confidently affirmed by the irreligious,

that the Founder of Christianity never existed, but is wholly the creation of symbolism and pietistic fancy. This preposterous opinion is now defended by no serious scholar, but it is still referred to with respect as if it were reasonably tenable by critics who know well its absurdity. Thus Professor Guignebert, who himself rejects it, observes that 'the position that Jesus had no historical existence is in itself a perfectly legitimate theory entitled to serious discussion'.[1] In this way it is insinuated that the Founder of Christianity belonged to the same category of mythical figures as the founders of the cults of Mithras or Isis. A shadow of dubiety is cast on the crucial and central fact which sustains the entire fabric of Christian faith and morals.

'It is the great distinguishing characteristic of Christianity', writes Dr. Rawlinson '(as contrasted, for example, with the so-called "Mystery Religions" of paganism, which in some respects superficially resemble it), that its Gospel was rooted in history, and the facts about Jesus were attested by contemporary witness.'[2]

Nothing is more certain than that the theory of a non-historical Jesus is quite baseless, and that apart from its polemical uses it would not command assent from any reasonable and educated man. Hardly less irrational and mischievous is the popular and highly patronized view which separates Jesus from the Christian society.

Ecclesiastical history is represented as the record of a continuing repudiation of the Founder's teaching. Yet the earliest documents which the Christian Church possesses are the Epistles of St. Paul, and they disclose in the Apostle a conviction that Christ was the 'founda-

[1] v. *Jesus*, p. 64.
[2] v. *St. Mark*, 'Westminster Commentaries', p. xiii.

tion' and 'head' of the Church; that He Himself had authorized the elaborate provision of the Christian Ministry; and that His words and appointments were finally authoritative for all Christians. He had Himself instituted the Holy Communion, given directions respecting Christian marriage, and authorized the maintenance of the Christian preachers. The whole system of organized Christianity had in St. Paul's belief a Divine origin, and was designed to serve a Divine purpose. Apostolic Christianity is unintelligible apart from the action of Jesus.

Dr. Matthews, the Dean of St. Paul's, in his notable presidential address to the Modern Churchmen's Union in Cambridge last August, emphasized the essential connexion between Christianity and the Church:

'The form-critics', he said, 'had at least reminded us that the Church had great importance in the earliest years of our religion, and that our knowledge of Jesus depended, if not upon its imagination, certainly upon its memory. Gospel and Church could not be understood in separation one from the other. At least it seemed beyond controversy that in the Pauline version of the Gospel the Church was an integral element.'[1]

The historical character of the Gospels is a vital concern for the student of Christian ethics, for it is precisely in the life and teaching of Jesus that he must find the supremely authoritative version of human duty. If the Evangelists' record be no more than the creation of posthumous idealization, its moral authority is destroyed. It belongs to the category of imaginative literature, and may take its place with other edifying fictions. The suggestion that the moral influence of

[1] v. *The Guardian*, August 30, 1935.

the life of Jesus is independent of its historical character may certainly be rejected. Professor Burkitt, in his brilliant and valuable volume, *The Gospel History and its Transmission*, has emphasized 'the witness borne by the Evangelists to the moral impression produced by Jesus Christ upon His followers', and has told us that 'the real miracle, which only escapes our notice because it is so familiar, is the irresistible vitality of the ethical teaching of the Gospel'.

'The Christian', he writes, 'has hardly need to claim more from the scientific historian than that the life of Jesus Christ on earth inspired the canonical Gospels, made the Evangelists write as they did, made the Gospels what they are.'[1]

It must not, however, be forgotten that we are only impressed by the Evangelists' testimony to Christ's character, life, and teaching in so far as we believe that testimony to be adequately grounded on knowledge of the facts. 'The irresistible vitality of the ethical teaching of the Gospel' has been throughout Christian history conditioned by the belief that 'the ethical teaching of the Gospel' was verily the teaching of Jesus and actually illustrated by His example. If it be agreed that the criticism of the New Testament disallows the historical character of the Gospels, brings into reasonable doubt almost every utterance attributed to Jesus, and demonstrates, or at least makes highly probable, that almost the whole of the teaching attributed to Him was fabricated by His followers, does any considering man seriously believe that 'the ethical teaching of the Gospel' will long retain its 'irresistible vitality'? If,

[1] p. 27.

moreover, the scepticism of the critics be suffered to extend even to the Person of the Founder of Christianity, and it become an open question whether in truth He ever existed at all, and, as I have said, such extremes of dubiety are certainly not unknown at the present time, does any one imagine that the Christian religion will succeed in retaining any vestige of moral influence? That moral influence has, indeed, been from the first amazing, but it has always hitherto been conditioned by the belief that the Gospels are in substance historically true, that Jesus really taught and acted as they assert, and that their pages do really present a portrait which belongs, not to the region of devotional fancy, but to that of genuine experience. So He taught, and so He lived, and so He died. Let that belief fail, and the influence which it has exercised cannot long survive. The momentum of the Christian tradition may delay the ultimate catastrophe, but cannot finally avert it. Morality, we know, is not necessarily Christian, and has older roots, but Christian morality as such stands or falls with the historical character of the Gospels which contain all that man can know about Jesus, and if Christianity be indeed, as few will deny, the most perfect outcome of man's religious development, then the fortunes of Christianity cannot be separated from those of religion itself, and the collapse of the distinctive Christian morality would imply nothing less formidable than the moral bankruptcy of the human race.

Two generations have passed since John Stuart Mill wrote the *Three Essays on Religion* which were published after his death in 1873. The passage in which he refers to the influence of the historic Jesus is so germane to my present argument, and so interesting in itself, that in spite of its length I transcribe it here. He has been speaking of the effect of the Christian belief in God, and thus he proceeds:

'Above all, the most valuable part of the effect on the character which Christianity has produced by holding up in a Divine Person a standard of excellence and a model for imitation, is available even to the absolute unbeliever and can never more be lost to humanity. For it is Christ rather than God, whom Christianity has held up to believers as the pattern of perfection for humanity. It is the God incarnate, more than the God of the Jews or of Nature, who being idealized has taken so great and salutary a hold on the modern mind. And whatever else may be taken away from us by rational criticism, Christ is still left; a unique figure, not more unlike all his precursors than all his followers, even those who had the direct benefit of his personal teaching. It is of no use to say that Christ as exhibited in the Gospels is not historical and that we know not how much of what is admirable has been superadded by the tradition of his followers. The tradition of followers suffices to insert any number of marvels, and may have inserted all the miracles which he is reputed to have wrought. But who among his disciples or among their proselytes was capable of inventing the sayings ascribed to Jesus or of imagining the life and character revealed in the Gospels? Certainly not the fishermen of Galilee; as certainly not St. Paul, whose character and idiosyncrasies were of a totally different sort; still less the early Christian writers in whom nothing is more evident than that the good which was in them was all derived, as they always professed that it was derived, from the higher source.

What *could* be added and interpolated by a disciple we may see in the mystical parts of the Gospel of St. John, matter imported from Philo and the Alexandrian Platonists and put into the mouth of the Saviour in long speeches about himself such as the other Gospels contain not the slightest vestige of, though pretended to have been delivered on occasions of the deepest interest and when his principal followers were all present; most prominently at the last supper. The East was full of men who could have stolen any quantity of this poor stuff, as the multitudinous Oriental sects of Gnostics afterwards did.

But about the life and sayings of Jesus there is a stamp of personal originality combined with profundity of insight which, if we abandon the idle expectation of finding scientific precision where something very different was aimed at, must place the Prophet of Nazareth, even in the estimation of those who have no belief in his inspiration, in the very first rank of the men of sublime genius of whom our species can boast. When this pre-eminent genius is combined with the qualities of probably the greatest moral reformer, and martyr to that mission, who ever existed upon earth, religion cannot be said to have made a bad choice in pitching on this man as the ideal representative and guide of humanity, nor, even now, would it be easy, even for an unbeliever, to find a better translation of the rule of virtue from the abstract into the concrete than to endeavour so to live that Christ would approve our lives.'[1]

Serious students of the Fourth Gospel are little likely to endorse Mill's contemptuous description of it, but, with this reservation, who can fail to be impressed by this estimate of the historic Jesus?

We may add to it the deliberate opinion of Professor Burkitt, who, after pointing out the factors which might be thought to detract from the historical authority of the Gospels, reaches the following conclusion:

'Yet, after all, the Portrait they draw remains essentially the same. Verse after verse, Saying after saying, might be quoted to you from the three Synoptic Gospels, and, unless you happened to have special knowledge or had given special atten-

[1] *Three Essays on Religion*, p. 253 f.

tion to such matters, you would be unable to say to which Gospel they really belonged. Morally, ethically, spiritually, they are all in the same plane. We cannot doubt that the common impression which they present of the way in which our Lord spoke, the style of His utterances, the manner of His discourse to rich and poor, to learned and unlearned, is based on true historical reminiscence.'[1]

The fatal weakness of all theories which deny the historical character of the New Testament is the impossibility of finding in the sub-apostolic age any writers who could be reasonably credited with its composition. Mill's challenge on this point cannot be met. Who that has been at the pains to read the so-called 'Apostolic Fathers', and remembers that grotesque compositions like 'the Shepherd of Hermas' and the 'Epistle of Barnabas' were so highly regarded by the Christians of the second century as to be accounted worthy of public reading in the churches, can tolerate the supposition that the New Testament was produced in the age which owned such men as spiritual leaders, and found such works spiritually precious? In the Preface to the *Apocryphal New Testament* the Provost of Eton dwells on the contrast in quality between the canonical and apocryphal literature. He claims with justice that a knowledge of the latter will disallow the popular assumption that 'it was only by accident or caprice' that these apocryphal writings, or some of them, were not included in the New Testament. 'The best answer to such loose talk', he writes, 'has always been, and is now, to produce the writings, and let them tell their own story.' Like the Tichborne

[1] v. *The Gospel History and its Transmission*, p. 216.

claimant in the witness-box, they are themselves the disproof of their pretensions. But their contribution to truth, though indirect and undesigned, is not unimportant, for they enable us to understand the generation which, it is absurdly suggested, could have produced the New Testament:

'They record the imaginations, hopes, and fears of the men who wrote them; they show what was acceptable to the unlearned Christians of the first ages, what interested them, what they admired, what ideals of conduct they cherished for this life, what they thought they would find in the next.'

The extent of the changes required by textual criticism is often greatly exaggerated. When the Revised New Testament was published in 1881, I well remember the eager expectation with which I compared it with the familiar Authorized Version, and how I was disappointed and half resentful at the relative unimportance of the changes. There had been so much discussion and controversy, that I had been prepared for something dramatic, and I found little to surprise, nothing to disturb. There were indeed numerous changes, some of which did not seem to me worth making, but of anything really important there was remarkably little. Canon Streeter has commented on the multitude and triviality of the variants which textual critics are concerned with:

'Between the Textus Receptus and Westcott and Hort, that is, practically between the Byzantine text and that of B, there are, in the Gospels alone, about 4000 differences. And the number of differences between the text of B and that of D would, I imagine, be quite twice as many. But no less remarkable is the infinitesimal character of the vast majority of these differences. For the most part they consist in variations in the relative order of words in a sentence, in the use of different prepositions, conjunctions, and particles, in differences in the preposition with which words are compounded, or in slight modifications of a grammatical nature. Indeed the great majority of them cannot be represented in an English translation.'[1]

The main service to truth which the textual critics have rendered, and it is no mean service, is to dissipate the suspicion that the sacred texts have, in the course of time, been seriously tampered with. One illustration of critical method may not be superfluous. The First Word from the Cross, 'Father, forgive them; for they know not what they do', is not found in many ancient manuscripts of the Third Gospel. If it ever formed part of that Gospel, it must have been deliberately omitted; if not, it must have been deliberately inserted. The critics are divided. Almost all would hold with Westcott and Hort that the words 'bear in themselves a sure witness to the truth of what they record', but how did it come about that they were omitted, or inserted? Some critics, like Harnack and Streeter, hold that the Early Church omitted them because they were too charitable, or because they seemed to contradict the witness of history to the fact that God had not forgiven the Jews. Others, like Creed, think that the Early Church inserted them, but hold none the less that they are entirely congruous with all we know of the character and habit of Jesus. They may not be properly 'historical' but they are true and luminous revelations of the Saviour's mind at that terrible crisis.

[1] v. *The Four Gospels*, p. 37.

It is apparent that these estimates of the probable motive of the second-century Church are contradictory. They are quite obviously mere individual impressions. Why should the Author of the terrific series of 'Woes' pronounced on the 'Scribes and Pharisees, Hypocrites', have refrained from pronouncing the curse of God on the enormous wickedness of His murderers? What security have we that those who placed these words of forgiveness in the dying Saviour's mouth were rightly interpreting His mind in that tremendous hour? Why should the most natural view not be also the right one, viz. that Jesus did Himself so speak, and that His words were treasured and transmitted? Their wonderful influence on Christian thought has unquestionably depended on this assumption, and is quite unintelligible on any other. We may be very sure that, if ever it came to be generally believed that these Words were not spoken by the Crucified, their moral power would not long survive.

In so far as form-criticism directs attention to factors which have unquestionably affected the composition of the Synoptic narratives, and which have not hitherto been adequately recognized by Christian students, its influence is salutary, and ought to be welcomed; but when it is offered as a sufficient explanation, not of the form merely but also of the substance of the Tradition, and as thus providing the key to the right understanding of the canonical versions of that Tradition, form-criticism can but lead to disastrous error. Only as genuinely historical documents can the Synoptic Gospels provide a foundation for an authoritative statement as to the essential content of Christian morality.

'Form-criticism', as it is presented by its thorough-going advocates, makes havoc of the tradition to which, Professor Lightfoot admits, 'immense weight and authority is rightly owing', for it all but annihilates the historical value of the Gospels. We move in a haze of symbols, conflicting tendencies, current conflicts. It is a modernized gnosticism to which we are led. A note of interrogation is set against every saying of Jesus, even the most original and the most characteristic, and the records of His deeds are so many creatures of mythical fancy and legend-framing art. The living Person of the Son of Man fades into a lifeless product of pietistic fancy or critical speculation. Professor Lightfoot, in the concluding paragraph of his *Bampton Lectures*, strikes a note which conflicts sharply with the joyous certitude of the New Testament. Not knowledge but a blank agnosticism is the student's reward:

'It seems that the form of the earthly no less than of the heavenly Christ is for the most part hidden from us. For all the inestimable value of the gospels, they yield us little more than a whisper of his voice; we trace in them but the outskirts of his way.'

To sum up. I regard the Synoptic Gospels as trust-worthy historical documents of the Apostolic age, and I shall not hesitate to depend on them for information as to the moral teaching of Jesus. These documents must be studied in the light of the time and place in which they were originally composed. When due allowance has been made for these circumstances, I cannot doubt their title to be accepted as honest records of fact.

Some emphatic words of an eminent Jewish scholar,

remarkable both for his learning and his candour, are worth remembering by those who are too easily led to accept the fashionable scepticism of our time. After stating that the difficulty of giving a complete life of Jesus arises 'not so much because of scarcity or credibility of material, but because we do not know the chronological order of his sayings or actions', Dr. Joseph Klausner proceeds:

'But to cast wholesale doubt on the historicity of the Synoptic Gospels becomes more impossible the more widely we study all the branches of Judaism during the period of the Second Temple. Notwithstanding all the efforts of the authors of the Gospels to stress the great opposition between Jesus and Pharisaic Judaism, every step he took, every thing he did, every word he spoke, all recall to us—chiefly by confirmation though sometimes by contradiction—the Palestine of his time and contemporary Jewish life and Pharisaic teaching.'[1]

[1] v. *Jesus of Nazareth*, 1927, p. 126.

III
THE JEWISH LEGACY

CHRISTIAN morality as we know it to-day is the result of a long process of development, in the course of which many contributions of varying origin, potency, and ethical quality have been assimilated. Throughout the whole process the dominant factor, which has absorbed and reshaped the most incongruous materials, was that which Christianity inherited from the parent system of Judaism. Jesus Himself, from Whom whatever is truly distinctive in Christian morality is derived, described His Mission as one of fulfilment. 'Think not', He said, 'that I came to destroy the law or the prophets. I came not to destroy, but to fulfil.'[1]

'About the word "fulfil" ($\pi\lambda\eta\rho\tilde{\omega}\sigma\alpha\iota$)', observes Hort, 'there is a certain ambiguity. But we may safely neglect the meaning which perhaps comes first to mind, that of personal obedience or performance, as we speak of the fulfilment of an injunction. The true meaning answers much more exactly to that destroying or undoing to which it is here formally opposed. It is to bring to fulness of completion, involving therefore a progress: it is not to keep a thing as it was.'[2]

Into the process of progressive development many elements have entered, but its course and character have been determined by the historic fact that its starting-point was the tradition of Israel. In ethics as in theology 'salvation is from the Jews'.

In this lecture we have to consider the character, content, and range of the morality which was taken over

[1] v. St. Matthew, v. 17.   [2] v. *Judaistic Christianity*, p. 15.

by the new religion. We remember that Jesus was a Jew, brought up religiously as such, and throughout His life living in obedience to the Jewish law; that He never moved beyond the frontiers of Palestine; that He based His teaching on the Jewish Scriptures, and delivered it for the most part in customary Jewish forms. Finally we remember that all His Apostles were Jews, and that the only Scriptures which they accepted as inspired were the canonical Scriptures of Israel. What, then, we ask, was the Jewish morality which was taken over by Christianity?

The current morality of Christ's contemporaries reflected the mingled experiences of a long national history. Political independence had been lost, and the wide dispersion of the Jews, which had been the consequence of their defeats, had brought them under influences which could not but affect potently both their theological beliefs and the practical morality which those beliefs inspired and conditioned. It had from the first been distinctive of Israel, that theology and morality were indissolubly united. This feature stamped Jewish morality with a unique and lofty character. The Creator was also the Author of the Moral Law, and, so the prophets had taught, had His witness in the human conscience. The true knowledge of God drew with it a right understanding of His Will, obedience to which was the essence of morality. Thus the Decalogue was not only the august symbol of Israel's religion, but also the authoritative summary of Israel's moral obligation. It proclaimed both duty to God and duty to man.

The downfall of the Jewish kingdom had created for the Jews a situation of the gravest difficulty, for with the

loss of the national independence had gone the destruction of the Temple and the forcible emigration of the
people. Exile would break many old links and fashion
many new ones. How should the scattered Jews living
in the midst of great civilized communities with different religious beliefs, different social customs, different
ethical standards, be enabled to retain uncontaminated
their monotheistic faith and their relatively severe
morality? When religion could no longer embody itself
in a local patriotism and utter its claims in the immemorial splendours of an established worship, how
should the subtle, assimilating power of circumstance
and environment be arrested, and some effective substitute for the old loyalties and disciplines be discovered? How, in short, should the individuality of
Israel be preserved intact under the strains and stresses
of national and ecclesiastical dissolution? Nor was this
the whole extent of the danger. Exile introduced the
Jews to a new intellectual world. In Babylonia, in
Persia, in the Hellenistic communities, in the Roman
Empire, they encountered ideas which conflicted sharply
with their ancestral beliefs. They found themselves
in daily contact with civilizations far more splendid and
elaborate than anything they had known in Palestine,
and they became familiar with an art and a literature
which transcended anything that they had hitherto
encountered. Josephus, when explaining the silence of
the Greek historians as to his ancient people, dwells on
the natural isolation of the Jews:

'Ours is not a maritime country; neither commerce nor the
intercourse which it promotes with the outside world has any
attraction for us. Our cities are built inland remote from the sea,

and we devote ourselves to the cultivation of the productive country with which we are blessed.'[1]

But the Dispersion perforce ended this natural isolation. The scattered Jews soon established themselves in prosperous colonies throughout the civilized world.

'They took up land,' writes Mr. Tarn, 'and were often employed as tax-collectors, but seldom did banking or money-lending and hardly ever occur as traders.'[2]

Their remarkable ability, and the attraction of their lofty faith, carried them everywhere. 'The Jews', writes Sir Samuel Dill, 'from the time of the first Caesar, had worked their way into every class of society.'[3]

Thus the Jews passed everywhere under influences which favoured the growth of an eclectic cosmopolitan temper far removed from the rigid provincial orthodoxy which prevailed in the mother-land. During the four centuries which preceded the Birth of Jesus, the consequences of the loss of political independence and the dispersion of the Jewish people had become apparent. Allegiance to the national monarch had been replaced by obedience to the Divine Law, and the Temple at Jerusalem had given place in religious influence to the synagogues throughout the world, wherever Jews were to be found. The sacrificial system administered by the priesthood in the Temple remained, and drew to itself the devotion of the nation, but that system was normally remote, and its effect on personal religion was relatively slight. The dominant influence in shaping the faith and morality of the Jews was that which was

[1] v. *Against Apion*, Book i.   [2] v. *Hellenistic Civilization*, p. 188.
[3] v. *Roman Society from Nero to Marcus Aurelius*, p. 83.

ever at hand. Effective guidance had passed from the central sacrificial system at Jerusalem to the recently established organization of the Scribes, that is, to those who were the students of the Law, and who expounded it in the synagogues every Sabbath. The famous sects of the Pharisees and Sadducees, whose rivalry gave distinctive character to Jewish politics and so deeply coloured the Synoptic narratives, found in the Temple and the Synagogue their respective instruments of influence. While the Pharisees controlled the Synagogue, the Sadducees controlled the Temple.

The Synagogue system, we learn from the New Testament, was firmly established in Galilee, where Jesus was brought up, and where, save for occasional visits to Jerusalem, He spent His whole life. He had been trained to attend the weekly services, and during His public ministry He was accustomed to avail Himself of the generous liberty which marked the action of the Jewish authorities. He taught in the synagogues without protest or hindrance. Now the Synagogue was pre-eminently an instrument of Biblical interpretation and moral teaching. The methods of Scriptural interpretation and ethical teaching which were adopted in the synagogues were those which are commonly described as Rabbinical. They attempted to provide a solution of the difficult problem which every ancient sacred literature presents to those who accept it as religiously authoritative, viz. the harmonizing of the inevitable crudity, theological and moral, of ancient scriptures with the accepted modern standards of faith and morality, and they offered an elaborated casuistry which professed to make it possible for the devout and obedient

Jew to bring his entire life under the control of his religious belief. We have to remember that the Rabbis, less fortunate than their modern successors, did not possess the knowledge with which religious students are now commonly equipped.

Ethnology and comparative religion did not yet illumine the study of religion and ethics. They could not apply the key of development to unlock the Scripture. They knew nothing of Biblical criticism, 'higher' or 'lower'. They were confronted by the sacred text in its naked crudity, divinely inspired, finally authoritative, and they had to discover some method by which, without derogating from its authority, they should be able to make it tolerable to men who had long outgrown its tribal conceptions of God and His demands on men. Accordingly they had recourse to the bold and dangerous theory of an 'Unwritten Torah', which with equal authority and convenient elasticity should stand beside the canonical writings, mitigating, correcting, and even disallowing the teaching which it professed only to explicate and adapt. The written law was rigid in form, and limited in range; but the unwritten tradition was neither. It could expand indefinitely as the exigencies of experience, or the general sentiment, or the intuitions of individuals might suggest. It did expand in course of time into the enormous mass of the Talmudic literature. The casuistry which was based on the 'Unwritten Torah' aspired to cover the whole area of human experience, and to equip the pious Jew with a complete manual of behaviour which should suffice for his guidance in all the myriad contingencies of life in the world.

Inevitably Rabbinical casuistry became, as at a far later time, under similar conditions, the casuistry of the medieval and Jesuit moralists became, over subtle, voluminous, morally enfeebling. The individual conscience, oppressed by the multitude of precise directions, lost perception of the governing principles, and became inadequate to its true and incommunicable function. It is indeed easy for the modern student to be unfair to the rabbis, and, in his unavoidable dislike of their cumbrous and arbitrary methods, to belittle their actual achievements. Yet these were certainly not inconsiderable. Within the period of time covered by the canonical scriptures it is apparent that, under the influence of the Prophets, there had been a notable advance in theology and ethics. We may not reasonably suppose that that advance was arrested when the prophetic succession ceased. On the contrary, there appear to be strong reasons for thinking that the period immediately preceding the Christian era did in some respects witness an important development in Jewish religion. The worship of the Synagogue was on a higher spiritual plane than that of the Temple; and the morality of the Jews, when brought by the coercions of history into direct relation with that of the Gentile world, was both emphasized and extended. In three main directions the development of Judaism may be perceived. In the first place, religion ceased to be regarded as essentially concerned with the community, and came to be recognized as primarily individual. There was in this respect a parallel between the Jew and the Greek. Individualism in the ancient world was the product of political disintegration. It was so with the Greeks when, after the conquests of Alexander, the self-governing city-state fell into decay. It was not less so with the Jews after the national state and the temple had perished. The teachings of Jeremiah and Ezekiel, which reflected their bitter experiences of national downfall and Babylonian exile, had been taken to heart, and the more devout and thoughtful Jews had come to realize that religion and morality are primarily personal, that a holy nation cannot really exist apart from holy citizens.

In the next place, following naturally from this personalizing of religion, there developed a belief in the life beyond the grave. For if, indeed, religion and morality found their expression in personal behaviour, then it followed that within the range of personal experience these must receive their proper vindication. During their long sojourn in Babylonia and as subjects of the Persian Empire the Jews could not have failed to gain knowledge of doctrines respecting a future life in which men would surely receive the due recompense of their earthly conduct. The persecution of Antiochus Epiphanes had multiplied martyrs; and every martyr had unwittingly but none the less effectively challenged the narrow ancestral creed. How could it be reconciled with the Justice of Jehovah that righteous Jews who had been loyal to His cause even unto death should pass unrecognized and unrewarded from the scenes of their witness? Belief in the Resurrection of individuals and a Final Judgement had become established elements of Jewish religion when Jesus was born.

Finally, Jewish religion in becoming personal could not remain merely Jewish. Its range was seen to be conterminous with moral activity, and that was wide as humanity itself. 'The spirit of man is the candle of the Lord' was an aphorism of Scripture which carried far. It followed that the Lord's claim and the possibility of responding to it must in some true sense be universal. The national election of Israel was increasingly conceived of in a broadly human context. Election was the Divine method of the world's redemption. The Jews were called and ordained to be the priests of mankind. But this larger conception of spiritual mission did not disallow or replace the older doctrine of national election. In the future as in the past, though with a cosmic reference, the Jews were to remain the privileged race, Jehovah's chosen people.

A twofold process disclosed itself—on the one hand, a deepening of the sense of the uniqueness of Judaism together with an almost fanatical insistence on whatever in it differentiated the Jews from the rest of mankind; and, on the other hand, an eager propagandism which aspired to Judaize mankind. 'To understand what Judaism was at the beginning of the Christian era it is necessary to bear in mind the twofold character of nationality and universality which had been inseparably impressed upon it by its history.'[1]

In the period immediately preceding the Christian era the Jews became indefatigable propagandists. Their missionary efforts were attended with considerable success. Large numbers of thoughtful Gentiles, to whom the absurdities of the reigning polytheism were intellectually repugnant, and whose consciences revolted against the vileness of pagan morals, were attracted by

[1] v. Moore, *Judaism*, i. 219.

the simple creed and high morality of the Jews. Every synagogue became a missionary centre, gathering about it those who professed admiration for Judaism, accepted the main lines of its creed, read with appreciation its sacred scriptures, frequented its religious assemblies, and subjected themselves in some measure to its discipline. In a remarkable passage Josephus claims that the homage of such partial acceptance was freely rendered to Jewish faith and practice:

'The masses have long since shown a keen desire to adopt our religious observances; and there is not one city, Greek or barbarian, nor a single nation, to which our custom of abstaining from work on the seventh day has not spread, and where the fasts, and the lighting of lamps and many of our prohibitions in the matter of food are not observed. Moreover, they attempt to imitate our unanimity, our liberal charities, our devoted labour in the crafts, our endurance under persecution on behalf of our laws. The greatest miracle of all is that our Law holds out no seductive bait of sensual pleasure, but has exercised this influence through its own inherent merits; and as God permeates the universe, so the Law has found its way among all mankind.'[1]

The treatise *Against Apion*, from which this passage is extracted, is thought to have been composed about the beginning of the second century, but it describes a situation which must have existed long before. Josephus is a writer whose statements must always be to some extent discounted by his situation, but he could hardly have expressed himself so confidently if he had not been sure of his ground.

In recent years great attention has been directed to

[1] v. *Against Apion*, ii. 282–4.

the remarkable literature which made its appearance
among the Jews during the distressful period between
the persecution of Antiochus Epiphanes and the beginning of the Christian era. This apocalyptic literature is
represented within the body of Jewish canonical Scripture by the Book of Daniel. It has been recovered from a
long oblivion by the labours of modern scholars, among
whom in Great Britain the late Dr. Charles was the
most conspicuous representative. These compositions
were written in Hebrew, but they have only survived
in Greek versions, a circumstance which may indicate
that they had but little circulation in Palestine. They
are concerned with the Divine Economy, emphasize
the moral requirements of Jewish religion, stimulate
patriotism by assurances of final triumph over the
Gentile oppressor, and foretell the course of the future
by means of mysterious and bizarre symbols. After the
strange literary fashion of the age, these apocalyptic
books are for the most part pseudo-epigraphical, being
attributed to famous individuals of the national past.
Most of them never gained admission to the Jewish
Canon of Scripture, and, indeed, owed their survival
mainly to Christian students, interested for polemical
reasons in Jewish compositions whose Messianic teaching accorded so easily with the current doctrine of
the Church. We are interested in them as providing
evidence of the morality which the Christian religion
found ready to its hand. They also have an apparent
bearing on the question how far we may rightly regard
the moral teaching of Jesus as original.

It is, perhaps, not wholly superfluous to enter a
caveat against the exaggerated language in which the

ethical teaching of these Jewish books is often described. We may take as a sufficient example the case of that apocryphal book which is confessedly the best illustration of such teaching. *The Testament of the Twelve Patriarchs* was written in Hebrew, if we accept the authority of Dr. Charles, between the years 109 and 106 B.C., thus preceding the life and teaching of Jesus by more than a century.

'The main, the overwhelming value of the Book', we are assured, 'lies in its ethical teaching, which has achieved a real immortality by influencing the thought and diction of the writers of the New Testament, and even those of our Lord. This ethical teaching, which is very much higher and purer than that of the Old Testament, is yet its true spiritual child, and helps to bridge the chasm that divides the ethics of the Old and New Testaments.'[1]

Dr. Travers Herford describes the book as 'a treasure of noble teaching, one conspicuous illustration of what Judaism could produce at its best'.[2] It is admitted that the book contains Christian interpolations, and this circumstance must induce a measure of caution in accepting its statements at face value, but we are assured by Dr. Charles that the interpolations are so clearly marked by their dogmatic character that they are easily detected, and that 'the only reasonable conclusion is that these ethical teachings belong to the original Testaments'.[3] Nevertheless, the moral quality of a book is not to be determined by a few lofty passages which may be but little representative of the composition as a whole. We must ask what is the final and cumulative

[1] v. Oxford ed. ii. 282.
[2] v. *Talmud and Apocrypha*, p. 236.   [3] v. Charles, op. cit., p. 291.

impression of the book, what would be its probable influence on a reader who had no special reason for separating the wheat from the chaff.

Regarded in this way, the lofty estimate of the *Testaments of the Twelve Patriarchs* is, perhaps, somewhat surprising. Taken as a whole the book is verbose, tiresome, and ill arranged. It is a long book, filling, with Dr. Charles's footnotes, no less than 64 of the large pages of the Oxford edition. Very few of these pages are concerned with the great ethical themes—Forgiveness, the Two Great Commandments, Universalism—which Dr. Charles enumerates, and he omits to point out the general effect of the context in which these subjects are presented. Thus the famous exhortation to forgiveness—'a unique passage in ancient literature on the subject' as Dr. Charles asserts, and worthy in his opinion to be placed alongside the teachings of Christ—hardly seems so impressive when read in its context. Following the plan of the book, the Patriarch Gad gives his dying admonitions to his descendants. He accuses himself of hating his brother Joseph, and being led by his hatred into the great wickedness of joining his brethren in the plot against Joseph's life. Accordingly he warns his descendants against hatred, and elaborates the ill consequences which follow from its indulgence. He offers himself as the illustration of his warnings.

'For God brought upon me a disease of the liver,[1] and had not the prayers of Jacob my father succoured me, it had hardly failed but my spirit had departed. For by what things a man transgresseth, by the same also is he punished. Since, therefor,

[1] According to ancient notions the liver was the seat of love, and of violent passions generally.

my liver was set mercilessly against Joseph, in my liver too I suffered mercilessly, and was judged for eleven months, for so long a time as I had been angry against Joseph.'

Then follows the famous passage on the subject of forgiveness. It runs thus in Dr. Charles's rendering:

'And now, my children, I exhort you, love ye each one his brother, and put away hatred from your hearts, love one another in deed, and in word, and in the inclination of the soul. For in the presence of my father I spake peaceably to Joseph; and when I had gone out, the spirit of hatred darkened my mind, and stirred up my soul to slay him. Love ye one another from the heart, and if a man sin against thee, speak peaceably to him, and in thy soul hold not guile; and if he repent and confess, forgive him. But if he deny it, do not get into a passion with him, lest catching the poison from thee he take to swearing and so thou sin doubly.'

Here follows a passage which is marked as an interpolation, and then the Testament proceeds:

'And though he deny it and yet have a sense of shame when reproved, give over reproving him. For he who denieth may repent so as not again to wrong thee; yea, he may also honour thee, and be at peace with thee. And if he be shameless and persist in his wrong-doing, even so forgive him from the heart, and leave to God the avenging.'

A paragraph warning against the envying of other men's good fortune follows, and then the Testament ends conventionally:

'Do ye also tell these things to your children, that they honour Judah and Levi, for from them shall the Lord raise up salvation to Israel. And when he had rested for a little while, he said again: My children, obey your father, and bury me near to my fathers. And he drew up his feet, and fell asleep in peace.'

'While this and similar passages read like genuine parts of the original work', observes Dr. Oesterley, 'the *possibility* that they may be Christian is not excluded.'[1] Without for one moment claiming the authority of an expert, I hold myself free as a mere student to express the view that this fine passage on forgiveness, if not actually a Christian interpolation, owes most of its impressiveness for modern readers to the Christian ideas which unwittingly they read into it. In any case, it is apparent that its ethical quality will turn on the point whether it is, or is not, limited in its application. The patriarch is pictured as addressing his children, and when he bids them 'love each one his brother', it is natural to suppose that he designs his counsel to have a limited reference. He has in mind the relations of Jews to fellow Jews, not of Jews to men as such. Moreover, this view of his meaning accords with the sharply accentuated nationalism of the book as a whole. It is inspired throughout by an intense nationalist sentiment, and although a vague sentence here and there appears to give the Gentiles some share in the ultimate triumph of righteousness, the general attitude towards Gentiles is one of hatred and loathing.

When we are invited to compare this apocryphal book with the New Testament in respect of its moral teaching, we cannot reasonably limit the comparison to selected passages which may not be really representative. We must form an opinion of the ethical quality of the book as a whole. There are some grave blemishes which cannot be omitted from a just estimate. The references to women in the Testaments are invariably

[1] v. *The Books of the Apocrypha*, p. 214.

dishonouring. They are presented as the cunning, pertinacious, unscrupulous temptresses of men. If this repulsive picture reflected an ascetic severity, it would at least be intelligible, but it obviously expresses nothing more respectable than that low estimate of the female sex distinctive of inferior cultures, which regards women as no more than the servitors of men's sensual indulgence, and the necessary instruments for providing them with offspring.

The detailed emphasis with which sins of impurity are dwelt upon gives an unpleasing colour to the book. Of the nine pages which contain the testament of Joseph no less than six are filled with a highly elaborated account of his experiences in the house of Potiphar! This unpleasant feature is the more surprising since, as we shall have occasion to notice, a most valuable part of the Jewish legacy of moral teaching which Christianity inherited was a relatively high standard of family life. How sharply does the unwholesome obsession with sexual sin in the Testaments contrast with the purity of the Gospels, and the reticence which marks the treatment of the subject in the New Testament!

There remains to be considered the light which the New Testament itself can cast on the Judaism of the first century. In his classic work on *Judaism*, a monument of massive learning and lucid exposition, Dr. Moore, of Harvard University, attaches high importance to the testimony of the New Testament.

'The Gospels themselves are the best witness to the religious and moral teaching of the synagogue in the middle forty years of the first century, and the not infrequent references, with approval or dissent, to the current Halakah are evidence of the rules approved in the schools of the Law and taught to the people. It is this relation between the Gospels and the teaching of the rabbis, whether tacitly assumed or criticised and controverted, which makes them the important source they are for a knowledge of the Judaism of their time, and on the other hand makes the rabbinical sources the important instrument they are for the understanding of the Gospels. The Gospels with the first part of the Acts of the Apostles are thus witnesses to authentic Jewish tradition, while the apocalypses (and the kindred element in the Gospels) represent groups, or at least tendencies, outside the main current of thought and life.'[1]

Dr. Travers Herford, whose authority is deservedly held in high regard, is more concerned with vindicating the trustworthiness of the picture of Jewish morality in the time of Christ which the rabbinical literature can provide. He points out with obvious justice that the general ignorance of Hebrew has hindered most English scholars from making full use of this literature, and he has placed all students of the New Testament under heavy obligations by exerting himself to place at their disposal his own extensive and accurate knowledge. He has to face what he calls 'the plausible objection very often made that the Rabbinic literature is almost entirely of later date than the New Testament period, and therefore cannot be used as a witness of what was current belief in the time of Jesus'. The objection, however, is not less sound than plausible. Without questioning the legitimacy of his argument, I must needs think that it is inadequate for his purpose. We may not safely or reasonably forget that between Jesus and the formulated Judaism of the rabbis there lies the tremendous crisis which, by destroying the Temple, brought to an end the

[1] v. *Judaism*, i. 132.

immemorial sacrificial system which the Temple had expressed, and, by blotting out the Jewish state from the map of the civilized world, gave a new and deeper significance to Jewish nationalism. The effect on Jewish thought must of necessity have been profound, but how far it has coloured the rabbinic tradition must be a matter of speculation.

In a previous lecture I have stated shortly the reasons which have led me to think that the New Testament is a genuine product of the first century and contains historical evidence of the first quality. Its authority, where it can be adduced, is, in my judgement, final. The circumstance that its authors were Christians does not appear to me to invalidate their evidence on matters of fact respecting which they may fairly be thought to have had full knowledge. If we would appraise justly the prevailing moral standard of the Jews of the first century, we may, I submit, accept with confidence the testimony of the New Testament. We know well enough that even the grossest moral confusions bred of superstition do not lack plausible theoretical apologies; but the test of a moral system must finally be found in the field of actual conduct. What was the moral quality of the society which had been disciplined by the Pharisees? How far was it able to secure the endorsement of Jesus?

On the whole, the impartial student of the New Testament will be favourably impressed by the picture of Jewish society which the Evangelists present. Jesus was evidently in substantial accord with the Galileans among whom He had been brought up. He did not find it necessary to challenge the general habit. No glaring

vices such as those which confronted St. Paul in the
Graeco-Roman cities moved Him to denunciation.
Fundamentally the morals of the Jewish community
were sound. The people were religious, industrious,
clean-living, law-abiding, self-respecting. The circumstance that He was able to move freely about the country,
welcomed in the synagogues, and everywhere listened
to with respect, is conclusive evidence that between
Himself and His contemporaries in Galilee there was
a fundamental harmony of faith and feeling. His
quarrel was with their nationalist prejudices, their
mundane obsessions, their literalism, and the perverted
moral perspective which confused their consciences.
The specimens of His teaching which have come down
to us confirm this account. For the most part they assume a fundamental harmony of moral presuppositions,
and build on it, as on a sure foundation, that larger and
loftier conception of religion and its practical expressions which He illustrated by His life. His teaching
was given in familiar language. It is said, no doubt with
some exaggeration, but certainly with substantial truth,
that 'parallels can be found in the Rabbinical literature
for perhaps as much as 90 per cent. of the recorded
sayings of Jesus'.[1] Klausner would almost claim that
Jesus was Himself a Pharisee, and insists that 'the most
conscious influence on Him was that same Pharisaism
through opposition to which Christianity came into
being.'[2] His favourite method of teaching by parable
was not original, but well established in the use of
Jewish teachers. In His hands, indeed, that method

[1] v. *Judaism in the New Testament*, by H. Travers Herford, p. 187.
[2] v. *Jesus of Nazareth*, p. 222.

acquired a range of spiritual reference and a perfection
of form which it has never attained before or since He
used it, but in adopting it He was following precedent,
and probably drawing on a fund of parabolic wisdom.
The originality of His teaching is to be perceived,
not in the novelty of His language or in His disdain
of conventional didactic methods, but in its spirit
and tendency. Here the difference between Jesus and
the Pharisees was apparent and complete. His was
a ministry of intellectual and moral enfranchisement,
which took up the witness of the greater prophets of
the nation and gave to it a just and noble development.
Thus He broke the paralysing bonds of Pharisaic
legalism, and released into action the imprisoned sympathies of men's hearts. The broad character of His
mission was significantly indicated at the beginning of
His public career as it is described by St. Luke. The
scene is pictured with dramatic power, and the narrative
suggests the vivid impressions of an eyewitness:

'And he came to Nazareth, where he had been brought up:
and he entered, as his custom was, into the synagogue on the
sabbath day, and stood up to read. And there was delivered
unto him the book of the prophet Isaiah. And he opened the
book, and found the place where it was written,

The Spirit of the Lord is upon me,
Because he anointed me to preach good tidings to the
poor:
He hath sent me to proclaim release to the captives,
And recovering of sight to the blind,
To set at liberty them that are bruised,
To proclaim the acceptable year of the Lord.

And he closed the book, and gave it back to the attendant, and
sat down: and the eyes of all in the synagogue were fastened on

him. And he began to say unto them, To-day hath this scripture been fulfilled in your ears.'[1]

His quarrel was with the religious teachers of the people who were primarily responsible for the popular notions of faith and duty—the Scribes and Pharisees. With these He came into open conflict, and upon these He pronounced censures of the utmost severity. The twenty-third chapter of the Gospel according to St. Matthew records the indictment which Jesus preferred against the spiritual leaders of the Jewish people. How far that indictment ought to be ascribed to Jesus Himself, and how far to disciples who had but an inadequate understanding of His mind, has been much debated by the critics. It is significant that it is prefaced by an emphatic recognition of the official authority of those whom it so sternly condemns. The disciples are bidden to attempt the difficult combination of public submission and private condemnation.

'Then spake Jesus to the multitudes and to his disciples, saying, The scribes and Pharisees sit on Moses' seat: all things therefore whatsoever they bid you, these do and observe: but do not ye after their works; for they say, and do not.'

There appears to be general agreement that the substance of the 'Seven Woes' belongs to the earliest element of the Synoptic tradition, so that its historical character cannot be reasonably questioned. It discloses what was the attitude which Jesus adopted towards the Pharisaism which He encountered. Was that attitude justified? Given the historical trustworthiness of the record, and the faithfulness of the portrait of Jesus

---

[1] St. Luke iv. 16–21.

which that record conveys, we cannot doubt that it was. 'It is not worth while', writes that learned and candid Jewish scholar, Klausner, 'to deny all these things and, like most Jewish scholars with an apologetic bias, assert that they are nothing but inventions.'[1] He insists, with reason, that the faults which Jesus denounced in the religious leaders of His time were precisely those which are likely to disclose themselves in every religious system, and which certainly have not been lacking in the Christian Church. He protests with justice against the assumption that 'the Scribes and Pharisees hypocrites' against whom Jesus pronounced the Seven Woes were true representatives of Judaism as a whole:

'What would be thought by Christian scholars were we to judge Christianity not by its Founder, nor its early fathers and saints who died a martyr's death, but by the many hypocritical and canting Christians who have flourished in every generation. A religion and a sect should be judged by the principles it expounds and by the best of its teachers rather than by its unworthy members: it should be judged by the best that it contains and not by the worst.'[2]

For our present purpose, however, the moral quality of the Scribes and Pharisees has little importance, nor are we much concerned with the critical discussion. The legacy of morality which Christianity inherited from Judaism was that which was taught in the synagogues, and illustrated in the lives of common folk. These were for the most part outside the formal disciplines of the Scribes and Pharisees, whose religious authority they owned. The rabbinic leaders retained their authority among the Jews, but for Christians it

[1] v. *Jesus of Nazareth*, p. 213.   [2] op. cit., p. 215.

had been finally disallowed by the sentence of Jesus. 'Rabbinism', says Dr. Travers Herford, 'is concentrated and intensified Judaism.' The 'common ground' of Jewish ethical teaching formed the starting-point both of Christian morality and of 'the colossal fabric reared by the Rabbinical teachers'. Jesus stood at the parting of the ways, and the two streams of moral development flowed in different directions, becoming as time passed ever more widely parted. The story of deepening alienation is pictured by the fortunes of the American rivers which, rising together in the Yellowstone Park, divide immediately, and move northwards and southwards: the one destined, after long wandering, to pour its swollen stream into the sub-arctic ocean, the other to discharge its mighty flood, replenished by a thousand tributaries, into the Gulf of Mexico:

> From the same cradle side,
>   From the same mother's knee,
> One to long darkness and the frozen tide,
>   One to the silver sea.

Rabbinism shrivelled into the negation of charity: Christianity became its confessed and inexhaustible spring.

IV

JESUS AND JUDAISM

CHRISTIANITY received the Jewish legacy of morality at the hands of Jesus. His teaching and His example confirmed, interpreted, corrected, and expanded the traditional doctrine of His nation. It was early observed with astonishment by His contemporaries that His tone and manner were without precedent. At the conclusion of the Sermon on the Mount we read that 'the multitudes were astonished at His teaching, for He taught them as one having authority, and not as their scribes'. What was there in the carriage and method of Jesus that gave His hearers this impression of unique authority? In the valuable *Studies in Pharisaism and the Gospels* by Mr. Abrahams this question is discussed at some length. He is not contented with the usual explanation which suggests that the populace were struck by the neglect of precedents which marked the teaching of Jesus, for he doubts whether the Talmudical method, 'with its scholastic adhesion to precedents', had been developed so early, and, in any case, points out that 'there was all along a popular exegesis besides the scholastic', and claims that 'Hillel, the greatest of the predecessors of Jesus, taught almost without reference to precedent'. But Jesus belonged to none of the existing Jewish parties, and, says Mr. Abrahams, 'it was perhaps just his eclecticism, his independence of any particular school, that is implied by the contrast between Jesus' teaching and that of the Scribes'. Here was a religious teacher who did not hesitate to speak in His own name, deliberately assuming the right to interpret and revise what was traditional and established. 'Ye have heard that it was said to them of old time', so ran His astonishing formula, 'but I say unto you'. Mr. Abrahams comments:

'Jesus spoke without reference to any mediate authority. To the Scribes it became an ever more sacred duty to cite the original authority for any saying, if it were consciously derived from another teacher. Such reference was an obligation which attained even Messianic import. "He who says a word in the name of its author brings Redemption to the world." Verify your quotations is C. Taylor's comment.'[1]

Here is the difference precisely stated. The Scribes rightly verified their quotations, because apart from those quotations they had no right to give any teaching at all. Jesus could ignore 'authorities' because He did not quote, but, in the full franchise of spiritual originality, could 'speak with authority'.

Professor Guignebert appears to take much the same view of the authority of Jesus which so impressed the hearers of His teaching:

'The meaning seems to be that he broke away—for good reason—from the form of teaching established in the schools: that he did not necessarily base his preaching upon a text of the Scriptures to be interpreted and commented upon: and that he did not cite the evidence of famous rabbis, but that his own inspiration was all he had need of, even when he appealed to the Book, and the freedom, the homeliness, and the spontaneity of his words were hampered by nothing, not even the attempt to organize them, because they were inspired and justified by an irresistible inner force.'[2]

[1] v. *Studies in Pharisaism and the Gospels*, 1st series, pp. 13–17.
[2] v. *Jesus*, p. 247.

Professor Guignebert is an extreme rationalist. He applies his critical principle (which we believe to be essentially unsound) so rigorously as to reduce the authentic tradition of Jesus preserved in the Synoptic Gospels to the most meagre proportions, yet even he cannot wholly escape the impression of a supreme spiritual master which that tradition conveys. He sees that Jesus cannot be fitted into any of the religious categories of His age, for He transcends them all. Belittlement and homage blend in his final conclusion:

'To sum up, Jesus appears to us as a belated scion of the Prophets. Such a description is the best explanation of the fact that while at heart as much a Jew as any man could be, he appears, even allowing for the misrepresentations of the Evangelists, to differ considerably from the various *types* into which Israel of that time seems at first sight to be divided. He is different from the Sadducee, the Pharisee, the Essene, the scribe, the zealot, the revolutionary always ready to fly to arms, the dreamer obsessed by his apocalyptic fantasy. Clearly his object was neither to destroy, nor properly speaking to reform, the Jewish religion, but to introduce into it as a predominant influence a certain spirit, the active principle, if we may so call it, of the profound faith which is in him, and of the supreme hope which he proclaims.'[1]

To students less hidebound by critical theory than the French savant this conclusion must needs appear halting and inadequate, but so far as it goes it is sound, and it properly implies far more than it actually says.

We must always bear in mind that the authority with which Christians from the first clothed the teachings of Jesus was far greater than any which the first hearers of those teachings could have imagined. To His

[1] v. *Jesus*, p. 312.

Galilean audiences He was at most a religious teacher, uniquely impressive and enigmatic, who disdained to use the familiar methods of winning attention to His words, but to the Christian congregations listening for the first time to the Synoptic Gospels, Jesus was a Divine Person, Who, in the words of His greatest disciple, the Apostle Paul, had been 'declared to be the Son of God with power, according to the spirit of holiness, by the resurrection of the dead'.[1] Between those first days of ministry in Galilee and the emergence of Christianity on the plane of history stood the awful events which concluded the life of Jesus, and these threw back on the previous ministry a significance and an authority which at the time it could not have possessed. For the serious student of history faith is a fact which can never be left out of reckoning. In this new attitude of submission and worship we have the key to Christian developments, theological and ethical. Every variant from the Jewish tradition which the Synoptic records contained, and which they ascribed to the direct influence of Jesus, acquired immediately an unquestioned title to Christian acceptance. Even Professor Guignebert permits himself to make an exception from the ruthless scepticism of his general attitude towards the Synoptic Gospels in favour of the moral teaching of Jesus. Here the developing orthodoxy of the Church, which, it is suggested, was destined to obliterate the history of Jesus almost completely, found little to object against:

'The development of the faith did not find all the teachings ascribed by the tradition to Jesus equally hampering. The

[1] Romans i. 4.

value of his precepts concerning morality and practical life, for instance, remained the same, or even increased, in proportion as emphasis on the deification of the Saviour increased.'[1]

Thus the Christian Church entered on its historic course with a twofold endowment of moral teaching, the Jewish legacy and the teaching of Jesus. The first was interpreted and expanded by the last. Original Christian morality was the synthesis of traditional Judaism and the teaching of Jesus. What, then, we must ask, did Jesus add to the moral tradition in which He had been brought up, and which He accepted as the foundation of His own teaching?

We, like His own contemporaries, are at once arrested on the threshold of our inquiry by the question raised by the manner of His moral teaching. In the strict sense He was neither a legislator nor a casuist, and if His words be treated with the preciseness which would be proper to laws and casuistic rules, they are likely to be dangerously misunderstood and misapplied. The scandals of Christian literalism are scattered thickly through Christian history. Both in ancient and in modern times the critics of Christianity have found in the contrast between the precepts of the Gospel and the normal habit of Christians material for sarcasm and denunciation. Julian the Apostate is said to have represented his anti-Christian measures as no more than reasonable attempts to recall Christians to the forgotten but indisputable obligations of their religion. On this hypocritical plea he could confiscate ecclesiastical property and forbid Christians to hold civil office. In modern times, at least since the time of Voltaire, the

[1] v. *Jesus*, p. 241.

popularity of the Quakers with the enemies of Christianity has not been unconnected with the desire to find in Quaker literalism a stick wherewith to beat the general body of Christian folk. Ascetics have ever been literalists, though their literalist exegesis of the Gospel has been as inconsistent as it has been confident. So strangely have they distorted the moral teaching of the Son of Man that the example of Him Who said of Himself that He 'came eating and drinking', mixing freely with His fellow men, and noted to be particularly at home with women and children, has been represented as requiring a severe self-exile from normal society. The imagination of Christendom has been kindled by the tender legend of St. Francis, who seemed to reproduce in medieval Italy the very details of the life of Jesus in ancient Palestine.

Quite recently a vast assembly in the Albert Hall in London was moved to enthusiasm by the passionate plea of an ascetic missionary that Christians should 'naked follow the naked Christ'. This fervour is not without moral value, but it is alien to the main tenor of Christian thinking and practice. It was not in that way that the Apostolic Church understood the teaching of Jesus. On this point the witness of St. Paul's Epistles is decisive. The Apostle himself was in his temperament and habit of life ascetic: he could appeal from the calumniators of his character to the evidence of a personal career which was notoriously filled with labour, privation, and persecution, but he definitely refused to offer himself as exemplary to his converts in that respect. On the contrary he bade them find in the experiences of normal life in society the sufficient instruments by which to demonstrate discipleship. His great dogmatic epistles have ever an epilogue of sober practical admonition. On two occasions he makes appeal to the authority of the Lord's personal directions, and in neither case is that supreme authority adduced on the side of asceticism. In the one, Jesus insists that Christians are not to make their profession a reason for repudiating the obligations of the marriage union;[1] in the other, the Lord ordains that the Church shall provide maintenance for the preachers of the Gospel.[2] To these we may add his quotation of a saying of Jesus in his address to the presbyters of Asia on the beach of Miletus, a saying which inculcates almsgiving, and implies the presupposition of almsgiving, viz. private property—'In all things I gave you an example, how that so labouring ye ought to help the weak, and to remember the words of the Lord Jesus, how He Himself said, It is more blessed to give than to receive.' Marriage, a settled ministry, separated for its work and maintained by the Church, almsgiving—these imply a Christian society which has accepted subordination to the normal conditions of life in the world. Christianity realized from the beginning that it was designed to be, not the private cultus of a small sect, but the religion of the human race.

We have already pointed out that Jesus was neither a legislator nor a casuist. He wrote nothing, and the knowledge of His teaching which has come down to us is contained in anonymous compositions, which, albeit, as we maintain, trustworthy authorities for the main lines of His life and witness, must be read with dis-

---

[1] 1 Cor. vii. 10, 11.   [2] v. 1 Cor. ix. 14.

crimination, if they are to be rightly understood. The amount of His teaching preserved by the Evangelists is not great.

'It has been computed', observes Professor Guignebert, 'that it would have taken no more than an hour for Jesus to utter all the *sayings* of his that we possess, and not more than six hours, the time required for two parliamentary speeches of average length, for him to deliver all the discourses attributed to him in the Gospels.'[1]

Happily it is the case that the sufficiency of ethical teaching has but slight relation to its extent. The modern community in which laws are the most numerous is notoriously that in which they are most despised and disregarded.

We may not, therefore, reasonably seek in the Gospels for laws and casuistic rules, but although these be wanting, we cannot fail to perceive what was the general attitude which Jesus adopted, the spirit which inspired His teaching, and the moral ideal which found expression in His life. The distinctiveness of His didactic method which amazed His hearers implied a rejection of the very basis of Pharisaism. 'What then really was the ground of opposition between Jesus and the Pharisees?' asks that doughty apologist of Pharisaism, Mr. Travers Herford, and he answers:

'In a sentence it was this:—he repudiated the whole system of the Halachah; and he criticized, and on occasion rejected, the Torah upon which the Halachah was based.'[2]

To postulate, as the Pharisees did, an 'unwritten Torah' which should stand alongside the Scripture as a coequal

---

[1] v. *Jesus*, p. 233.
[2] *Judaism in the New Testament Period*, p. 205.

authority was in effect to subject the Scripture to that authority, and, since the limits and the practical application of the 'unwritten Torah' were committed to the Scribes, their position, which was that of the Pharisees, did really, as on a memorable occasion Jesus asserted, 'make the word of God of none effect'.

Judaism did but illustrate the common fortune of all religions which have recourse to unwritten tradition to harmonize Scriptures held to be Divine with the irresistible and multiplying requirements of life. The general law has nowhere been more strikingly illustrated than in the case of Christianity. The Roman Catholic Church, following the precedent of the rabbis, has placed tradition alongside the Scripture as a coequal authority. In the event of a conflict between the text and the tradition the victory must always lie with the latter, since it speaks with a more recent and more relevant authority. Inasmuch as the Canon of Scripture is closed, no mitigating epilogue can be added, and since the authority of Scripture is Divine, no correcting gloss can be allowed. But tradition is more accommodating, and not less authoritative. It grows with a thousand circumstances, and is as manysided as the needs it aspires to satisfy. Moreover, since its transmission and formulation are vested in the society whose tradition it is, there is no avoiding the consequence that the Scripture must become completely subordinated to the tradition. The dogma of papal infallibility, which marks the high-water mark of traditional supremacy over the written word, provides a luminous instance of Christian rabbinism.

It is to be noted that the experience of Jesus did not

qualify Him for the rôle with which Christians have so often insisted on crediting Him. He lived and died in an obscure and backward part of the Roman Empire. He belonged to a humble class, and spoke Aramaic, which was the current popular speech of His fellow Galileans, and, like the Celtic tongue which has lingered in the Highlands, in Wales, and in western parts of Ireland, formed, for those who had no other, a barricade against the wider culture of the age. He had not been educated in any of the recognized centres of learning; He had not pursued any avocation which would widen His outlook, and bring Him into personal contact with the greater movements of the civilized world; when He entered on His public ministry as a religious teacher He found the main sphere of His activity among the simple and unlettered rustics and fisherfolk of His native Galilee. All this did not provide what might be called the normal equipment for a lawgiver and a moral philosopher. How different has been the secular framework within which the greater moral teachers have shaped and delivered their doctrine! The founder of Buddhism came of a noble stock, and garnered his knowledge of mankind from varied experience and extensive travel. Confucius was an educated man who had been employed in public affairs and was familiar with royal courts. Mohammed had a chequered career, which brought him into touch with all sorts and conditions of men, and compelled him to face the problems of society and government. Socrates lived in Athens during its brief golden age. Plato, Aristotle, Seneca, St. Paul, Marcus Aurelius, St. Augustine—all thought and taught under conditions which could not but give them exceptional opportunities for studying human nature, and becoming acquainted with the amazing variety of human circumstance. It would be easy to multiply illustrations of the general rule that the greater moral teachers of the world have been assisted in their task by the secular framework of their lives. With Jesus the case was far otherwise. It was neither as a lawgiver nor as a moral philosopher that He would so influence the ethical development of mankind as to 'make all things new'. He accepted the current morality of His nation, which was that which the Scribes had deduced from the Scriptures, and which was expounded in the synagogues every Sabbath. Of this morality the Pharisees were the most conspicuous, consistent, and respected representatives. The Synoptic Gospels are unintelligible apart from their Jewish background, and at every point the teaching of Jesus presupposes that of the Scribes and Pharisees.

Klausner hardly exaggerates when he says that

'throughout the Gospels there is not one item of ethical teaching which cannot be paralleled either in the Old Testament, the Apocrypha, or in the Talmudic and Midrashic literature of the period near to the time of Jesus.'[1]

Klausner, however, is too honest a writer not to admit that, though the items separately may be paralleled, the combination is unique:

'But there is a new thing in the Gospels. Jesus, who concerned himself with neither *Halakha* nor the secular knowledge requisite for *Halakha*, nor (except to a limited extent) with scriptural exposition—Jesus gathered together and, so to speak, condensed and concentrated ethical teachings in such a fashion

[1] *Jesus of Nazareth*, p. 384.

as to make them more prominent than in the *Talmudic Haggada* and the *Midrashim*, where they are interspersed among more commonplace discussions and worthless matter. Even in the Old Testament, and particularly in the Pentateuch, where moral teaching is so prominent, and so purged, and so lofty, this teaching is yet mingled with ceremonial laws or matters of civil and communal interest which also include ideas of vengeance and harshest reproval . . . but the ethical teachings of the Gospel, on the contrary, came from one man only, and are, every one, stamped with the same peculiar hall-mark. A man like Jesus, for whom the ethical ideal was everything, was something hitherto unheard of in the Judaism of the day.'[1]

In three particulars of supreme importance Jesus broke away from the ethical tradition in which He had been reared. He disallowed its national limitations, its mechanical conception of human duty, and its unworthy treatment of women. In addition to this direct teaching Jesus set out an ideal of personal character which conflicted with the reigning conventions of His time and race, and He illustrated this ideal in Himself.

I. It is difficult for a modern student to realize how intense and pervading was the national conviction of incommunicable spiritual privilege which inspired the Judaism of the first century of our era. Jewish apologists are often carried by their polemical ardour to base on occasional quotations from Jewish literature a claim that no superiority attached to the teaching of Jesus. When, however, these quotations are seen in their context, and considered in the light of the general doctrine, they are found to provide no adequate basis for this contention. I have already quoted the candid admission of a learned foreign Jew as to the true unique-

[1] v. ibid., p. 389.

ness in its totality of the ethical teaching of Jesus. Let me quote another learned Jew, one of our own speech and nation. Dr. Claude Montefiore, to whom all serious students of the New Testament are so deeply indebted, has discussed this question at considerable length. He writes as a Jew, and no Christian would accept some of his judgements on the teaching of Jesus, but his conclusions are decisive:

'I think Rabbinic teaching *was* defective about the love of the foreigner and the idolater, and that Jesus might very well have said, "You all consider your neighbour to be only your fellow-Jew, but I tell you that the neighbour whom you are to love includes all men, the Roman and the Greek and the Syrian no less than the Jew." That would by no means have been needless teaching. . . . Jesus says: "You have heard that it was said, Thou shalt love thy neighbour and hate thine enemy." To this statement, as we know, the Jewish critics reply that nowhere is it stated in the Law or in the Old Testament that "thou shalt hate thine enemy". On the contrary, passages can be quoted to the opposite effect, if by "loving" "doing good to" is meant, and by "hating" "doing evil". But *these* passages certainly refer to the Israelite, not the foreigner or the idolater. If, then, Jesus bids his disciples, in contradistinction to current teaching, or to the teaching of the Law and of the Old Testament, to love their enemies, he must be referring, not to the Israelite but to the foreigner.

'The Jewish critic is obviously right when he says that there is no passage in the Old Testament which says, "Thou shalt hate thine enemy." He is also obviously right when he refers to passages like Exodus xxiii. 4, 5, or Proverbs xxv. 21, xx. 22. Nevertheless, if one were to take the Old Testament as a whole, I am not so sure that one can honestly say that its general teaching is very definite on the love of enemies, even of Israelite enemies. Still less can it be said that it is so when the enemies, though Israelite, are conceived to be the enemies of the "pious" party, to whom the speaker or writer belongs. For this view the Psalms bear witness, so that even, in the noblest of all the Psalms, we get the familiar verses, "Surely thou wilt slay the wicked, O God; depart from me, therefore, ye bloodthirsty men. Do not I hate them, O Lord, that hate thee? I hate them with perfect hatred: I count them mine enemies." Though the Psalmist makes the order: God's enemies, *therefore* mine, he was probably half deceived; the order was equally, or even primarily, my enemies, *therefore* God's. And there is no reason to believe that the Psalmist is here alluding to foreigners. It is against such teaching that Jesus . . . may very well have protested in Matt. v. 43.'[1]

The exclusive temper, which found such frank expression in the canonical Scriptures, had been intensified by the political experiences of the Jewish nation during the age which preceded the Christian era. It gives distinctive colour to the Apocalyptic writings, and in the later literature of the Talmud reflects the fierce resentments born of the terrific calamities in which the national polity finally collapsed.

We have an example of the power of national distress to generate a fierce national spirit in Germany at the present time. It requires but the change of a few words to make Professor Nygren's description of the genesis of the almost demented nationalism which now dominates the mind of Germany suitable for describing the state of feeling in Palestine in the time of Jesus.

'The common distress has soldered the people together, and brought about a quite new solidarity and feeling of cohesion. They have adopted the Nation, and they have adopted it as

[1] v. *Rabbinic Literature and Gospel Teachings*, by C. G. Montefiore, p. 62 f.

something holy—nay, as the Holy of Holies. The holiness of people and race has become the absolute value. This race passion has gone all over Germany as a revival, and the peculiar thing is that it has in an equal degree fettered Christians and non-Christians. Even to many Christians this experience of one's own people has been something so overpowering that it puts Christianity in the shade. Under full sail Germany is running into this new paganism. It cannot be denied that to great multitudes the deification of their own race is taking the place of religion.'[1]

Among the Jews, however, this national passion had deep roots in religion. We may be sure that it prevailed among the contemporaries of Jesus, and that the universalist spirit which pervaded His teaching was perceived to be in sharp contrast to the current doctrine of Jewish orthodoxy. It follows that, in spite of frequent and sometimes surprising agreements, the total impression made by the Gospels on a candid reader differs *toto caelo* from that made by the Jewish writings which can be compared with them.

II. Jesus broke with Pharisaism on the cardinal point of its mechanical conception of human duty. In doing so He reverted to the position which the Prophets of Israel, whose teachings He must often have listened to in the synagogue at Nazareth, had taken up towards the established religious system of their time. With increased insistence and more august authority, He echoed the protests of Isaiah and Amos against an established religion which had parted company with fundamental morality, and, in its emphasis on ritual and ceremonial obligations, had destroyed the true perspectives of human duty. The great passage in the

[1] v. *The Church Controversy in Germany*, by Anders Nygren, 1934, p. 87.

Gospel according to St. Mark, in which Jesus exposes the morally stultifying effect of the Rabbinic version of Jewish religion, must be quoted in full. It stands on record as the supreme exposition of ethical religion, and it presents a picture, drawn we cannot doubt by an eye-witness, of Jesus in direct conflict with the orthodoxy of His time.

'And there are gathered together unto him the Pharisees, and certain of the scribes, which had come from Jerusalem, and had seen that some of his disciples ate their bread with defiled, that is, unwashen, hands. For the Pharisees, and all the Jews, except they wash their hands diligently, eat not, holding the tradition of the elders: and when they come from the marketplace, except they wash themselves, they eat not: and many other things there be, which they have received to hold, washings of cups, and pots, and brasen vessels. And the Pharisees and the scribes ask him, Why walk not thy disciples according to the tradition of the elders, but eat their bread with defiled hands? And he said unto them, Well did Isaiah prophesy of you hypocrites, as it is written,

This people honoureth me with their lips,

But their heart is far from me.

But in vain do they worship me,

Teaching as their doctrines the precepts of men.

Ye leave the commandment of God, and hold fast the tradition of men. And he said unto them, Full well do ye reject the commandment of God, that ye may keep your tradition. For Moses said, Honour thy father and thy mother; and, He that speaketh evil of father or mother, let him die the death: but ye say, If a man shall say to his father or his mother, That wherewith thou mightest have been profited by me is Corban, that is to say, Given to God; ye no longer suffer him to do aught for his father or his mother; making void the word of God by your tradition, which ye have delivered: and many such like things ye do. And he called to him the multitude again, and said unto them, Hear me all of you, and understand: there is nothing from without the man, that going into him can defile him: but the things which proceed out of the man are those that defile the man. And when he was entered into the house from the multitude, his disciples asked of him the parable. And he saith unto them, Are ye so without understanding also? Perceive ye not, that whatsoever from without goeth into the man, it cannot defile him; because it goeth not into his heart, but into his belly, and goeth out into the draught? This he said, making all meats clean. And he said, That which proceedeth out of the man, that defileth the man. For from within, out of the heart of men, evil thoughts proceed, fornications, thefts, murders, adulteries, covetings, wickednesses, deceit, lasciviousness, an evil eye, railing, pride, foolishness: all these evil things proceed from within, and defile the man.'[1]

Jewish scholars have objected that this passage from the Gospel gives an unfair, and even wholly misleading, version of Rabbinic teaching, and we may concede that the remarkable insistence on filial duty, which marks the moral teaching of the Talmud, justifies the view that the particular instance which occasioned the pronouncement of Jesus was not representative of Judaism. We know too little of the actual situation with which Jesus was confronted to pronounce dogmatically on the likelihood of such casuistry as He condemned at that time and place, and certainly such language as Dr. Travers Herford permits himself to use when commenting on this episode appears to me altogether unwarrantable. But none can dispute either the tendency of Rabbinism unduly to magnify the religious importance of ritual and ceremonial requirements, or the danger of

[1] v. St. Mark vii. 1–23.

moral lopsidedness implicit in that tendency, or the immense mischiefs which from this source have flowed to religion, not merely Jewish but Christian. Indeed the tendency, and its baleful consequences, are the parasites of religion itself.

Montefiore concludes a careful, and by no means wholly favourable, criticism of the passage I have quoted with the following verdict:

'Looking back upon the whole incident after 1900 years, we see that while both parties had a certain right upon their side, though neither could persuade the other, Jesus was more profoundly right and more essentially true. The future was with him, not with the Rabbis and Pharisees. His principle would gradually win the day. It represented a higher and purer conception of religion than the opposite principle which is embodied in the Pentateuchal law. Liberal Judaism has consciously accepted it. Jesus himself, with his keen moral and religious intuitions, went straight to the essential truths of religion.'[1]

The difference between the teaching of Jesus and the orthodox Judaism of His time was particularly apparent in connexion with the Sabbath. This was a matter which carried to the very heart of Jewish religion. 'The two fundamental observances of Judaism are circumcision and the sabbath', and of these for obvious reasons the Sabbath was the more important. Piety blended with patriotism in clothing the Sabbath with unique and sovereign claim. Exile had emphasized its significance, and martyrdom had dignified its observance.

'For the Jews colonized in Babylonia or scattered in other lands, the sabbath alone of all the sacred calendar remained,

---

[1] v. *The Synoptic Gospels*, i. 176.

and its importance was thus greatly enhanced. It was the one observance historically associated with the cultus that could still be maintained wherever there were Jews, and the observance of it was the most conspicuous sign of allegiance to the national God and the institutions of their fathers.'[1]

About this supreme institution the Rabbis had set the hedge of abundant regulations, and a complicated casuistry grew up, which tended to obscure in the general mind the original character and intention of the Sabbath law. It is apparent on the face of the Synoptic record that nothing in the behaviour of Jesus more exasperated the Pharisees than His treatment of the Sabbath. Abrahams, in his learned and interesting note on 'the Sabbath', argues that the Pharisees, while holding stiffly to the traditional requirements, were substantially in agreement with Jesus on the grand principle that 'The sabbath was made for man and not man for the sabbath', and that, in deference to that principle, they authorized breaches of the sabbatic law in certain contingencies. 'The principle that the Sabbath law was in certain emergencies to be disregarded was universally admitted, the only dispute was as to the precise Pentateuchal text by which the laxity might be justified.' But is it not precisely on that very point that the essential difference between Jesus and the Pharisees comes to light? Ought the fulfilment of the evident requirements of mercy to be made subordinate to the discovery of an appropriate Pentateuchal text? In face of human need ought a benevolent man to 'search the scriptures', and not rather to give immediate obedience to the promptings of his heart? When the ruler of the

[1] v. Moore, *Judaism*, ii. 23.

synagogue, witnessing the healing of the paralysed woman who for eighteen years 'had been bowed together, and could in no wise lift herself up', was 'moved with indignation because Jesus had healed on the sabbath', and bade the people seek relief from their distress on some other day than the Sabbath, he was raising the very issue between spiritual and legal conceptions of religion. The rules of the Pharisees admitted many reasonable exceptions, but always within the limits of their hard theory of legal obligation.

'But', concludes Abrahams, 'Jesus went further. No act of mercy, whether the need pressed or not, was to be intermitted because of the Sabbath. This is an intelligible position, but the Pharisaic position was as intelligible, and it was consonant with the whole idea of the Sabbath rest. For there are many categories of acts, clearly servile, and yet which might be brought within the definition of the merciful, thus first invading, and finally destroying, the day set aside for repose and communion with God. The Pharisees permitted, nay required, the performance of all necessary works of mercy, but refused to extend the licence too indiscriminately, and never reconciled themselves to the theory that in general the performance of a duty justified the infringement of a prohibition. Whatever may be urged from other points of view against the Rabbinic treatment of the Sabbath, and much may be so urged, it is just on the subjects in dispute in the Gospels that their withers are entirely unwrung.'[1]

If, however, the duty in question be a moral obligation, and it can be nothing less when it has reference to helping the afflicted, then to disregard it in deference to a legal obligation involves the very fault with which

[1] v. Abrahams, *Studies in Pharisaism and the Gospels*, 1st series, p. 135.

Jesus charged the Pharisees when He said that 'they rejected the commandment of God that they might keep their tradition'. For Him, as for Wordsworth, Duty was 'the stern Daughter of the Voice of God'. To the anxious questionings of Pharisaic scrupulosity He would have made answer in the words of the prophet's reply to Balak, king of Moab: 'He hath shewed thee, O man, what is good; and what doth the Lord require of thee, but to do justly, and to love mercy, and to walk humbly with thy God?'

The mind of Jesus with respect to the ritual and ceremonial laws, of which the law of the Sabbath was the most important, is, perhaps, disclosed in the episode which finds a place in the remarkable manuscript of the Greek Testament preserved at Cambridge, and known from its donor's name as Codex Bezae. This interpolation is thought by many eminent critical scholars, including my predecessor, Bishop Westcott, to embody a genuine tradition of Christ's words. It follows St. Luke vi. 4, and runs thus:

'The same day, having seen one working on the Sabbath, He said to him: "O man, if thou knowest what thou doest, thou art blessed, but if thou knowest not, thou art accursed, and a transgressor of the Law."'

Dean Plumtre, who regards the narrative as authentic, remarks: 'It brings out with a marvellous force the distinction between the conscious transgression of a law recognized as still binding, and the assertion of higher law as superseding the lower.' If the man had so fully grasped the Divine intention of the Sabbath law, viz. the provision of a discipline, by which men might be led to a complete consecration of their lives, as for himself to be able to dispense with the observance of that law, he was blessed indeed, but if, unconscious or oblivious of the Divine Intention, he was insolently disregarding the commandment, he was verily immersed in deep guilt, 'accursed and a transgressor of the law'. In the opening paragraphs of his famous *Dissertation on the Christian Ministry* Bishop Lightfoot has suggested this explanation of the singular combination in Christianity of a religious theory which renders all mediate disciplines of order and worship superfluous, with the organization of both by the Apostolic Founders of the Christian Church:

'The celebration of the first day in the week at once, the institution of annual festivals afterwards, were seen to be necessary to stimulate and direct the devotion of the believers. The appointment of definite places of meeting in the earliest days, the erection of special buildings for worship at a later date, were found indispensable to the working of the Church. But the Apostles never lost sight of the idea in their teaching. They proclaimed loudly that "God dwelleth not in temples made with hands". They indignantly denounced those who "observed days and months and seasons and years". This language is not satisfied by supposing that they condemned only the temple-worship in the one case, that they reprobated only Jewish sabbaths and new moons in the other. It was against the false principle that they waged war; the principle which exalted the means into an end, and gave an absolute intrinsic value to subordinate aids and expedients. These aids and expedients, for his own sake and for the good of the society to which he belonged, a Christian could not afford to hold lightly or neglect. But they were no part of the *essence* of God's message to man in the Gospel: they must not be allowed to obscure the idea of Christian worship.'[1]

[1] v. *Philippians*, p. 184.

The Pharisees, as Jesus saw them, had lost sight of the original purpose of the Sabbath in their zeal for its due observance, and were stifling devotion by their numerous and detailed regulations.

III. Jesus broke away from the habit of Jewish society, and implicitly condemned the orthodox Jewish doctrine, by His treatment of women and by His teaching with respect to marriage and divorce. It was the accepted view of antiquity that woman is naturally inferior to man, and among orientals this inferiority has always been emphasized in direct connexion with sexual function. Alone in antiquity the people of Israel maintained a relatively high standard of sexual morality. The monotheistic religion, which was their distinctive possession, implied acceptance of a congruous moral law, and the fact that the Syro-Phoenician religions were bound up with the grossest sexual licence compelled in the Israelites anxious and continuing precautions against corruption. 'On the whole', writes von Döllinger, 'the social status of the woman (in Israel) was a lower one than among the Germans, and a higher one than among the Greeks.'[1] Sexual morality never fell among the Jews to the same abyss of degradation as among other oriental peoples. Jehovah was the Holy One of Israel, and His worship could not tolerate the abominations which marked the cults of Syria and Babylon. The influence of the prophets was thrown steadily on the side of purity, and this influence was powerfully assisted by the patriotic reaction against Hellenistic pressure. One of the 'three deadly sins' in Judaism was incest, a term which 'was extended to comprehend all illegitimate

[1] v. *The Gentile and the Jew*, ii. 361.

intercourse between men and women, and the various
abuses and perversions of sexual instinct'.[1] Moore does
not scruple to describe 'the social and religious position
of woman in Judaism' as 'itself a moral achievement,
and fundamental in the morals of the Jewish family'.[2]
But, as von Döllinger observes, 'the value and consequence of the female sex was wholly in marriage and
maternity.' Moore says substantially the same when
he tells us that 'her place was in the home of her
father till she was married, then in that of her husband
as wife, mother, and housekeeper. For emancipated
women there was in the ancient world only one
calling.'[3] Woman as woman had no claim on respect,
only as serviceable to the needs and interests of her
male relations.

It cannot be disputed that the Jews were frankly
oriental in their view of women as such. In the Jewish
liturgy the men thank God that they have not been
created women. Thus in the heart of the synagogue
worship the inferiority of the female sex is proclaimed.
To some extent their orientalism was corrected by the
high estimate in which family life was held by the Jews,
but they always built the discipline of the household on
the foundation of man's inherent superiority, not on that
of the essential equality of the partners in the marriage
union. We shall deal at greater length with this aspect
of the subject when, in a later lecture, we come to
the subject of the Christian law of marriage. Montefiore's comment on the answer which Jesus is reported
to have returned to the question about divorce which

---

[1] v. Moore, *Judaism*, ii. 267.   [2] v. ibid., p. 131.
[3] v. ibid., p. 126.

the Pharisees addressed to him states the Jewish position with characteristic frankness:

'This passage is one of the most important in the Gospels.
In no other point was the opposition of Jesus to the Rabbinic
law of profounder significance. The religious position of woman
and the law of divorce form the least attractive feature in the
Rabbinical system. If the general status of women among
the Jews has, nevertheless, been tolerably satisfactory, this is
scarcely because of their laws, but in spite of them. The
unerring ethical instinct of Jesus led him to put his finger upon
the weak spots and sore places of the established religion. Of
all such weak spots and sore places this was the weakest and
the sorest. And the weakest and the sorest it still remains. The
reform, or rather the renouncement, of the Orientalisms in
the laws about women is one of the greatest necessities of
orthodox Judaism.'[1]

The attitude of friendliness towards women which
Jesus maintained, and the prominent place which they
took in His life, contrasted sharply with the habit of
the Rabbis. Even His own disciples were astonished.
When they found Him holding converse with the
woman of Samaria by Jacob's well, we are told by
the Fourth Evangelist that 'they marvelled that he was
speaking with a woman'.[2] Bishop Westcott, commenting on this verse, quotes the Rabbinic sayings that 'a
man should not salute a woman in a public place, not
even his own wife', and that it was 'better that the words
of the law should be burnt than delivered to women'.
Such opinions did not spring from an ascetic dualism
which regarded the flesh as intrinsically evil, and the
sexual impulse as the very climax of fleshly appetite,
for ascetic views were utterly alien to Jewish modes of

[1] v. *The Synoptic Gospels*, i. 235.   [2] St. John iv. 27.

thinking. But this contempt for woman, and her
exclusion from the greater acts of Jewish religion,
expressed the normal oriental contempt for the female
sex. Closely connected with His treatment of women,
indeed, inseparable from it, were His love of children
and the evident pleasure which He found in their
company. It was an honourable feature of Judaism
that it held childhood in high regard, and made admirable rules for the education of boys. Nevertheless it is
excessive to say with Abrahams that 'Jesus' loving regard
for the young' was 'fully in accord with the Jewish
spirit'. The disciples were fairly representative of their
generation when they moved their Master to indignation
by 'rebuking' those who brought little children unto
Him.

To sum up. Jesus delivered the current Jewish
morality to His disciples transformed in three cardinal
particulars. It was national: He made it universal. Its
perspectives were wrong: He rectified them, presenting
human duty in the true order of its obligation. It was
unequal in its treatment of the sexes: He abolished that
inequality, bringing the female sex frankly and fully
within the social covenant, and making an end of
limitations which were both unnatural and degrading.
Thus He made good His claim, not to destroy but to
fulfil the Law of Moses.

V

THE NON-CHRISTIAN WORLD

SO long as Christianity remained within the sphere of Judaism, where indeed it had the aspect of a new Jewish sect, Christians and Jews were morally in substantial agreement. Both received the Decalogue as the Divinely revealed summary of essential morality. Both accepted the canonical Scriptures as the source of moral teaching. Jesus had ever in His teaching taken for granted the established morality which yet by that teaching He would transform. There was no quarrel between Him and His contemporaries in this regard. When, however, St. Paul carried Christianity beyond the frontiers of Palestine, and laid the foundations of a Catholic Church in the cities of the Empire, a new situation was created. There was no longer an accepted morality which Christians could without hesitation adopt as their own. The lines of human obligation were otherwise drawn than in their map of duty. At once they realized the sharp discord between the Church and the World which was implicit in their religion, found expression in a thousand differences, and would in course of time fill Christian history with the glorious tragedies of martyrdom. Christianity was essentially a way of life, and, as such, it carried those who walked in it from the high road of the general 'use and wont'. Christians were not, like the Jews, protected by a national character, and therefore recognized by the imperial law, and, albeit repulsive, yet intelligible to the imperial populations.

The large tolerance of polytheism was patient of almost limitless eccentricities of creed and conduct, and, though the exclusiveness of Jewish religion strained that tolerance almost to breaking point, still the national character provided an explanation which was not wholly unsatisfactory. But the Christians could offer no such intelligible excuse for themselves. They were both repugnant and enigmatic. While they were apparently and aggressively distinctive, they could advance none of the familiar pleas for moral distinctiveness. There is but a short step from moral distinctiveness to unpopularity, and it was soon taken. Christians were speedily immersed in extreme and general odium. The worst interpretation was given to their unquestionable oddity. Tacitus, describing the Neronian persecution, tells us that it was not the ridiculous accusation of arson which told against the Christians, but the vague, inflaming suggestion that they were essentially hostile to society. It was *odium humani generis* which was the fatal vice of Christians in pagan eyes. The full extent of the change in their position was not indeed immediately apparent, for the Apostle in his missionary efforts was able to avail himself of the synagogue system. He entered into the succession of the liberal Jewish teachers. It would not, perhaps, be excessive to say that Christianity garnered the harvest of the earlier Jewish sowing, and absorbed into itself that universalist element which had been so conspicuous in pre-Christian Judaism, and has been so completely absent in the later Judaism of the Rabbis. This will explain a phenomenon which has often attracted attention, and is at first sight perplexing, viz. the fact that Christianity seems to have left no trace on the Judaism which rejected it. In Jewish religion there had coexisted in an uneasy combination two elements, nationalist and universalist, and these by the advent of Christianity were sharply and finally sundered. Jesus stood at the parting of the ways. Under His banner universalist Judaism ranged itself. Nationalist Judaism refused to accept Him, entrenched itself in its traditional exclusiveness, and passed into history as the Judaism of the Talmud.

It is to be noted that the very circumstances which exposed Christians to misunderstandings and even persecutions from which Jews were exempt did also facilitate and assist their evangelistic efforts. In taking up the missionary work of the Hellenistic Jews the Christian Evangelists had some great advantages. They were unhampered by a national claim; they were not required to insist on the repulsive admission rite of circumcision; they did not subject their converts to a multitude of tiresome and inconvenient restrictions. At the same time they possessed the features of Judaism which had most attracted thoughtful and devout non-Jews, its monotheism, its lofty morality, its simple and reasonable worship, its sacred literature.

Within the range of synagogue propaganda the morality of Judaism was known and generally accepted, but when, with the closing of the synagogues to the Christian preachers, the Gospel was introduced to the general body of the Graeco-Roman population, that morality wore an arresting aspect of novelty. In the famous fifteenth chapter of the *Decline and Fall* Gibbon assigns as the fourth of the five 'secondary causes of the rapid growth of the Christian Church' its moral superiority, 'the reformation of manners which was introduced into the world by the preaching of the gospel'.

At first, indeed, Christianity, especially in the West, was regarded with the gravest suspicion by the imperial authorities. The absenteeism from social intercourse, imposed on the primitive believers by the pervasive and corrupting polytheism which coloured the general life, was, we have said, interpreted in the worst possible sense. It is, perhaps, not the least impressive evidence of the foulness of society that so perverted a judgement should have been so often and so confidently passed on behaviour which, though unfamiliar and unpleasing, was innocent and laudable. The Apologists addressed themselves with energy and eloquence to the disproof of the horrible accusations which darkened the popular mind. How far their compositions were read by those to whom they were addressed we cannot know. It is not probable that the writings of obscure and unpopular sectaries would have arrested the attention of the rulers of the Roman Empire. This circumstance, however, in no degree detracts from their value as revelations of the state of public opinion. The Apologists disclose the situation which actually confronted them; and the arguments which they formulated were those which were actually urged, and did finally prevail. Hadrian or Antoninus Pius may never have read the Apology which Aristides addressed to him, but those of his subjects who were in personal contact with the professors of the new religion knew its truth, and felt its power. In reading apologies we may not forget their purpose. They leave out of the picture which they present those features which would lessen its impressiveness, and even throw doubt on its fidelity. But even so no serious student of the early centuries will question the substantial truth of the Christian claim.

Dr. von Dobschütz begins his investigation on *Christian Life in the Primitive Church* by quoting the language of Aristides. It is the completest picture of practical Christianity in the second century which has survived, and its fidelity to fact is confirmed by the verdict of history. We may with advantage have it in front of us. It runs thus:

'The Christians have received the commandments [of the Lord Jesus Christ], which they have engraved on their minds and keep in the hope and expectation of the world to come; wherefore, they do not commit adultery or fornication, they do not bear false witness, they do not deny a deposit, nor covet what is not theirs. They honour father and mother: they do good to their neighbours, and when they are judges they judge uprightly. They do not worship idols made in the form of man; and whatever they do not wish that others should do to them, they do not practice towards others: they do not eat of food consecrated to idols, for they are undefiled: those who grieve them they comfort, and make them their friends; they do good to their enemies; their wives, O King, are pure as virgins, and their daughters modest; their men abstain from all unlawful wedlock and from all impurity, in the hope of the recompense to come in another world; if any of them have bondmen, bond-women, or children, they persuade these to become Christians for the love that they have towards them; and when they have become so they call them without distinction brethren. They do not worship strange gods; they walk in all humility and kindness, and falsehood is not found among them. They love one another. From the widows they do not turn away their countenance: they rescue the orphan from him who does him violence; he who has gives to him who has not, without grudging; and when they see a stranger, they bring him to their dwellings, and rejoice over him as over a true brother; for they do not call themselves brothers after the flesh, but after the Spirit and in God. When one of their poor passes away from the world, and any of them sees it, then he provides for his burial according to his ability; and if they hear that any of their number is imprisoned or oppressed for the name of their Messiah, all of them provide for his needs, and, if it is possible, they deliver him.

'If there is among them some one poor and needy, and they have not an abundance of necessaries, they fast two or three days that they may supply his want with necessary food. They observe scrupulously the commandments of their Messiah; they live honestly and soberly, as the Lord their God commands them, thanking Him always for food and drink, and all other blessings. And if any righteous person of their number passes away from the world, they rejoice and give thanks to God, and they follow his body, as if he were moving from one place to another. When a child is born to any one of them, they praise God, and if again it chance to die in its infancy, they praise God exceedingly, as for one who has passed through the world without sins. If, on the other hand, they see that one of their number has died in his ungodliness, or in his sins, they weep bitterly and sigh, as over one who is about to go to punishment.

'As men who know God, they ask from Him what is proper for Him to give and for them to receive. Thus they complete their lifetime. And because they acknowledge the goodnesses of God towards them, lo! therein consists all the beauty that is in the world.

'The good deeds, however, which they do, they do not proclaim in the ears of the multitude, and they take care that no one shall perceive them. They conceal their gift, as one who has found a treasure and hides it. Thus they labour to become righteous as those who expect to receive the fulfilment of Christ's promises in the life eternal.'[1]

[1] v. von Dobschütz, l.c., Introduction, pp. xxv f.

Let it be frankly conceded that this is an idealization of the facts, and that the writer has evidently written with a view to correcting some current criticisms of his religion. We may not doubt that there were many shadows, for human life at its highest is never without them, and, in the second century as in every other, virtue was closely pressed by hypocrisy. But the facts which Aristides idealized were sufficiently impressive, and hypocrisy, even when most gross and afflicting, has ever the character of homage paid to virtue. The virtue of these early Christians was arrestingly novel in that 'hard pagan world' of the Empire.

It is certainly true that no feature of the new religion impressed thoughtful pagan observers so much as the severe standard of personal morality which it required in its professors. There is, perhaps, a note of surprise in the language of Pliny when he reports to the Emperor Trajan what he had ascertained to be the teaching of the Christians whom the law proscribed, and public opinion vilified:

'They maintained that the amount of their fault or error was this, that it was their habit on a fixed day to assemble before daylight and sing by turns a hymn to Christ as a god: and that they bound themselves with an oath, not for any crime, but not to commit theft or robbery or adultery, not to break their word, and not to deny a deposit when demanded. After this was done, their custom was to depart, and meet together to take food, but ordinary and harmless food; and even this, (they said,) they had given up doing after the issue of my edict, by which in accordance with your commands I had forbidden the existence of clubs. On this I considered it the more necessary to find out from two maid-servants who were called deaconesses (ministrae), and that by torments, how far this was true: but I discovered nothing else than a wicked and arrogant superstition.'[1]

The moral superiority of Christians, as we have said, was a favourite theme of the Apologists, who were concerned with removing the heavy cloud of suspicion under which Christianity existed. Especially they appealed to Christian conduct as demonstrating the civic value which a conscientious refusal to worship the reigning Emperor seemed so plainly to disallow. This, they claimed, was the standing miracle which proved the truth of Christian witness. In themselves, by the familiar habit of their lives, Christians illustrated the character and power of their religion. We have already quoted Aristides. Not less impressive is St. Justin Martyr, who, writing about the year A.D. 150, describes the effect of conversion:

'We who were once used to rejoice in fornication, now only cleave to chastity: we who once practised magical arts, have now consecrated ourselves to the good and unbegotten God: we who beyond everything loved gain and property, now bring even what we have into the common fund, and share it with the needy: we who once were haters and murderers of one another, and because our customs were different would have no common hearth with strangers, do now, since Christ's manifestation, eat together with them, and pray for our enemies, we seek to persuade those who hate us unjustly, so that they may order their lives according to Christ's glorious doctrine, and attain to the joyful hope of receiving like blessings with us from God, the Lord of all.'[2]

[1] Pliny's Letter is printed and translated in the convenient *Selections from Early Writers illustrative of Church History to the Time of Constantine*, by the late Professor Gwatkin. London, 1893.
[2] c. xiv.

We are reminded of the language which St. Paul had, a century earlier, addressed to the converted Greeks of Corinth. For them also conversion had implied moral transformation. In the Epistle to the Corinthians, as in the famous first chapter of the Epistle to the Romans, the Apostle represents the society of the Roman Empire as sunken in extreme moral debasement. In this respect St. Paul is thoroughly representative. The contrast between the 'Church' and the 'World' is drawn in the sharpest lines by the inspired writers. We cannot wonder that Christians gave the impression of anti-social moroseness when their attitude towards their neighbours was shaped by such admonitions as those of St. John:

'Love not the world, neither the things that are in the world. If any man love the world, the love of the Father is not in him. For all that is in the world, the lust of the flesh, and the lust of the eyes, and the vainglory of life, is not of the Father, but is of the world. And the world passeth away, and the lust thereof: but he that doeth the will of God abideth for ever.'[1]

How far, we cannot but ask, was such language justified by the facts? How far ought we to discount it as expressing the ancestral prejudice of the Jew, and the precipitate judgement of the neophyte? Could not as black an indictment be drawn against the civilization of modern Christendom? Is there anything in the satires of Juvenal more profoundly significant of moral debasement than the tragedy of the Lindbergh baby's fate? Were not the Christians disqualified by their social obscurity, their lack of culture, and the inevitable

----

[1] v. 1 John ii. 15–17.

prejudices born of their harsh fortune, for the task of passing a verdict on their contemporaries?

Any serious attempt to compare the civilization of the past with that of the present must needs be embarrassed by great difficulty. When the point of the comparison is practical morality the embarrassment will be greatest. We ourselves are members of the modern civilized society which we seek to appraise, and we can bring the key of our personal experience to the task of interpreting the facts within our knowledge. When we examine the civilized societies of antiquity, this key is not available. Then we can only approach the subject from outside, and must perforce draw on our faculty of historic imagination for the interpretation of our material. And that material is woefully limited. Take the case before us. How limited are our materials at best! We have a mass of information, but curiously little knowledge. There is the literature, mostly written by and for the members of a small educated minority. 'The great writers of antiquity', observes Dr. Edwyn Bevan, 'wrote for grandees and for men, and knew and cared very little about the ways of small people or of women. They never really studied what we call "the human document".'[1]

Satirists and philosophers are unsafe guides when popular thought and practice are in question. The first find their favourite material in follies and crimes which are sensational aberrations from what is normal and respected. The last are concerned with speculations which may, or may not, influence the behaviour of common folk. The dramatists, whose acknowledged

[1] v. *The Church's Task under the Roman Empire*, p. 95.

task is to present and analyse the current life, stripping off its disguises of convention, and exposing the unacknowledged principles and objectives which these have screened, are more illuminating, but for the most part they cast their light on but a small part of the ancient society. Legislation can tell us something respecting whatever came under the view of statesmen and judges. The memorials of ancient religion, literary, liturgical, and monumental, can teach us much about what men believed and aspired after, but the secret of the power of the dead religions lies in their graves. In recent years, thanks to the labours of a multitude of scholars, we have learned much about the social and economic life of the Empire, and are able to picture it in considerable detail, but we are still much in the dark as to the normal modes of its thinking, and the moral standards which it accepted. In fact, all our information put together provides but a pitiably insufficient basis for any complete or trustworthy estimate of the civilized morality which prevailed in the Graeco-Roman society of the pagan Empire. 'Mere information is of no value as a means towards understanding', observes Count Keyserling with characteristic exaggeration, but also with substantial truth.[1]

The ancients did not possess our principal sources of information. They lacked exact statistics, and did not share the anxious curiosity of modern social students as to all matters concerning the health and habits of the multitude. They did not possess anything properly equivalent to popular education, for, though the imperial government interested itself in schools and

[1] v. *America Set Free*, p. 20.

universities, these were limited to a small part of the population.

'Good education on Greco-Roman lines', writes Rostovtzeff, 'was certainly a privilege of the higher classes only, and when the emperors of the second century decided to pay the salaries of the teachers in the public schools out of the *fiscus*, their intention was, not to educate the proletariate, but to help the city *bourgeoisie* in its effort to secure a fair education for the rising generation.'[1]

There was no cheap press, nor anything comparable with modern fiction. The immense and various machinery of social redemption, which is the most impressive and honourable feature of Christendom, had hardly any parallel in the ancient world, which was not pricked in conscience by the evils of its life. Thus the critic of modern civilization has at his disposal a mass of testimony, superior in quality to, and in quantity far more extensive than, any which the student of ancient civilization can possess. This circumstance, perhaps, tends to obscure the worst features of the pre-Christian civilization. We are apt to form our estimate of it from its surviving literature and monuments, and these may not be, I incline to think that probably they are not, representative of the general life. Time has destroyed much, and what it has destroyed is not likely to have been what was best worth preserving. The considering observer of the Roman aqueducts, walls, circuses, villas, tombs, temples, and theatres, must needs be impressed, almost overwhelmed, by the power and majesty of imperial Rome, but he does not so readily perceive the moral background of those

[1] v. *Social and Economic History of the Empire*, p. 178.

stupendous works, the abominable cruelty, the cynical oppression, the pride, uncleanness, and tyranny. The Roman Empire was not regarded by its victims with sentiments of admiration. There was a solid justification in fact for the words of fierce hatred which Tacitus places in the mouth of Galcacus, on the eve of the battle in which Caledonian freedom fell before the legions of Agricola. His bitter description of the Romans discloses the seamy side of that Pax Romana which inspired the patriotic verse of Vergil and Claudian, and that description is certainly supported by the history of the process by which it was established:

'Harriers of the world, now that earth fails their all-devastating hands, they probe even the sea: if their enemy have wealth, they have greed; if he be poor, they are ambitious; East nor West has glutted them; alone of mankind they behold with the same passion of concupiscence waste alike and want. To plunder, butcher, steal, these things they misname empire: they make a desolation and they call it peace.'[1]

If it be objected that not even the brutal aggression of ancient Rome insulted justice more grossly than the new-born imperialism of Mussolini's Italy, we must needs admit the fact, but at the same time point out the novel and profoundly suggestive circumstance that the latter is proceeding under the formulated condemnation of civilized mankind.

For the most part the classical literature, which has been the foundation of European culture, is a literature of masterpieces. We may fairly doubt whether this literature is really representative of the moral and intellectual level of ancient society. We know how small

[1] v. Agricola, c. xxx.

among ourselves is the circulation of the best books compared with that of the more or less ephemeral produc-
tions which are morally and intellectually inferior. In
short, while the worst features of contemporary civilization are those which are most likely to be pressed on
our attention, the best features of ancient civilization
are those which have survived the 'changes and chances'
of Time, and now most easily determine our verdict.
Nevertheless, a careful study of the surviving monuments of antiquity will go far to correct the favourable
conception of personal and social morality which a cur-
sory survey might be likely to convey.

If we would form a just estimate of ancient society,
we need not depend on the testimony, inadequately
informed and inevitably prejudiced, of its victims,
whether Jewish or Christian. The classical literature,
when carefully studied, provides ample justification for
an unfavourable verdict. In the actual circumstances
of the Empire, how could extensive moral corruption
have been averted? All the well-authenticated conditions and symptoms of moral decline were present—
protracted war, sudden breaking down of political and
social conventions, widely spread scepticism along with
a rank growth of popular superstition, economic dislocation involving sharp social cleavages, vast riches
and limitless indigence and squalor, a rapidly declining birth-rate, and unspeakable private vices. A
recent Hulsean lecturer, Mr. H. G. Wood, has compared the Roman Empire, not unfitly, to the United
States of America as a 'melting-pot' of diverse races
and creeds. Melting-pots are not schools of virtue.
In them the blending of incongruities ever works out

in the debasing of types. A low and a lowering level of morals is the hall-mark of such societies.

It was not for lack of moral teachers that the ancient world had fallen into such degradation. The greatest thinkers of Greece had devoted themselves to ethics, and they have remained the masters of moral science ever since. Civilized thinking on the problems of human conduct will never be able to dispense with the recorded reflections of Socrates, Plato, and Aristotle. The later schools of Zeno and Epicurus 'concentrated their energies on ethics', and both have powerfully influenced the course and character of European morals. It was certainly not without justification that St. Jerome could describe St. Paul's contemporary, the Stoic philosopher-statesman, as 'noster Seneca'.

The classical literature was well known to educated Christians in antiquity, and they came into frequent contact with their best pagan contemporaries. They were not blind to the moral excellence which they encountered. St. Ambrose, for instance, 'evinced a lively interest in the ethical teachings of the ancients', and 'was prepared to admit that a great deal of this ethical material was valuable'. He and other Christian thinkers sought an explanation of the astonishing phenomenon of sound ethical teaching united to gross religious error in 'the daring hypothesis that all that was best in pagan teaching was plagiarized from the Sacred Scriptures'.[1] Nevertheless, when all allowance had been made for such moral elements as pagan life and literature disclosed, the broad facts could not be con-

[1] v. Homes Dudden, *The Life and Times of St. Ambrose*, i. 15.

cealed. Pagan philosophy was morally powerless to cleanse and elevate the habits of pagan society.

All the ancient thinkers laboured under certain grave disadvantages to which both Jews and Christians were not subject. Their conception of human nature was faulty: the conditions of human intercourse which they assumed as normal were in fact highly artificial: the range of their political experience was perilously restricted; above all, their religion was divorced from morality, and their philosophies, if religious at all, were not sufficiently religious to be morally effective. In varying measures these disadvantages vitiate the ethical doctrine of all the ancient thinkers and imprint on their teaching the stamp of a disabling inadequacy.

The Christian claim to moral superiority appears to have been well founded. In the very interesting inquiry to which reference has been made Dr. von Dobschütz has discussed 'the actual effects which the impulse proceeding from the Gospel produced', and seeks to discover 'not the ethical teaching of primitive Christianity but its real morals'. His conclusion is as decisive as it is favourable. Christianity, in his opinion, made good its claim to enable in its professors a higher standard of morality than that which the non-Christian world could exhibit. The humblest and least esteemed members of society were living like philosophers. The fact was too evident to be reasonably questioned. Gibbon was certainly right in counting it among the reasons why Christianity succeeded in winning acceptance in the teeth of philosophic contempt, the vested interest of polytheism, the suspicions of despotism, and the blind fanaticism of the unlettered multitude.

If, indeed, the actual conduct of Christians be contrasted with their theoretical character, and the measure of their moral attainment be set against the Divine assistances to which they claimed to have access, the spectacle presented by Christianity in every age, not excepting the first, must be allowed to be deeply disappointing. The discord is extreme and intolerable.

The aged Pope in Browning's great poem asks himself an inevitable question:

> And is this little all that was to be?
> Where is the gloriously-decisive change,
> Metamorphosis the immeasurable
> Of human clay to divine gold, we looked
> Should, in some poor sort, justify its price?
> Had an adept of the mere Rosy Cross
> Spent his life to consummate the Great Work,
> Would not we start to see the stuff it touched
> Yield not a grain more than the vulgar got
> By the old smelting-process years ago?
> If this were sad to see in just the sage
> Who should profess so much, perform no more,
> What is it when suspected in that Power,
> Who undertook to make and made the world,
> Devised and did effect man, body and soul,
> Ordained salvation for them both, and yet—
> Well, is the thing we see, salvation?

The postulate of the Incarnation at one end of Christian history and the current morality of Christendom at the other suggests, perhaps, the gravest difficulty to faith which Christians have to reckon with. That postulate the Gifford Lecturer is not free to make: and the difficulty which it involves for the orthodox Christian lies outside his concern. It is sufficient for our

argument to take account of the fact that Christianity
brought into the ancient world a higher standard of
personal morality, and by doing so justified the claim
which its apologists advanced against their opponents
and persecutors.

The opening paragraph of the chapter on 'The
Pagan Empire' in Lecky's well-known *History of European Morals* indicates the radical weakness of ancient
morality.

'One of the first facts', he says, 'that must strike a student
who examines the ethical teaching of the ancient civilizations is
how imperfectly that teaching was represented, and how feebly
it was influenced by the popular creed. The moral ideas had
at no time been sought in the actions of the gods, and long before
the triumph of Christianity, polytheism had ceased to have any
great influence upon the more cultivated intellects of mankind.'

Religion was at the same time morally impotent and
intellectually contemptible. It commanded the allegiance neither of the general conscience nor of the cultivated mind. Philosophers might deride the popular
mythology, but they acquiesced in, and even defended,
the worst aberrations of the popular conscience. The
golden age of ancient philosophy was in some important
respects morally infamous, and the grosser scandals
of antiquity—slavery, infanticide, sexual perversion,
suicide, and the bloody shows of the arena—flourished
in a society which held philosophers in high regard.
Christian morality in such a social environment as the
Roman Empire provided could not but wear an offen-
sively alien aspect and acquire an inevitably ascetic
character. For at every point it conflicted with the
prevailing habit, and the Christian's indispensable

contacts with his neighbours brought him under the pressure of continuing moral temptation.

Readers of Cardinal Newman's beautiful romance, *Callista*, will be familiar with the description of the pagan city of Sicca as it appeared to a Christian youth on the eve of the Decian persecution. I think the description is as historically justified as it is vividly drawn. The young Christian is pictured as entering a place on whose very walls iniquity was written. He moves forward 'amid sights which now shock and now allure':

'Fearful sights—not here and there, but on the stateliest structures and in the meanest hovels, in public offices and private houses, in central spots and at the corners of the streets, in bazaars and shops and house-doors, in the rudest workmanship and in the highest art, in letters or in emblems or in paintings—the insignia and the pomp of Satan and of Belial, of a reign of corruption and a revel of idolatry which you can neither endure nor escape. Wherever you go it is all the same; in the police-court on the right, in the military station on the left, in the crowd around the temple, in the procession with its victims and its worshippers who walk to music, in the language of the noisy market-people; wherever you go, you are accosted, confronted, publicly, shamelessly, now as if a precept of religion, now as if a homage to nature, by all which, as a Christian, you shrink from and abjure.'[1]

Newman was a master of rhetoric, and his natural temperament was ascetic. There is rhetorical exaggeration in this picture and the colouring of asceticism, but I think that few will be disposed to question its substantial justice. Modern India would perhaps provide a similar picture of moral corruption prevailing, penetrating, subtly pervasive.

[1] v. *Callista, A Tale of the Third Century*, chapter x.

In these circumstances the value of the Church as a disciplinary and didactic institution cannot be over-stated. When we remember that the converts were mostly drawn from the humbler ranks of society, that they were peculiarly helpless in face of private oppression and public prejudice, that their own ignorance and inbred prejudices were for ever co-operating with these external pressures to draw them back into the errors and vices from which Christianity had released them, we can see that nothing short of the strong discipline of the Church and the holding power of an intense consciousness of its fellowship could have secured the survival of Christian standards and ideals of conduct.

Polytheistic religion was linked so closely with sexual licence that in Christian eyes the two were inseparable. Thus were associated a stern intolerance of idolatry and an excessive exaltation of chastity which were the roots from which in course of time grew the twin scandals of Christian persecution and Christian asceticism. No scandals have weighed more heavily on the credit of Christianity, and none had a more respectable origin. The penitential system of the primitive Church, which impresses the modern student as excessively severe, and indeed could hardly ever have been more than theoretical, is only intelligible when it is regarded as the military discipline of the Christian society necessitated by the conditions of active warfare and justified by the result of the campaign. In a world which had lost hold of personal morality the Christian Church vindicated, as it were by violence, the existence and authority of a moral law, and stamped on the Christian conscience an ineradicable sense of sin. How considerable has been the achievement of Christianity is largely obscured by the fact that history concerns itself little with that hidden sphere, in which individual character is shaped and men's standards and ideals of duty are determined. Yet the quality of civilization and the atmosphere of society depend finally on nothing else. Much, e.g. infanticide, slavery, and religious prostitution, was normal and unquestioned in the world illumined by Plato and his master Socrates which, in our modern world, is almost inconceivable. There has been nothing less than a revolution in the moral sphere, and that revolution is the achievement of Christianity. Polytheistic religion was corporate and official, the concern of the community, the race, the nation, the state, never, outside the Jewish sphere, of the individual. When Peter and John, 'unlearned and ignorant men', standing before the Sanhedrin of their nation, met its prohibition of their witness by the bold declaration, 'Whether it be right in the sight of God to hearken unto you rather than unto God, judge ye: for we cannot but speak the things which we saw and heard', they formulated a principle ultimately fatal to all tyrannies, as well secular as spiritual. The situation in which the Christians found themselves, when confronted by the requirement of the Roman State that they should supplement their Christian worship by conforming to the official cultus of the reigning Emperor, forced them to realize the magnitude of the personal claim which their religion implied. Civic obedience for them could never be unlimited. They could never give to Caesar an unconditioned allegiance. 'We must obey God rather

than men' was a formula of spiritual revolt. It claimed
for individual conviction a final authority, and owned in
the private conscience 'the aboriginal Vicar of Christ'.

To sum up. The non-Jewish environment shaped
Christian morality mainly by the reactions which it
provoked. Its pervading licentiousness strengthened
the ascetic tendencies in Christianity and associated
them with ascetic tendencies which were not properly
Christian. Its persecuting intolerance developed a
kindred temper within the Christian society, and facilitated the disposition to use coercion in its own interest, which later developed into the worst scandals of
Christian history. At the same time persecution
deepened the consciousness of fraternity among the
members of the Christian fellowship, and enriched the
moral tradition by noble examples of self-abnegating
heroism.

Christianity did not come unscathed out of its conflict
with Paganism. The morality of the triumphant Christians of the fourth century was in some respects inferior
to that of the persecuted Christians of the first. The
deterioration was mournfully acknowledged by friends,
and exultantly emphasized by foes; but there was gain
as well as loss. Prejudices were abandoned as well as
principles obscured. Sympathies were enlarged in some
directions, if they were narrowed in others. The moral
tradition of Paganism was not altogether worthless. It
had some contributions of value to make to the ethical
treasure of mankind. The conversion of the Empire,
although largely nominal, did make possible the progressive Christianization of society.

It is the unfortunate and unscientific habit of many

modern writers to pay no attention to the reports of Christian missions. If they would examine those documents, they would find themselves confronted by a record of moral achievement not inferior to that which impressed the 'hard, pagan world' of antiquity. The pessimistic note too often dominant in references to the future of the Christian religion would be rebuked by the evidence of actual experience. In Asia and Africa to-day, as in the Roman Empire long ago, Christianity would be seen to be a moral force raising the life of individuals and societies to a higher plane.

The text from the Fourth Gospel—*Ego veni ut vitam habeant*—which Bishop Westcott, an enthusiast for foreign missions, caused to be inscribed on his grave in the chapel of Auckland Castle, and which is the key to his social teaching, declares tersely the normal and distinctive effect of Christianity. It is life on every level of human activity, a quickening of natural faculty, a direction of human effort, an exaltation of human ideals. *Ego veni ut vitam habeant.* Such it was in the ancient world, and such it is still in the modern.

VI

CHRISTIAN MORALITY IN HISTORY

THE range and character of original Christian morality were mainly determined by three factors —the tradition of Judaism, the teaching of Jesus, and the influence of Graeco-Roman society. From the first, Christianity received the conception of a moral law expressing the Will of a Righteous God, and, in its essential contents, declared in the Decalogue. From the second, Christianity derived freedom from national limitations, a new and larger understanding of moral obligation, and, above all, a supreme embodiment of personal morality in its Founder. From the third, Christianity, by an inevitable reaction from its social environment, learned to emphasize the necessity of ascetical discipline, to assert the final authority of the private conscience, and to magnify the function and claim of the Christian fellowship. Of these three main constituents of Christian morality, the last, reaction to social environment, is distinctive in this respect, that it continues to operate. The legacy of Judaism was once for all received from the past. The teaching and example of Jesus were given at a specific time and place, and are on record in the unalterable text of the Gospels. But the shaping influence of environment continues still to affect the moral judgements and practice of Christians, and will continue to do so as long as the world lasts. Thus Christian morality, while rooted in the past, ever possesses a provisional character, and absorbs into itself new elements from an ever novel experience. It is less a finished product than something still in making, and the factory in which it is gradually fashioned is history. For history is the record of unceasing change. Always new situations are emerging, and these ever involve a challenge to social use and wont. Principles, indeed, must needs be unalterable, but not their applications in practice. Indeed the very proof of the soundness of principles is the fact that they are found to be relevant to ever novel conditions of life in a world which never continues in one stay. Precedents are rarely safe, never sufficient, guides to human conduct.

'Christianity,' to quote the words of Dr. Kenneth Saunders in his illuminating volume, *Ideals of East and West*, 'is still in the making, and its ethic could no more be once and for all delivered to the saints than the full implications of its Master's life and death'.[1] The historical character of Christianity is not only guaranteed by the fact that it is rooted in a human life of which the record has been preserved, but also in the fact that its significance has been disclosed gradually, and still continues to be disclosed, in experience. It is both original and eclectic. The facts can only be justly perceived when their full significance has become apparent. In this sense the historian may adopt Count Keyserling's formula that 'in the domain of life significance creates the facts'.[2]

We must be on our guard against exaggeration. In borrowing the vocabulary of the Greek philosophers Christianity did not wholly, if at all, take over the ideas which that vocabulary had conveyed. In conforming to

[1] v. *The Ideals of East and West*, by Kenneth Saunders, Litt.D., p. 223. Cambridge University Press.   [2] v. *America Set Free*, p. 90.

established social forms, and even in adopting the imperial system as the model of its own organization, Christianity did not forfeit or renounce its own distinctive quality. It is only by the violent process of separating the Christian religion from the historic society in which it has been embodied, and by which it has been diffused among men, that we can recognize anything more than a dubious half-truth in Dr. Inge's statement that 'the Christian Church was the last great creative achievement of the classical culture'. For the classical culture had certainly nothing to do with the creation of the society which did, confessedly, to a large extent shape its system on Graeco-Roman models. Such shaping of ecclesiastical system by the non-Christian environment may be freely admitted, but certainly no more. As with the framework of the Christian society, so with its moral teaching. To say with Dr. Inge in the well-known volume, *The Legacy of Greece*, that 'early Christian ethics . . . were mainly Stoical', and that 'the Stoical ethics were taken over by Christianity' is surely to use the language of dangerous exaggeration. Nor is it easily reconcilable with the same writer's language a little later in the same essay:

'The Gospel was, as S. Paul said, a new creation. It is most significant that it at once introduced a new ethical terminology. The Greek words which we translate love (or charity), joy, peace, hope, humility, are no part of the stock-in-trade of Greek moralists before Christ. Men do not coin new words for old ideas. Taken as a whole the Gospel is profoundly original; and a Christian can find strong evidence for his belief that in Christ a revelation was made to humanity at large, in which the religion of the Spirit, in its purest and most universal form, was for the first time presented to mankind.'

The relation of Christianity and Stoicism has been discussed with characteristic thoroughness by Bishop Lightfoot in the essay, 'St. Paul and Seneca', which he appended to his well-known edition of the Epistle to the Philippians: 'It is difficult to estimate,' he says, 'and, perhaps, not very easy to overrate, the extent to which Stoic philosophy had leavened the moral vocabulary of the civilized world at the time of the Christian era.'[1] St. Paul, as his birth and early nurture at Tarsus, which was a notable centre of Stoic teaching, make probable, and as his speech at Athens seems to demonstrate, was not unacquainted with Stoic writings. His epistles abound in expressions which suggest Stoic influences. But, when we pass from language to the meanings which it bears, the contrast between Stoicism and the doctrine of the Christian Apostle is seen to be complete. Epictetus was a better theologian than Seneca, and Marcus Aurelius a better teacher of morality. Both the slave and the emperor were nobler men; but neither was a typical Stoic. The harsh and narrow-minded Cato was 'the most perfect type of the school'.

'It is interesting', writes Bishop Lightfoot, 'to note the language in which these two latest and noblest representatives of Stoicism refer to the Christians. Once and once only is the now numerous and rapidly growing sect mentioned by either philosopher, and in each case dismissed curtly with an expression of contempt. "Is it possible", asks Epictetus, "that a man may be so disposed under these circumstances from madness, or from habit like the Galileans, and can no one learn by reason and demonstration that God has made all things which are in the world?" "This readiness to die", writes M. Aurelius, "should follow from individual judgement, not from sheer obstinacy as

[1] v. *Philippians*, p. 303.

with the Christians, but after due considerations and with dignity and without scenic display (ἀτραγῳδῶς), so as to convince others also." The justice of such contemptuous allusions may be tested by the simple and touching narrative of the deaths of this very emperor's victims, of the Gallic martyrs at Vienne and Lyons: and the appeal may confidently be made to the impartial judgement of mankind to decide whether there was more scenic display or more genuine obstinacy in their last moments, than in the much vaunted suicide of Cato and Cato's imitators.'[1]

The fallacy of supposing that, because Christianity made use of the ethical vocabulary which Stoicism had minted, it therefore 'took over' the Stoic morality, so that 'Christian ethics were mainly Stoical', is sufficiently exposed by the total lack of understanding and sympathy which are here exhibited. The spirit of Christianity and the spirit of Stoicism are as wide apart as love is from pride.

Of all the Christian Fathers Saint Ambrose was the most deeply influenced by the moral teaching of the Pagan writers. His debt to Cicero and the Stoics is apparent, but it does not extend to the substance of his ethical doctrine.

'Ambrose, in fact', observes his latest biographer, 'has taken the virtues admired by paganism and refashioned them into something new and Christian. It is only the retention of the classical terminology which hinders us from perceiving instantly the revolutionary nature of the change so unobtrusively accomplished.'[2]

While the influence of the non-Christian environment on the Christian society was certainly considerable, it is, perhaps, even more important to remember that the contact between the two affected both. There has

[1] v. ibid., p. 318.
[2] v. Homes Dudden, *The Life and Times of St. Ambrose*, ii. 530.

ever been a reciprocity of influence between the Church and the World. Always the effect of Christianity on its secular environment is twofold, stimulating and corrective. It emphasizes the characteristic features of the human material upon which it works, and at the same time it introduces a new principle which finally modifies, and even transforms, them. Thus it endorses and consecrates the virtues of submission, bidding the Christian slave accept his servitude, rendering faithful service to his owner 'as to the Lord and not to men', and requiring the Christian subject of Caesar to discern in the Roman State the divinely appointed instrument on earth of God's Order and Justice. But, at the same time, it teaches the Christian slave that he is 'the Lord's freedman', a citizen of the New Jerusalem which is free, and an equal member of the Family of God; and it requires the Christian free man to condition his obedience to Caesar by his duty to another and diviner Lord. Time passed, and the situation of Christians changed dramatically. From being the victims of Power, they became its possessors. Christianity accepted and blessed autocracy. The Christian Augustus wielded all, and more than all the power of his pagan predecessors, and he abated nothing of their magnificence; but, along with these legacies of paganism, he accepted the character of a disciple, owned himself a member of the Christian Church, and as such subject to its discipline. The supremacy of the moral law as understood in the Church was acknowledged, and despotism was shadowed and chastened by the certainty of Divine judgement. The union of pagan tradition and Christian principle worked out in a gradual transformation of the whole conception of power. When St. Ambrose publicly barred the Emperor Theodosius from entering the cathedral of Milan, and put him to open penance for the savage massacre at Thessalonica, he made apparent to the world that, as Christ's minister, he represented an authority, viewless and weaponless, which not even Augustus at the height of his pomp and power could successfully withstand. The lesson had to be taught afresh, under novel conditions of infinite difficulty, to the barbarians who established themselves within the Roman Empire. Always the same twofold process is to be perceived. On the one hand, Christianity accepts with disconcerting facility secular procedures which are apparently and even grossly incongruous with itself; on the other hand, Christianity introduces a new spirit into life, and silently shapes society into conformity with its own principles and standards.

The key to the strange paradoxes of Medieval Christianity is in this twofold process of accommodation and innovation. Christianity, in the phrase of St. Paul, 'became all things to all men that it might by all means save some'. Assimilation and transformation, the first the condition of the last, are the distinguishing features of development in Christian morality. We may say of Christ's religion as it is disclosed in history what was said at the first of Christ Himself in His career on earth, 'the light shineth in the darkness: and the darkness apprehended it not'. The paradox was most apparent where the accommodation was closest and most arresting, viz. in the sphere of ecclesiastical politics. Christianity was from the first organized as a society, and by natural stages, swiftly traversed, the society acquired complete social equipment, administrative, legislative, disciplinary. The Catholic Church has its place in human history as an organization, shaped under secular conditions, forming secular connexions, and bound into contemporary secular society by many interests and ambitions. Bryce, in his well-known volume on *The Holy Roman Empire*, has described the process by which the Christian society modelled its system so closely on that of the imperial state that the Church and the Empire appeared in the eyes of the barbarians inseparable. 'Christianity as well as civilization became conterminous with the Roman Empire. To be a Roman was to be a Christian: and this idea soon passed into the converse. To be a Christian was to be a Roman.' Institutions respond to environment more slowly than individuals because they have larger responsibilities and longer experience. Hence the greater scandals of ecclesiastical history, but hence also the large service which explains and in some sense excuses them. Institutional Christianity does not wholly merit the unpopularity into which it has fallen. In our impatience of the Church's reluctance to admit the necessity of changes in its moral code, we are in some danger of forgetting its vigilant wardship of the principles which no moral code that is rightly described as Christian can violate. It is inevitable that the official morality of the Church should tend to lag behind the morality of the best Christians, for such official morality must needs have been formulated in the past, under conditions which cannot have remained unchanged, and may even have altogether ceased.

[1] v. *Holy Roman Empire*, p. 12.

It may fall out, therefore, that official morality, expressed in canons and casuistries, has become obsolescent or actually obsolete. In that event, a breach will have opened between the morality which is established and authoritative, and that of individual Christians. The history of religion is marked by recurrent crises of acute internal dissension when authority, challenged and rebelled against, becomes tyrannous, and its victims, misunderstood and treated harshly, become lopsided and sectarian. Nevertheless, it is through this troubled and scandalous historic process that the Light gains upon the Darkness and Christian morality is developed.

Nor is it only in the understanding of Christian duty that there has been advance. The range of Christian obligation has been enlarged, as now one, and now another, department of social action has been brought under the control of Christian principles. Ideally there never have been recognized any limitations of the Christian claim. 'Whatsoever ye do,' writes St. Paul, 'in word or in deed, do all in the name of the Lord Jesus',[1] a requirement which cannot mean less than that life, in the totality of its activities, is to be regarded as subject to Christ's law. But the full implications of Christian duty were only gradually perceived. The conquest of life was a slow process, and we may be sure that its completion is yet distant. Moreover, the pace of moral advance has been strangely unequal. The governing principles of Christian morality have indeed been fixed once for all, but the circumstances of human life, the far-extending ramifications of individual responsibility, and the measures of human knowledge

[1] Colossians iii. 17.

U

vary almost infinitely, and the practical applications of those principles must needs reflect the fact. The facile surrender of Christianity to secular influences is not wholly explicable by the timidity, sycophancy, and ambition of Christians, though all these have had their place in the process. If there has been much to justify the mournful censures of saints and the jubilant scorn of the open enemy, there has also been much to justify the generous receptiveness of the Church. The large-minded exhortation of the Apostle gives the key to much in Christian history which lends itself to a facile misunderstanding: 'Every creature of God is good, and nothing is to be rejected, if it be received with thanksgiving.'[1]

Christianity seeks the audience of men for a message which it affirms to be of universal import, and therefore it must go to men where they may be found, grouped in their natural divisions of race and language, and ordered diversely as their several histories have determined. Thus in the interest of its mission Christianity becomes, in its external aspects, imitative and, so to say, parasitic. It takes its stand on the actual plane of nature in order that it may raise it. In truth Christian history ever illustrates the law of all moral and spiritual advance, which St. Paul formulated: 'That is not first which is spiritual, but that which is natural; then that which is spiritual.'[2]

Christian morality, if it indeed be potentially universal, and as such entitled to be regarded as natural, must include within itself whatever elements in the world's life are ethically sound, and therefore congruous

[1] v. 1 Timothy iv. 4.   [2] v. 1 Corinthians xv. 46.

with its own principles. It may not be isolated from the march of humanity, since that also is an inspired thing. The slow evolution of mankind out of the primeval state of non-moral animalism into the richly humane life of civilized society has enshrined a Divine purpose, and disclosed a Divine energy. Since man is so framed that he must live in society if he is to live at all, social needs and social influences must play an increasing part in his development. That development is itself the witness of God in the universe. The Divine Wisdom is described in the Old Testament as the source of civilized order: 'By me kings reign, and princes decree justice. By me princes rule, and nobles, even all the judges of the earth.' The physical creation is His work, but in the society of men He finds His chosen dwelling-place: 'When he [i.e. Jehovah] marked out the foundations of the earth: then I [i.e. Wisdom] was by him, as a master workman: and I was daily his delight, rejoicing always before him: rejoicing in his habitable earth; and my delight was with the sons of men.'[1] Christianity did not inaugurate the action of the Spirit of God in the affairs of men. It interpreted, exalted, purified, stimulated, and completed whatever in the world was congruous with itself. As in the pre-Christian ages so it is now, and so it shall ever be. God is in history, through all its changes and chances fulfilling the purpose of His Providence, and Christian morality garners the truth which He makes known, and discerns the guidance which He gives. The field of His action is co-extensive with creation, and man, as man, is His commissioned prophet. From the Christian point of view there is no

[1] v. Proverbs viii. 15, 16, 29-31.

importance in the distinction so often drawn between Christianity and Hellenism, as if in some sense they were rivals for the glory of being the creators of modern civilization. For the two streams, though so different in course and character, had ultimately the same Source, and their final blending was in the circumstances of history entirely natural.

The concluding paragraph of Dr. Hort's famous Lectures on *The Christian Ecclesia* contains a warning which has a wider relevance than his argument required. In morals as in polity much was left over for the gradual determinations of history:

'In this as in so many other things is seen the futility of endeavouring to make the Apostolic history into a set of authoritative precedents, to be rigorously copied without regard to time and place, thus turning the Gospel into a second Levitical code. The Apostolic age is full of embodiments of purposes and principles of the most instructive kind: but the responsibility of choosing the means was left for ever to the Ecclesia itself, and to each Ecclesia, guided by ancient precedent on the one hand and adaptation to present and future needs on the other. The lesson-book of the Ecclesia, and of every Ecclesia, is not a law but a history.'[1]

'The lesson-book is not a law but a history.' Those words might well be written at the head of every treatise on Christian morality, for they give the key to the process by which it is what it is. The claim that Christian morality is properly described as natural, that is, competent to express the moral demand for all sorts and conditions of men, is really bound up with its power to grow, to hold the allegiance of the human

[1] v. *The Christian Ecclesia*, p. 232.

conscience in every variety of circumstance and at every stage of culture, to keep pace with the waxing knowledge and widening experience of mankind, and thus to vindicate for its essential principles their right to Divine authority.

. The naturalness of Christian morality, implicit in its essential character as the expression of the Creator's Will for His creatures, disallows the mechanical literalism which has sought to press the language of the Gospel into the precise definition of Christian duty, and thus to stamp on Christianity the aspect of an unnatural and impracticable idealism. This obstinate error, which has so often disturbed the minds of Christian men and sharpened the pens of their critics, is sufficiently corrected by the New Testament itself. There is little trace of such literalism in the age when the memory of Jesus was recent. The Apostolic epistles, which include the oldest documents of the Christian society, deal largely with the moral obligations of discipleship but ever take for granted that these grow out of normal situations. Apart from the brief description of the voluntary communism of the Church in Jerusalem which is said to have followed the outpouring of the Spirit on the day of Pentecost, there is nothing in the book of the Acts which suggests that the first believers regarded themselves as bound to a literal understanding of their Master's words, and His own example disallowed it. In any case, the stern teaching of experience was swift to rebuke the unreflecting enthusiasm of the converts. The experiment in voluntary communism ended in failure, and the Church in Jerusalem soon found itself dependent on the charity of the more prosperous

churches which St. Paul had established outside Palestine. Christianity entered on its history without the
handicap of bondage to any specific economic system.
Its principles are indeed more congruous with some
economic systems than with others, but they can find
effective expression in all. It does not concern itself
directly with economic systems, which may be left
to the shaping forces of history: it has a higher rôle.
It can establish fraternity between the slave and his
owner, and equality between the serf and his lord. No
system which the greed and ambition of men has
created will be able to prohibit its glorious paradoxes;
so that finally, by its subtle, pervading power it will
undercut the ancient tyrannies of the world, and vindicate for itself the character of the great Enfranchisement.
Slavery has nearly passed: the crudities of feudalism
are little more than a memory: the gross paradoxes of
industrialism are passing. 'With freedom has Christ
set us free.' Christianity entered on its career unpledged
to systems, economic or social or political, but endowed
with a unique genius of assimilation which, under the
aspect of almost limitless subordination, carried the
promise and potency of vast changes.

It is this unique genius of assimilation which distinguishes Christianity from every other religion. It
possesses in unequalled measure the power to appropriate, absorb, and apply the lessons of an ever widening and varied experience. Adaptation to its secular
environment has been the historic condition of ecclesiastical development, and Christianity now carries the
garnered wealth of centuries of history. The mighty
mingled flood which finally pours itself into the ocean

bears faint resemblance to the tiny stream from the fontal spring far distant in the mountains, but its connexion is certain, its continuity is unbroken, and its essential character is unaltered. That is no inapt picture of Christian morality and its relation to the Gospel.

This amazing power of adaptation to circumstance is not unlimited. It is always conditioned by the original and essential principles which are embodied in the Founder's life and teaching. These have operated, and will ever operate, as the test of legitimate ethical development. The norms of right human conduct are on record in the Gospel, which provides a final court of appeal against the delusive casuistries of history. Civilization and Christianity are not to be identified, though they run a parallel course and both have ultimately the same Divine Author. A perfect civilization and a rightly apprehended Christianity would harmonize, for the kind of social conduct required by Christianity is identical with that which the health and permanence of civilization demand. Every corruption of society which the history of mankind has disclosed is found to be ultimately traceable to a repudiation of the Christian principles of social intercourse. And every anti-social doctrine and policy which the Christian Church has maintained is found to be ultimately traceable to some departure from the essential principles of the religion which the Christian Church professes and, alas, too often profanes. But, however closely they may be associated, civilization and Christianity are inviolably distinct. This important but easily forgotten truth is admirably stated by Dean Church in a great sermon preached before the University of

Oxford in 1868, and published in the volume, *The Gifts of Civilisation*:

'Civilisation cannot be said to be the same thing as the influence of Christianity, or to be purely a result derived from it; for these tendencies to moral improvement existed before Christianity, and showed themselves by unequivocal signs, however much they were thwarted, neutralised, or at last destroyed. There are certain great virtues which social life loudly calls for, and tends to foster; which as thought grows and purposes widen, are felt more clearly to be the true and imperative conditions of all human action. Civilisation, whether or not it presupposes and assists in keeping in view another life, arranges primarily and directly for this one; and these virtues it produces in increasing force and perfection, as its fruit and test. It is no disparagement to that which we believe to be as infinitely greater than civilisation as the future destiny of man is greater than his present state, to acknowledge gladly that these beneficial tendencies were originally implanted in society by the author of society. But the effect has been, that alongside of the influence of Christianity has grown up another influence, not independent of it, yet not identical with it; owing much—it would be bold to limit *how* much—to Christianity, yet having roots of its own; not in its own nature hostile to religion, yet moving on a separate line; sometimes wearing the guise of a rival, sometimes of a suspicious and uncongenial associate, with diverging aims and incommensurate views; but always, even when most friendly, with principles and methods of its own. It has many names, and perhaps none of them happy ones; but it is that power, distinct from religion, however much it may be affected by it, which shapes our polity, and makes our laws, and rules in our tribunals, and sets the standard in literature, and impregnates our whole social atmosphere.'[1]

Civilization develops a morality of its own, limited in

[1] v. *The Gifts of Civilisation*, p. 98.

its requirements, sanctioned by its conventions, enforced by its laws, and this morality has a higher
character than it claims. It reflects the purpose of the
Creator, and attests the influence of His Spirit. But,
though accepted by Christianity and incorporated in
its scheme of human duty, it remains essentially distinct.
There is a significant agreement in the content of
civilized morality. Since, as Aristotle said, 'Man is a
political animal', he must needs live in society with
others, and by that fact be brought under the control of
the conditions which determine social life. A certain
surrender of individual independence, a certain restraint
of private ambitions, a certain control of personal
desires are indispensable to any continuing association
with others. Only so can society cohere and continue:
only in such wise can men live together. Mr. H. L.
Mencken writes truly on the agreement of mankind
on such articles of association:

'All of the really basic varieties of moral good have been
esteemed as such since the memory of mankind runneth not
to the contrary, and all of the basic wickednesses have been
reprehended. . . . The five fundamental prohibitions of the
Decalogue—those levelled at murder, theft, trespass, adultery
and false witness—are to be found in every moral system ever
heard of, and seem to be almost universally supported by human
opinion.'[1]

These five fundamental prohibitions of the Decalogue
are precisely those which social life itself necessitates.
Murder, theft, trespass, adultery, and false witness are
obviously incompatible with the harmony of society,
and, if suffered to prevail therein, would assuredly

----

[1] v. *Treatise on Right and Wrong*, pp. 5, 6.

bring about its dissolution. Therefore, as life in society develops and men are bound together by the multiplying links of civilization, these types of individual behaviour are everywhere condemned and legally punished. The root of the universality of their prohibition lies in the universality of the conditions under which they are seen to be intolerable. When, however, from the morality which is shaped by automatic motives, that is, by the considerations which are imposed on men from without by the conditions under which they must needs live together in society, we turn to the morality which is dictated by motives which are imposed on men from within, which they think out for themselves, we find that we are confronted by an amazing variety. *Quot homines, tot sententiae.* It is here that the so-called revealed religions exercise their formidable authority over men's minds for good and for evil. Here the measure of men's knowledge and the quality of their ideals are reflected in their laws, customs, and policies. Here specific civilizations are shaped, and here specific civilizations must be judged.

The root of the distinction between Christian morality and civilized morality lies in the hidden sphere of motives and sanctions. The same conduct may spring from different motives, and be enforced by different sanctions. The motives and sanctions of civilization are other than those of Christianity, and do not extend to types and descriptions of conduct which fall within the ambit of Christian morals. The point on which we insist, as implied in the statement that Christian morality is natural, is the agreement between the conduct which Christianity requires and that which human civilization at its best insists upon. Christianity is in human society a moral influence which stimulates every element in it which is properly described as natural. This is the reason why Christian civilization has become the norm of modern civilization. In India, in China, in Japan there are distinctive civilizations which have flowered richly in art and literature, and still succeed in holding the allegiance of numerous communities. But all are 'cribbed, cabined, and confined' within local and racial conditions. It is inconceivable that they should win acceptance in Europe and America. Christian civilization alone has the strength, range, and elasticity which make universal adoption ulti- mately inevitable. Whether when so adopted it will retain its ancestral connexion with Christianity may be doubted, but about the connexion there can be no question.

The civilization of Christendom may be compared to a lake into which there is ever passing a stream of living water. As long as that stream flows freely, the lake remains fresh and wholesome: but if that stream should be blocked, and the inflow of living water be made to cease, the lake will speedily become stagnant, noisome, and pestiferous. A dechristianized civiliza- tion will lose its contact with Nature, and be set on a course of progressive moral deterioration. In their admiration for the secular achievements and almost limitless secular promise of modern civilization, men readily forget the unseen conditions of its soundness and permanence. Some observations of the late Lord Bryce in the concluding chapter of his monumental work on *Modern Democracies* indicate an apprehension which few considering students of our modern world will be able to escape:

'The question of the permanence of democracy resolves itself into the question of whether mankind is growing in wisdom and virtue, and with that comes the question of what Religion will be in the future, since it has been for the finer and more sensitive spirits the motive power behind Morality. Governments that have ruled by Force and Fear have been able to live without moral sanctions, or to make their subjects believe that those sanctions consecrated them, but no free government has ever yet so lived and thriven, for it is by reverence for the Powers Unseen and Eternal which impose those sanctions, that the powers of evil have been, however imperfectly, kept at bay and the fabric of society held together.'[1]

Christian morality, being rooted in the Will of the Creator, and having its witness in the human spirit, is natural to man as man. It exalts its professors by emphasizing precisely those elements in them which are distinctively human. Since, as the Sage of Israel says, 'The Spirit of Man is the candle of the Lord', to follow the leadings of the human spirit is to be placed on an ascending path of moral advance. The so-called natural religions, which deified the powers of the physical universe and, by title of those fleshly appetites common to man and beast, held their professors in bondage to what in themselves was least truly human, could not but condemn men to a process of moral declension. See what a paradox the history of religion presents! The fatal ambiguity in the word 'natural' explains the facility with which Religion, the source,

[1] v. *Modern Democracies*, vol. ii, p. 666.

sustenance, and sanction of morality, has been made too often the instrument of its extremest degradation. In view of the vast evils of superstition, how often have thoughtful men echoed the bitter words of Lucretius,

'Tantum religio potuit suadere malorum.'

Perverted beliefs about God draw in their train procedures which insult the reason and wound the heart. Who, reflecting on these fruits of religion, will not sympathize with Plutarch in his preference of atheism to superstition?

'What say you? The man who does not believe in the existence of the gods is unholy? And is not he who believes in such gods as the superstitious believe in a partner to opinions far more unholy? Why, for my part, I should prefer that men should say about me that I have never been born at all, and there is no Plutarch, rather than that they should say "Plutarch is an inconstant fickle person, quick-tempered, vindictive over little accidents, pained at trifles. If you invite others to dinner and leave him out, or if you haven't the time and don't go to call on him, or fail to speak to him when you see him, he will set his teeth into your body and bite it through, or he will get hold of your little child and beat him to death, or he will turn the beast that he owns into your crops and spoil your harvest."'[1]

For the religious man all turns ultimately on his theology, for his theology will draw a congruous morality in its train. Christianity, following and expanding the theology of Judaism, held that man's nature is essentially spiritual. In the Sermon on the Mount Jesus summed up His moral teaching in the pregnant declaration: 'Ye therefore shall be perfect, as your heavenly Father is perfect.' So assured was He

[1] v. *On Superstition*, 10. Babbitt's translation in Loeb's edition.

on this fundamental point of the kinship of man with His Creator that He found the evidence for God's benevolence in the instinctive kindness of men. 'If ye, then, being evil, know how to give good gifts unto your children, how much more shall your Father which is in heaven give good things to them that ask him?'

The naturalness of Christian morality is disclosed by its exaltation of those relationships which we distinguish as natural—the union of the sexes in marriage, the dependence of children on parents, the obligation of parents towards children, the fellowship of the family. How profoundly significant is the position which the Fifth Commandment holds in the Decalogue! It is the link between the two Tables of the Law. In it religion and morality are united. From it flow the great constituents of social duty. The Home, clothed with supernatural sanctions, is the source of all the subordinations and disciplines which are summed up in social obligation. The Divine Law which authenticates parental authority and filial piety is the 'first commandment with promise', for it enshrines the very principle of social stability, apart from which civilization is ultimately impossible.

A few weeks ago I read in the *Manchester Guardian* (August 6, 1935) what seemed to be a careful report of a speech by an eminent publicist whose services to social science are universally recognized, Lord Passfield, still better known to us as Sidney Webb. He was describing to the Fabian Summer School the impressions made on him during a recent visit to Russia:

'We were witnessing the emergence of a new civilization as different from Western civilization as that was from Islam and

Buddhism. It was certainly the biggest thing that had happened in Europe since the Renaissance.'

Lord Passfield described the rule of the Bolsheviks as 'a most extraordinary success':

'The country was relatively prosperous, and there had been no unemployment for the last five years.... The average Russian workman was getting a livelihood and standard of comfort, education and treatment in sickness much better than that of the two million English workmen who are on the dole. The Russian working class families and a large proportion of the collective farm peasants were better off than the lowest grade of our population.'

Similar roseate pictures of life in Soviet Russia are now common, and all appear to have two distinguishing features. On the one hand, they dwell almost exclusively on those elements of human life which lie within the control of the State, omitting all reference to the 'imponderables' which lie outside that control, and do yet finally determine the quality of civilization; and, on the other hand, they are invariably drawn by those whose acquaintance with Russia is brief and superficial, and whose opinions are significantly harmonious with their known hopes and desires. It suffices to observe that they conflict sharply with descriptions which have recently been published by men long resident in Russia (e.g. Mr. Chamberlin in his luminous volume, *Russia's Iron Age*) whose acquaintance with the facts must be far greater than any which even the most observant and discriminating student could gain in the course of a brief visit.

Be the material state of the Russians what it may, I am concerned with the moral situation which the

Bolsheviks have created, and which provides the unseen foundations of whatsoever genuine civilization they can create. Lord Passfield proceeds:

'People born since the revolution had grown up with no sense of sin and largely without a sense of the supernatural.'

If the postulate of the Gifford Trust be true, that is, if man be essentially religious, and theology a natural product of his thinking, then to destroy the sense of sin, which in every man attests the travail of his spirit, and to banish the sense of the supernatural, which in every man is the witness of his immortality, must mean the doing such violence to man's nature as ultimately to ensure his uttermost undoing. Moreover, if the chequered annals of mankind carry any lesson from the past to the present, surely it is that which the philosopher Coleridge tersely expressed in the aphorism, 'Not without celestial observations can even terrestrial charts be accurately constructed.'

NOTE:—Since this lecture was written there has appeared the important book, *Soviet Communism: a New Civilisation?* by Sidney and Beatrice Webb. 2 vols. (Longmans, Green & Co.) I have added in an appendix a careful examination of this work.   H. D.

VII
THE DEVELOPMENT OF CHRISTIAN MORALITY

IN a previous lecture we dwelt on the unique ability of the Christian religion to adapt itself to its secular environment and to assimilate whatever ethically sound elements that environment contained. But we emphasized the fact that, while this adaptation has been the historic condition of ecclesiastical development, it has never destroyed the essential distinction between civilization and Christianity. We pointed out that the two might be intimately associated, so intimately as to suggest an actual identity, and we claimed that an ideal civilization would be entirely harmonious with Christianity. The history of Christendom, we suggested, has disclosed varying relations between them, sometimes a harmony so complete as almost to obliterate difference, and sometimes a discord so extreme as almost to prohibit agreement. Establishment and persecution stand side by side in the record. The one would absorb the Christian Society, the other would destroy it. Both assume that its essential individuality is intolerable. Nevertheless we insisted that the soundness of civilization was measured by the extent of its agreement with Christianity, and we pressed the significance of the fact that the specifically Christian civilization has become in the modern world the norm of civilization itself, as justifying our contention, that Christian morality is uniquely entitled to be described as natural. In the present lecture we propose to consider the fact, the character, and the significance of development in Christian morality.

The morality of the medieval Church, of the early Christian centuries, even of the Apostolic age as it is disclosed in the New Testament, impresses the candid student as in some respects definitely lower than that which modern Christians exhibit and acknowledge. It is not merely a question of a less developed civilization, but of a real change of mind. The excesses of asceticism and the violences of intolerance which darken the annals of the Christian Church, and provide the adversary of Christianity with the materials for his weightiest indictment, are explicable, largely, if not wholly, as the creatures of a semi-civilized phase of social development. Christianity did but reflect the crudities of current pagan dualism and the cruelty of pagan tyranny. The roots of ascetic extravagance and religious persecution grew elsewhere than in the soil of Christianity, though in that soil they grew with unique rapidity and luxuriance. Christianity, as it realized itself in a kinder environment, threw aside these extraneous disfigurements. The modern Christian repudiates both dualistic asceticism and religious persecution, but he still believes with the ascetic that discipline is an essential element in a rightly ordered human life, and he still holds with the persecutor that orthodoxy, that is, accurate thinking in religion and ethics, is of supreme importance. In becoming civilized he has cast aside uncivilized conceptions of asceticism and orthodoxy, while retaining his hold on both. The content of his morality is unchanged, only he sees its practical requirements otherwise than he did. He has been carried forward on the waxing stream of developing culture. In the light of modern science he interprets many things far otherwise than, in the false light of an unsound and often irrelevant theology, his religious ancestors perforce interpreted them. The change in his attitude has been determined by new knowledge and by the teaching of experience, not by any alteration in the basal assumptions of his moral belief. When St. Paul asks, as if his question could only receive a negative answer, 'Is it for the oxen that God careth?' and, when we remember that the questioner is none other than the author of the glorious hymn on Love in the thirteenth chapter of the first Epistle to the Corinthians, we cannot but see that, in his attitude towards animals, St. Paul was on a definitely lower level than the modern Christian who is eagerly concerned to secure humane treatment for bird and beast, and who looks with suspicion and even hostility on the popular sports which involve the suffering and death of sentient creatures. Plutarch was on a higher moral level than St. Paul in this matter of the treatment of animals. In his biography of Cato the Elder he dwells with indignant disgust on the famous Roman's harshness to his slaves and animals, and he expresses his own view:

'We should not treat living creatures like shoes or pots or pans, casting them aside when they are bruised and worn out with service, but, if for no other reason, for the sake of practice in kindness to our fellow men, we should accustom ourselves to mildness and gentleness in our dealings with other creatures. I would not sell even an ox that had worked for me, just because he was old, much less an elderly man, removing him from his habitual place and customary life, as if it were from his native land, for a paltry price, useless as he is to those who sell him and as he will be to those who buy him. But Cato, exulting as it were in such things, says that he left in Spain even the horse which had carried him through his consular campaign, that he might not tax the city with the cost of its transportation. Whether, now, these things should be set down to greatness of spirit or littleness of mind, is an open question.'[1]

Plutarch, as he is revealed in his writings, was a singularly generous and high-minded man, and certainly not typical of the society to which he belonged. The highly developed civilization of the Graeco-Roman world had no feeling for the sufferings of animals. The popularity and persistence of the hideous spectacles in the arena demonstrate its callousness. I do not think that civilization as such would ever concern itself with the moral obligations which condition our treatment of animals. If, therefore, humanitarian sentiment, from the influence of which not even animals are shut out, has become a distinctive note of modernly civilized communities, we can hardly be mistaken in ascribing the fact to the theory and practice of Christian morality.

Plutarch, in the true spirit of the Greek moralists, bases his kindness to animals on his own moral interest, that thereby he may train himself in kindness to men. St. Paul, like the true Jew he was, bases his argument on what he mistakenly assumes to be congruous with the character of God. It seemed to his thinking unworthy of Jehovah to concern Himself with the distresses of animals. In fact Plutarch's conclusion was Christian, while his premises were Greek. St. Paul's conclusion was based on a defective theology. In his indifference

---

[1] v. *Lives*, Cato Major, in Loeb's Classics, Perrin's translation.

to the claims of animals as such, he stood with the pre-Christian world. Christian morality has endorsed the attitude of the Greek moralist and disallowed that of the Christian Apostle.

Take another illustration. Who has not felt astonishment and repugnance when reading the passage in St. Augustine's *Confessions* in which he narrates his heartless dismissal of the faithful woman who for years had been his wife in all but name, and had borne him a dearly loved son? He dwells on his own distress, but has never a word for hers, and states how, unable to wait two years until the girl whom he had arranged to marry was old enough for marriage, he provided himself with another concubine:

'Home again went she into Africa (vowing to thee never to know man more), leaving a bastard son with me, which I had begotten of her. But unhappy I, who had not the heart to imitate a woman, impatient now of all delay—quickly procured another.'[1]

His own conscience seems never to have troubled him; his saintly mother, who was eager for his marriage, acquiesced in, if she did not even encourage, his brutality. St. Augustine, we remember, is, perhaps, next to St. Paul, the most illustrious figure in the undivided Church, and the most influential of Christian thinkers. His strong and winning personality has impressed itself deeply on Christian thought, both ethical and theological. He remains a potent force to this day. His *Confessions*, from which we have quoted, are counted among the spiritual classics of Christendom, nay of humanity. How is it explicable that he could

[1] v. *Confessions*, vi. 15.

treat a loyal woman so basely? Clearly the standard of morality in the matter of man's treatment of women has been notably advanced since his time.

If, then, we take a general view of Christian history, and seek to formulate some theory which shall interpret the incongruous and even contradictory witness which it seems to deliver, we cannot resist the conclusion that Christian morality as we conceive of it in the twentieth century includes much which was absent from Christian morality as it was conceived in the first. Nor need this surprise us. The modes in which the Christian religion was carried into men's acceptance, and the conditions under which it was established, were so various, that the effect on the religion itself could not but be very great. It were, indeed, hardly an exaggeration to say that, in the process of expansion, Christian morality received almost as much as it gave. Christianity has enlarged its dominion by a method not wholly unlike that which has been adopted by the imperialist statesmen of modern Europe. First, large territories inhabited by semi-civilized or barbarous peoples are annexed as protectorates or spheres of influence. Next, a gradual process of education and assimilation is inaugurated in order effectively to civilize the new populations. Thus, in course of time, a new type of citizen is created in which the standing requirements of civic allegiance are blended with elements drawn from the older cultures. This result represents a genuine development of the civic ideal, a development which may be upwards or downwards, involving in the one case a real enrichment of that ideal, and in the other as real an impoverishment. For development ever carries the burden of the alternative—either progress or degeneration. In the blending of diverse elements in the crucible of history, sometimes the lower prevail and sometimes the higher. The final outcome of the process is something definitely lower or definitely higher than the unblended constituents. Christian morality has developed variously, illustrating the general law, here maturing nobly, there degenerating grossly. Christendom, the sphere of its development, exhibits arresting instances of both tendencies. Nowhere have the distinctive vices of pre-Christian types, racial and cultural, been displayed more patently, and nowhere have the distinctive virtues been more nobly expressed. The servility of the Asiatic, the emotionalism of the African, the chicanery and sycophancy of the Greek, the ruthless imperialism of the Roman, the crude violence and wayward sentimentalism of the Teuton, —all have asserted themselves within the Christian sphere, and gained therein a superlative emphasis. All the familiar types known to human experience are at their best, and worst, in their Christian versions. Sovereign and subject, statesman and prelate, lawyer and merchant, thinker and artist, casuist and ecclesiastic, teacher and student, trader and workmen, husband and wife, child and patriot—within Christendom, in the bracing atmosphere of Christian individualism, all are at their best, and worst.

In the process of moral development we may distinguish three principal factors—the influence of the human material on which Christianity has had to work, the pressure of circumstances forcing the Christian conscience to face new situations, and the increase of knowledge, disallowing old precedents, and compelling new assumptions. These must be more carefully considered.

I. *The Human Material.* The world in which Christianity was preached was an old world, with long traditions, strongly entrenched customs, distinctive racial types, immemorial institutions, and the all pervading habit of an advanced and articulated culture. Behind the first preachers was the inheritance of Judaism, and their version of morality, as we have it in the canonical literature, is dominated by the fact. St. Paul, the leading figure of the Apostolic age, and not unfairly described as the founder of the Church's ethical and theological system, was himself a pupil of the Rabbis. His education at the feet of Gamaliel has coloured his moral teaching as well as his modes of theological argument. But the Rabbinic morality was not wholly congruous with the mind of Christ, and, as the Jewish tradition waned and the principles of Christianity found freer expression in the larger society of the Graeco-Roman world, the incongruity became increasingly apparent. The Rabbinic colouring grew fainter, Jewish Christianity failed and passed, and Christian morality absorbed new elements from the non-Jewish converts. The Jewish material gave place very speedily to the Greek and the Roman, which prevailed in the ancient civilized world, and, when that world foundered in the storms of barbarian invasion, these were succeeded by the distinctive elements of the modern civilized world, Teutonic, Celtic, and Slavonic. Within the last two centuries Christianity has begun to tell effectively on the highly distinctive human material of Asia and Africa, and it is already apparent that this will follow the general rule. Every one of these varieties of the common human material has had a fashioning influence on the religion which has succeeded in bringing them all under its penetrating and disciplinary influence.

The intense individualism of the Jew, the secularist habit of the Greek, the masterful legalism of the Latin, the strong family life of the Teuton, the clannishness of the Celt, the corporate almost impersonal temper of the Slav, the half-disclosed idiosyncrasies of the Asiatic and the African survive in their Christian versions, and contribute distinctive elements to the Christian ethic which is always in process of becoming, never something finished and complete.

We have already said that behind the original preaching of Christianity there was the inheritance of Judaism. In the Old Testament, which the Christian Church took over from the Jews, there was expressed a version of morality which was frankly Jewish, and as such not wholly congruous with Christian principles nor wholly adequate to Christian needs. Very soon the Church took the momentous step of adding a Christian supplement to the Jewish Scriptures. The New Testament was given a place alongside the Old as part of the Christian's Bible, and by a logical necessity became the primary factor within it. One result was far-reaching in its effect. The teaching of the Apostles acquired the fixed and final authority of canonical Scripture. As such it was immune from criticism, and placed on an equal level of importance throughout. Little account was taken of the circumstances in which that teaching had been originally given, and thus elements in it which

have no essential permanence, and are properly regarded as temporary, reflecting rather the inevitable
prejudices of ancestral Judaism than the frank application of Christian principles, became clothed with an
undeserved finality, which has clouded and confused
the Christian conscience ever since.

No human material has been more distinctive than
the Jewish. To this day the indestructible individuality
of the Jewish people constitutes an insoluble problem
for statesmen. Through the canonical literature, which
in origin and history was Jewish, Christian morality
received a Jewish colour which it still retains.

An illustration is provided by the Christian treatment of women. On this subject the teaching of Jesus
was not entirely welcome, nor indeed wholly intelligible
to His followers, of whom the greatest hardly seems to
have accorded with it. St. Paul, we may not forget,
was not quite in the same position as the other disciples.
He was not like the older apostles an uneducated man,
nor had he shared that personal contact with Jesus
which at once commended and in some measure interpreted His words. He could not possess their naïve
receptivity. The graduate of a Jewish university could
hardly be as the unlettered peasants of Galilee.

It is impossible to read St. Paul's Epistles without
perceiving that he is sometimes more Rabbinic than
Christian. Not always, for he rises above Rabbinism
when he declares that the enfranchisement which Jesus
has secured for humanity prevails even over the barrier
of sex: 'There can be neither Jew nor Greek, there can be
neither bond nor free, there can be no male and female.'[1]

[1] v. Galatians, iii. 28.

Postponing to a later lecture our consideration of the
Christian attitude towards the problems of sex, it is
sufficient for our present purpose to point to the exceptional, and in some respects excessive, influence of the
Jewish factor on the development of sexual morality in
Christendom as providing the most conspicuous illustration of the effect which the human material has had on
the religion which has fashioned it. This is a continuing
phenomenon in Christian experience. As nationality
has developed in modern Christendom, and uttered
itself in language and literature, in social use and
political institutions, in local patriotism and economic
habit, in art and architecture, so it has told subtly yet
potently on religion. Every nation has its own well-
marked version of Christianity, and places its own
emphasis on the various elements of Christian morality.
The spiritual heroes are racy of the soil. Only Italy
could have produced a St. Francis or a Savonarola;
only France a St. Louis, a Maid of Orleans, a Blaise
Pascal, or a St. Francis Xavier; only Germany a Luther
or a Zinzendorf; only Spain a St. Dominic or a St.
Ignatius Loyola; only England an Alfred, a Sir Thomas
More, an Elizabeth Fry, or a General Gordon; only
Scotland a John Knox, a Dr. Chalmers, or a David
Livingstone. The ethical distinctiveness of the moral
types, so apparent in the famous persons, is represented
on lower levels of prominence by all sorts and conditions
of men. Nor may we reasonably suppose that the future
will in this respect differ from the past. The unassimi-
lated treasures of humanity are indefinitely great. As
the sharply marked ethnical types of Asia and Africa
pass under the influence, at once stimulating and

disciplinary, of Christianity, they also will tell potently on Christian conceptions of faith and duty. A genuinely Catholic Christianity which has incorporated into its dominion the distinctive genius of the Japanese, the Chinese, the Hindu, the Arab, and the African will be vastly richer and nobler than any version of Christ's religion which the world has hitherto known. All the ethical treasures of humanity will finally find complete and permanent expression in Christian morality.

II. *The Pressure of Circumstances* forcing the Christian conscience to face new situations, and to determine ethical requirements with respect to them.

The student of the Apostolic age will not fail to observe that the founders of the Christian society were little embarrassed by fixed regulations imposed in advance of the circumstances to which they would be properly relevant. In a previous lecture we quoted a luminous sentence from Dr. Hort's writings to the effect that 'not a law but a history' has been 'the lesson-book of the Ecclesia'. Here we must emphasize the effect of experience in drawing out the ethical implications of Christianity. Even so crucial an issue as the admission of Gentiles to the Church on equal terms with Jews was not determined until an actual situation forced the Apostles to confront it. St. Peter, to whom it was made known by a vision that he 'must call no man common or unclean', and who in deference to that Divine admonition sanctioned and defended the baptism of the Roman centurion Cornelius, was unable to maintain his liberal attitude, and drew upon himself by his vacillating behaviour the stern rebuke of St. Paul. The extreme hostility which the Christian Jews exhibited towards St. Paul shows how startling to the first believers appeared that equality in Christ which is now the very assumption of Christian thought. The circumstances in which the converts of the Apostles were actually living dictated the character and limited the range of the morality which they were required to acknowledge. Christians then formed an obscure and unpopular sect living in the midst of a pagan society despotically governed, and based on the institution of slavery. There was no practical reason why they should contemplate such civic obligations as we, the members of a free self-governing democracy, must needs contemplate. Obedience to the State and an honest fulfilment of social obligations within the limits prescribed by their Christian profession exhausted the actual obligations of the Christian subject of the Roman Caesar.

The character of the State has changed, and that change has involved a corresponding change in the conception of civic duty. The obligations of a good citizen in a free self-governing democracy are essentially different from those of a good citizen in an autocratically governed empire. Responsibility inheres in power, and precisely because democracy invests the individual citizen with larger power, it binds on him also a larger responsibility. In fact the citizen's obligation has been extended, and now includes what was once the autocrat's monopoly, namely, responsibility for the system and policy of the State itself. Therefore the free citizen of a democracy has to enlarge his conception of moral obligation by including within it a more extended area of social behaviour, and, as a Christian, he has to discover the bearing of discipleship on his civic duty, and to apply the principles of his religion to the novel and multiplying activities of citizenship. He cannot, as Pilate vainly essayed to do, wash his hands of responsibility for the public policies which as a citizen he had a hand in shaping. He cannot divest himself of his Christian character when he enters the polling booth; for, though the methods of government must in some respects differ from those of private duty, yet the principles of morality are immutable, and the grand objective of all rightful human action is the same. Nor does the case differ when the argument is transferred from the political to the economic plane, though the area within which individual action can tell effectively on economic conditions is far more limited than it is pleasant to admit. Here also we can see that there has been advance.

Feudalism was ethically on a higher level than the slave-based societies of antiquity; and industrialism, as it has been known in the past, was certainly on a higher ethical level than feudalism. Confessedly there has been a change for the worse; and industrialism under the conditions with which we are familiar, and in the monstrous forms which, notably in America, it has taken, is plainly challenging the Christian conscience, and calling with ever-growing insistence for some drastic revision of the traditional working morality of Christendom. How long the monstrous economic structure will survive the disappearance of its moral sanctions remains to be seen. Here we emphasize the apparent fact that Christian morality to-day goes deeper and carries farther than in the past. St. Paul, in the circumstances of his age, could satisfy his conscience by sending the fugitive slave Onesimus back to his master with a request that he should be treated kindly as a brother in Christ, but it is inconceivable that if the Apostle had been living now he would thus have accepted, without challenge or criticism, a social institution which itself involved a flagrant violation of Christian fraternity. The whole question of Christian obligation is now debated on a higher level. There has been a genuine development of Christian morality, so that what was tolerable, and as it seemed inevitable, to the best Christian of the Apostolic age would be repugnant to the average Christian of modern times. The effective cause of the change has been the change of circumstances which has compelled Christians to read their duty in a new light. The change has been dictated by non-moral causes. Experience has demonstrated the economic disadvantages of slavery, and men in their own selfish interest have been led to abandon it. But the important fact is that the change is seen by Christians, not to conflict with the principles of their religion, but to be properly required by their application. They find themselves under no necessity of explaining away the demands of Christian morality by some elaborate casuistry, but, on the contrary, they are enabled to see their duty more clearly in the absence of the obscuring prejudices of economic doctrine and secular advantage. How different is the situation of the Mohammedan or the Hindu! The rising standards of civilization compel an ever wider breach with the moral requirements of their religions. What the late Lord Cromer held of Mohammedanism, that it could with difficulty provide a possible basis for modern civilization because of its religious attitude towards slavery and the female sex,[1] may be said, *mutatis mutandis*, of the other non-Christian religions. The ethical development of mankind does not in their case, as in the case of Christianity, bring out their true principles into freer expression and more illuminating prominence, but strikes the principles themselves with an obsoleteness which is apparent, extreme, and irrecoverable.

It is to be noted that the development of Christian morality under the pressure of circumstances is to be clearly distinguished from those politic accommodations to extraordinary situations which have been made repeatedly in Christian history, and never made without bringing the Christian religion into grave discredit. Development draws out the principles into new applications, and thus discloses the inspired activity of the Christian spirit. Politic accommodations obscure the principles, and may even contradict them altogether. They imply, not the fresh activity of the Christian spirit, but its inertness, the pressure of mundane interest, the timidity or ambition of individuals, and the low-toned casuistry of Erastianism.

A notable example of such politic accommodation is provided by the melancholy history of the American slave trade. Why was it that the Christian churches so generally acquiesced in, and even defended, the enslavement of the negroes? Partly, zealous men were led to 'do evil that good might come'. They sought to remove the practical difficulties in the way of evangelizing the slaves, which were raised by the fears and suspicions of the slave-owners. They argued that Christian baptism

---

[1] v. *Modern Egypt*, vol. ii, ch. xxxiv.

need not imply the freedom of the baptized, and that slave-holding was not necessarily incompatible with the Christian profession. The classic instance of Philemon was ready to their hand. Mostly the reasons for complaisance were less respectable. The black skin, repulsive aspect, and crude savagery of the negroes made it plausible to draw a distinction between them and the rest of mankind. Their spiritual interest was supposed to be served by their being brought, albeit with violence, within the sphere of Christian influences. Thus even good men like Whitfield were led to recognize the merciful provision of Divine Providence in an institution which in its essence and practical expressions was an impudent violation of Divine Law! The material interest of the British colonies seemed to necessitate the maintenance of slavery, which was energetically defended by British statesmen on that ground. Such pleas were able to silence the protests, if not wholly to satisfy the consciences, of Christian men. Even so genuine a Christian and so clear-sighted a thinker as Bishop Butler could not wholly emancipate himself from such sophistries, though he yielded with evident reluctance and distress of mind. In the sermon to the Society for the Propagation of the Gospel in Foreign Parts, preached in 1739, Butler refers to the case of the negroes in America. His language reflects the embarrassment of the preacher, for it oscillates between an acknowledgement of the negroes' wrongs and an apology for their continuance:

'Of these our colonies, the slaves ought to be considered as inferior members, and therefore to be treated as members of them: and not merely as cattle or goods, the property of their masters. Nor can the highest property, possible to be acquired in these servants, cancel the obligation to take care of their religious instruction. Despicable as they may appear in our eyes, they are the creatures of God, and of the race of mankind for whom Christ died: and it is inexcusable to keep them in ignorance of the end for which they were made, and the means whereby they may become partakers of the general redemption. On the contrary, if the necessity of the case requires, that they may be treated with the very utmost rigour, that humanity will at all permit, as they certainly are; and, for our advantage, made as miserable as they well can be in the present world; this surely heightens our obligation to put them into as advantageous a situation as we are able, with regard to another.'[1]

In these sentences we catch the note of sardonic humour which is characteristic of Butler when he is deeply moved. He acquiesces in an accommodation which he feels to be wrong, and consciously accepts, on the plea of practical necessity, a lowering of the level of Christian morality. Fifty years ago in East London I used to hear the preachers of atheism make great play with a book containing a collection of pronouncements by American preachers in favour of slavery. They offered it to their hearers as an authorized exposition of Christian morality. In so doing they were mistaking for legitimate development what was really no more than a temporary and unwarrantable accommodation to circumstances.

I am disposed to think that the root of the ecclesiastical malady historically known as 'Erastianism' is to be found in accommodation. In the circumstances of their time, the leaders of Christianity find themselves in a situation which seems to place religious liberty, and the opportunities of religious work, in the hands of the

[1] v. *Works*, ed. Bernard, i. 209.

secular power. They readily make a virtue of necessity, and disguise their complaisance under some plausible plea of spiritual duty. Apologies for establishment in principle are commonly justifications of some specific establishment. Thus Hooker, in his *Ecclesiastical Polity*, defends the arrangements of the Elizabethan Settlement, and Warburton, in the *Alliance between Church and State*, does as much for the depraved version of the same which flourished under George II. In earlier times, when power was vested in monarchs, the personal piety of the sovereign might disguise the real character of the deference which he could count upon, but the root of it was ever the same—an accommodation to a specific situation. Hierarchies, as well Catholic as Protestant, are persistently parasitic, prompt to offer homage to power, and fertile in theories to justify it. Erastianism is no true development of Christian morality.

Such accommodations invariably have the character of politic abatements of the full ethical demand. They imply a temporary suspension of Christian morality in deference to urgent practical requirements. They apply the dangerous aphorism, *Necessitas non habet legem*, and the consequences are what might be expected. We may compare them with those suspensions of the Habeas Corpus Act which are authorized in such situations of civil disturbance as may imperil the stability of the State. Unhappily such accommodations, which can only be defended, if defended at all, by their temporary character, are but too likely to take rank as precedents, and in that capacity to wield an influence on subsequent practice which is irrational, mischievous, and extensive. This permanent lowering of moral standards is a far greater evil than immediate scandal, though it is less easily perceived and less frequently realized.

Generally it may be said that the pressure of circumstances has influenced the development of Christian morality by determining the emphasis which the Christian society has placed on the several parts of its ethical demand. The conditions under which the Christians lived in the pagan empire compelled them to withdraw as far as possible from contact with general society, to sustain with patience the oppressions of authority, and to disarm by persistence in confessedly virtuous behaviour the obstinate prejudices of the multitude. With the conversion of Constantine, the situation changed dramatically. The Church emerged from obscurity, and came out into the strong light of establishment. Christians were suddenly called upon to resist the novel temptations of social consequence, and to accept the unaccustomed responsibilities of governing power. The situation was rendered all the more difficult by the fact that the Christian Church included in its membership no more than a minority of the population. Paganism was roughly handled, but it died hard, if indeed it can be truly said to have died at all. The morality which the Christian Empire forced on the masses was a strange amalgam of old and new. With the downfall of the Roman Empire, and the establishment within its area of the Teutonic Kingdoms, the Church found itself confronted with the necessity, no longer of Christianizing populations, which, though pagan, were anciently civilized, but of civilizing on Christian lines communities which were both pagan and uncivilized. How difficult, intermittent, and embarrassed the process was may be seen in the record of Gregory of Tours, which is an amazing picture of the conflict between Christianity and barbarism. The crudest vices stand alongside the noblest virtues. Emphasis was necessarily placed on elementary morality, the issues of the human against the bestial in man. The Penitentials, which are so distinctive a feature of the age, were largely concerned with those sins of violence and sensuality which dominate barbarian life.

III. *The Increase of Knowledge disallowing old precedents and compelling new assumptions.* Christianity claims to be the natural religion of mankind. It may adopt the famous sentiment of the Roman poet,

Humani nihil a me alienum puto.[1]

As the true version of man's essential self, it must needs accept, assimilate, and absorb every element of truth which is disclosed in the slow upward movement of humanity. Just because Christianity is essentially not racial, nor local, nor secular, but truly human, it possesses this unique power of incorporating into its version of truth every genuine increase of man's knowledge, and including in its version of duty every obligation that is properly universal and permanent. Unembarrassed by the intellectual paradoxes of polytheistic theology and the moral confusions of dualistic philosophy, the Christian religion requires its professors to regard nature with reverence as the instrument of its Creator's self-revelation, and history with profound interest as the ordained sphere of Divine Providence. At the same

[1] Terence, *Heaut.* I. i. 24.

time, its sublime assumption that man is essentially
akin to his Maker, that 'the spirit of man is the candle
of the Lord', that the intuitions of man's conscience
are rightly clothed with the august character of Divine
intimations, and that the working of the Spirit of God
is most fully apparent in that civilized order which
is the most distinctive and beneficent achievement of
man's genius—this sublime assumption of man's kindred
with God has wonderfully stimulated the higher human
faculties, and predisposed men to accept the revelations
of science and the ventures of secular progress.

We have here the key to what is perhaps the most
amazing of the enigmas with which human experience
is filled. Why is it that Christianity, the 'other worldly'
religion *par excellence*, whose professors describe themselves with obvious fitness as 'strangers and pilgrims'
on the earth, whose most illustrious representatives
have been saints and martyrs, whose members live by
faith, and in an unsympathetic or even hostile environment, 'endure as seeing Him who is invisible', is housed
in the Christendom we see—wealthy, luxurious, arrogant? Why is it that a religion which despises this
world and pictures it as the mere vestibule and training
ground of another in which alone life is real, rich, and
abiding, has yet moved men to the most impressive and
sustained demonstrations of human courage, power, and
persistence, and has in the course of centuries created
for its secular vesture the most elaborate, powerful,
beneficent, and enduring of all the civilizations known
to human record? Students of antiquity have dwelt
frequently on the note of despondency, even of despair,
which is audible in its literature, and gave a prevailingly

sombre colour to its life. Against this background of diffused and dominant pessimism the professors of Christianity presented an arresting spectacle of jubilant hope, untiring activity, habitual cheerfulness, and confidence. Dr. Hort held that the secret of the difference lay in the Christian belief that by His Resurrection Christ had validated human effort, and guaranteed the permanence of human achievement. Our Lord's Resurrection, he says,

'reversed every doom of every kind of death, and thus annulled the hopelessness which must settle down on every one who thinks out seriously what is involved in the universal empire of death. It was by the faith in the Resurrection that mankind was enabled to renew its youth.'[1]

In these words the great Cambridge scholar is but echoing the thought of the Christian Apostle, when at the conclusion of his long argument for resurrection, so familiar to English folk as part of the lesson appointed in the Burial Service, he calls his readers to eager and hopeful effort: 'Wherefore, my beloved brethren, be ye stedfast, unmoveable, always abounding in the work of the Lord, forasmuch as ye know that your labour is not vain in the Lord.' 'Vain' means 'empty' or 'futile'. The Christian, St. Paul suggests, knows that the external aspect of things gives no trustworthy account of their real character and importance, that the true standard by which values are to be determined was disclosed in the life of the Master, that the final vindication of effort is not found here but hereafter, that 'the things that are seen are temporal but the things which are not seen

[1] v. *The First Epistle of St. Peter*, p. 34.

are eternal'. It needs not that I should remind you that this inspiring and invigorating influence of Christian faith on mundane life has often been obscured, and even denied, by the obscurantist obsessions of fanaticism and the morbid absorptions of asceticism. But we are here concerned with the inherent ability of Christ's religion to embrace new knowledge, and thus to enlarge and enrich the content of its morality. That precisely within Christendom, that is, within the social order which the Christian religion has shaped and coloured, the mighty fabric of modern science has come into being and developed, is a fact which cannot be ignored or explained away, and which has a valid place in our present argument. We may recognize frankly that we owe the elements of physical science to the thinkers of ancient Greece, and yet the question remains and must be answered—Why was it that only within Christendom did that classical inheritance become fruitful? I have already pointed out that the quality of the human material which Christianity had to handle told subtly and potently on its own ethical system. We may concede much to the distinctive idiosyncrasies of the European nations, which form the constituents of modern Christendom; but, even so, those nations were cradled and nurtured by the Catholic Church, and the raw material of their natural potency was fashioned and directed by Christianity. If there had not been something in that religion which was friendly to intellectual progress, which stimulated scientific inquiry, and predisposed men to accept truth and to weave it into the fabric of their thought, the Greek heritage of mental freedom and scientific investigation would have had no better fortunes within the Christian sphere than they had within the Mohammedan. The suggested comparison is certainly not unfair to the religion of Mohammed, for the populations of the Eastern Empire which fell under the power of the Khalifs were, in far richer measure than those of the Western Empire which came under the rule of the Teutonic barbarians, the inheritors of Greek culture. The Arabians were too few to do more than establish themselves as rulers, and to impose their creed on their subjects. Accordingly, the difference between the fortunes of Greek culture in the East and in the West cannot be explained by the difference in ethnical quality between the Semite and the Teuton. Not race but religion gives the key to the history of civilization both in Christian and in Mohammedan countries. Christianity is morally, aesthetically, intellectually stimulating. Mohammedanism is a religion of stagnation and decline. The one has created a civilization, the other has destroyed one; and such substitutes for what it ruined as it has provided have achieved little and promise nothing.

The paradoxical aspect of Christian history may easily blind the student to its true significance. It is, indeed, difficult to overstate the strangeness of the paradox. Christianity is the religion of peace, yet it has occasioned more, and more destructive, wars than any other: it is the religion of truth, yet no forms of falsehood have been more subtle and depraving than those which its casuists have imagined and defended: it is the religion of humility, and yet the extreme expressions of human pride have been seen in its ordained exponents: it is the religion of love, yet no persecutions have been more relentless and persistent than those organized in its professed interest: it is the religion of freedom, and yet no type and measure of bondage, social, political, and economic, have been absent from Christendom: it is the religion of spiritual franchise, yet nowhere else has sacerdotal pretension been more extravagant, or superstition more abject. It is surely nowise astonishing that ecclesiastical history has been an armoury from which the assailants of Christianity have drawn their deadliest weapons. The words, sombre and even threatening as they are, which the Founder of Christianity addressed to His disciples in the Sermon on the Mount, may well serve as a summary of Christian history:

'Ye are the salt of the earth: but if the salt have lost its savour, wherewith shall it be salted? it is thenceforth good for nothing, but to be cast out and trodden under foot of men.'

Nevertheless, throughout this history of extreme and sinister paradox, the true genius of the religion was ceaselessly operative, here moving the stirring protests of individual heroes, and there steadily creating a Christian conscience in the masses of Christendom. In due time there comes some notable apocalypse of the Christian spirit, lifting the whole level of general morality, and proscribing some ancient iniquity as for ever exiled from Christian acceptance. The motto of the student of ecclesiastical history should be *Finem respice*, 'look to the end'. Instead of dwelling on the immense scandals, look at the situation which has followed them. The Christian society learns the lessons of its own failures. The scandals of the past are acknowledged and lamented. The sophistries by which they were justified are detected. The errors which occasioned them are repudiated. Modern Christianity bears a steady and strengthening witness to the moral ideal which Jesus proclaimed and which Jesus embodied. The familiar cycle is traversed from vehement opposition to authoritative endorsement. In due course the novel truth, tested in the fire of conflict and purged of incidental error, takes its rightful place in the general scheme, and Christian morality is found to have been disentangled from some compromising misconceptions, and brought to bear more effectively on a still larger area of human action.

VIII

SEXUAL MORALITY

IN the present lecture and in the three following lectures I propose to consider Christian morality as it determines human conduct with respect to certain matters which now are greatly exercising the minds of thoughtful men in every civilized community, and which enter in varying measures of prominence into the open repudiation of the Christian tradition of duty which is now general and, as many think, advancing. The most intimate and the most public concerns of the individual are affected by the view he takes of Sex, Race, Economics, and Civic obligation. It is precisely on these subjects that there is an apparent, and perhaps a widening, breach between the conduct which Christianity requires and that which is now common among non-Christians. If, indeed, this be the situation, and there is a fundamental dissidence between the traditional morality of Christendom and the accepted standards and procedures of modern society, it needs no argument to demonstrate that an open conflict between them is finally unavoidable. To some extent, perhaps, it may be the case that the Christian view on these questions is misconceived, opinions being regarded as representative and authoritative which are properly no more than sectional and unauthorized; and, to some extent, it is certainly the case that the modern alternatives to the Christian tradition are no more than essays on which the verdict of experience has not yet been passed. Nevertheless, when full allowance has been made both for misunderstandings of the Christian demand and for the experimental character of its rivals, there does undoubtedly remain an area within which a direct conflict between the two conceptions of human duty must be frankly acknowledged: and, with respect to this, it is the contention of these lectures that Christian morality is alone genuinely natural, and alone carries the promise of a true human development, alike of the individual and of society.

We are concerned in this lecture with the questions connected with the natural fact of Sex, admittedly the ultimate root of many, perhaps most, of the constituent elements of civilization. The whole issue of personal morality may be said, not excessively, to be bound up with the treatment of sexual relations. In this connexion Christianity has been often and vehemently denounced as irrationally and mischievously ascetic. It is important to consider this accusation with some care.

Asceticism simply means training determined by purpose. The word was transferred from the sphere of athletics to that of ethics. St. Paul had pictured the Christian life as a race in the arena, run under the familiar conditions. Training or discipline entered from the first into the Christian conception of morality. In this regard, of course, Christianity was nowise exceptional, though it is not to be denied that the Christian doctrine of 'original sin' gave to asceticism a distinctive character and gravity.

Asceticism is inseparable from deliberate moral effort, and since religion as it emerges from mere naturalism requires and stimulates moral effort, asceticism may be truly said to be integral to religion itself. Accordingly, in one form or another, asceticism enters into all the higher forms of religion, and in the history of the highest it has played a great part. No criticism of historic Christianity has been more weightily urged than that which is based on its ascetic character. Thus Lecky accumulates an indictment. Asceticism, he says, altered 'the proportion of virtues', giving to an unnatural chastity the primacy which in the New Testament is assigned to love: it emphasized disastrously the depravity of human nature, and invested the life of virtue with a sombreness which was both excessive and unwholesome: it cast a profound discredit on the domestic virtues, and dragged down the female sex into a deep and pervasive degradation. This criticism, considered in the light of Christian history, cannot be fairly said to be without large justification. Nevertheless it is more plausible than sound. It does not discriminate between the requirements of the Christian religion and the mistaken estimates of those requirements which have too often dominated Christian thought and determined Christian action. It fails to distinguish between the asceticism of self-discipline and the asceticism of self-mutilation, between that which aims at bringing the body under control and that which aspires to belittle, suppress, and, in a sense, annihilate the body. The one vindicates, the other destroys, the rightful balance of human nature. This distinction is essential if the ascetic character of Christian morality is to be rightly understood. Christianity is unquestionably ascetic in the one sense, and as unquestionably non-ascetic in the other. Its doctrine of original sin requires self-discipline: its doctrine of the essential goodness of human nature authenticates self-expression. The two activities are complementary. In common parlance, however, asceticism is understood to mean, not that reasonable self-control which is determined in the interest of nature, but an arbitrary suppression of properly natural instincts. In traditional usage an ascetic is a monk. We are concerned with the normal habit of Christians, not with the special disciplines of solitaries and conventuals.

We have seen that the original constituents of Christian morality were largely derived from Judaism, and that Judaism was effectually protected against irrational asceticism by its creed, which was inviolably monotheistic. In Israel faith and morality were indissolubly united. Irrational or self-annihilating asceticism has ever been the concomitant of dualistic conceptions of human nature. For dualism postulates an original and integral contradiction within human nature itself, and thus provides a key to that enigma of moral conflict which is the very hall-mark of humanity. It assumes an ultimate and irremovable divergence between the physical and the moral constituents of human nature, presenting the one as the normal and natural adversary of the other, to be suppressed and destroyed, never to be disciplined and brought into natural harmony. Jewish religion required, not the suppression but the consecration of the material factor. 'The earth is the Lord's and the fulness thereof' was the assumption of its ethical doctrine. Thus the Jews stood firmly for the unity of man's life and the universality of God's empire. Their dream of final felicity took shape in the vision of a completely consecrated universe, when 'the earth should be full of the knowledge of the Lord,

as the waters cover the sea'. The prophet Zechariah
conceives of the ultimate triumph of Israel in terms of
an all-penetrating dedication to Jehovah:

'In that day shall there be upon the bells of the horses, HOLY
UNTO THE LORD; and the pots in the Lord's house shall be like
the bowls before the altar. Yea, every pot in Jerusalem and in
Judah shall be holy unto the Lord of hosts; and all they that
sacrifice shall come and take of them, and seethe therein: and
in that day there shall be no more a Canaanite in the house of the
Lord of hosts.'[1]

The anti-ascetical tradition of Judaism was confirmed
and illustrated by the Founder of Christianity. His
manner of life was such as to lend a certain plausibility
to the prejudiced comments of His contemporaries.
'The Son of man is come eating and drinking; and ye
say, Behold, a gluttonous man, and a wine-bibber, a
friend of publicans and sinners!' None the less there
was much in the life and teaching of Jesus which could
not but provide a foundation for ascetical developments
in the Christian society. He was Himself unmarried,
and He called His disciples to the renunciation of
domestic claims in the interest of the Kingdom which
He proclaimed. In the cause of that Kingdom He laid
down His life in the shame and sorrow of universal
desertion. The Cross became the significantly inevitable symbol of His service, and an ascetical habit of life
seemed to be inseparable from any tolerable interpretation of the 'Imitatio Christi'. Renunciation of secular
comfort and advantage in the interest of the spiritual
Kingdom has clothed with an ascetical character the
lives of multitudes of devoted believers, but obviously

[1] v. Zechariah, xiv. 20, 21.

such renunciation could not be universal. The mass of Christians were neither missionaries nor martyrs. Their discipleship had to express itself in the normal situations of secular life—in home, business, society, and politics. Their problem was the ancient problem, coeval and coextensive with moral life itself. How to vindicate for the spirit its rightful authority over the flesh, how to preserve the freedom of the self amid the enslaving forces of mundane life, how to garner the whole harvest of natural faculty in the teeth of the depraving tendencies of inherited bias—these were the questions which the Christian had to answer in the light of his new beliefs.

Asceticism in the interest of personal character, the asceticism of moral discipline, became an apparent necessity if, indeed, any effective answer was to be found. The issue became immediately urgent as the Christian convert on the morrow of his conversion, when the fresh fervour which had carried him to his fateful decision had given place to a calmer mood, reviewed the situation into which he had come. There, on the one side, was the mighty, pervasive, and continuing impact of the non-Christian society to which he was bound by so many links of tradition and interest, and here, on the other, the stern, inexorable demand of the new religion, which exposed, rebuked, and condemned all that former familiar habit, and to which, he had come to see, he must at all hazards be true. The awful language of the Sermon on the Mount acquired a direct and cogent relevance:

'If thy right eye causeth thee to stumble, pluck it out, and cast it from thee: for it is profitable for thee that one of thy members should perish, and not thy whole body be cast into hell.

And if thy right hand causeth thee to stumble, cut it off, and cast it from thee: for it is profitable for thee that one of thy members should perish, and not thy whole body go into hell.'[1]

We have, in an earlier lecture, dwelt on the reaction of primitive Christianity to the foulness of ancient society. It gave a powerful impetus to the ascetic influences of very mingled origin and value which bore on the Christian society and coloured its thought. Here it is important to notice that Christianity, in emphasizing the necessity of ascetical discipline in the interest of moral freedom, was in line with the highest philosophic tradition of antiquity. But there was this essential difference, that, while morality was by the ancients associated with philosophy, it was by the Christians made integral to religion.

Dr. Percy Gardner has well pointed out the inherent weakness of philosophical morality, and the reason:

'The great defect of all systems of ethics based on reason and contemplation is that they comparatively seldom lead to vigorous action. Psychology easily explains this when it shews that by its very nature contemplative thought is an impediment to action. Thought can only come in when action is delayed and thwarted. And in the same way thought is hostile to emotion, which is the element which gives energy and force to action. For such reasons ethical philosophy must always influence the educated few rather than the many.'[2]

Not philosophy but religion was the source of morality among the disciples of Jesus. Within the Christian society virtue was no longer the achievement of the intellectual few, but the possession of the uncultured many. Very significant is the astonishment which the

[1] v. St. Matthew v. 29, 30.
[2] v. *The Practical Basis of Christian Ethics*, p. 107.

thoughtful pagans expressed when confronted by the lofty behaviour of Christians, who for the most part were humble working folk lying outside the accepted limits of virtuous living.

'The ancient world had arrived,' writes Harnack, 'by all the routes of its complicated development, at the bitterest criticism of and disgust at its own existence; but in no other faith was religion itself as effectively combined with asceticism, in none did the latter come so powerfully to the front, yet in none did it submit itself so pliably to Church government, as in Catholicism.'[1]

Asceticism within the Christian sphere is not to be interpreted by the extravagances of the solitaries of the Thebaid and the pillar-saints of Asia Minor, nor yet by the half hysterical language of eminent individuals. These are best understood as expressing that dualistic view of human nature which, though the very negation of Christian faith, did yet beyond question affect potently and unwholesomely the thought and practice of the early Church. Living in a highly artificial and mainly hostile framework of circumstance it is no matter for wonder that the proportions of Christian thinking were distorted and life was seen in false perspectives. The true, normal, and continuing purpose of Christian asceticism was directed to the discipline of ordinary Christians, living in the world, and, in face of its aggressive and prevailing wickedness, maintaining the Christian standard of life. St. Paul's appeal to the Philippians draws the picture of Christians in society:

'Do all things without murmurings and disputings; that ye may be blameless and harmless, children of God without blemish in the midst of a crooked and perverse generation,

[1] v. *History of Dogma*, iii. 127.

among whom ye are seen as lights in the world, holding forth the word of life.'[1]

The issue of asceticism, as well dualistic as disciplinary, has ever been, and still is, raised most insistently and conspicuously in connexion with sexual life, for not only is the sexual passion the most energetic and unmanageable of all the physical appetites, but its influence on social intercourse, on aesthetic development, and on religious life is profound, pervasive, and far-reaching. Accordingly, the necessity of its effective control is apparent as well in the interest of the individual as in that of society. How shall the sexual passion be correlated with the insistent pressure of personal claim and the colder but greater requirement of social cohesion and continuance? How shall self-respect be reconciled with self-expression? How shall private indulgence be subordinated to public interest? How shall the immediate pressures of physical appetite be held in check by the more lasting needs of mind and spirit? Such questions disclose the decisive character of the sexual issue. It is the core of personal morality. Thus for apparent reasons it was in the region of sex-life that asceticism most powerfully affected the morality of Christianity.

'At bottom,' writes Harnack, 'only a single point was dealt with, abstinence from sexual relationships; everything else was secondary: for he who had renounced these, found nothing hard. Renunciation of the servile yoke of sin (servile peccati jugum discutere) was the watchword of Christians, and an extraordinary unanimity prevailed as to the meaning of this watchword, whether we turn to the Coptic porter, or the learned Greek

---

[1] v. Philippians ii. 14, 15.

teacher, to the Bishop of Hippo, or Jerome the Roman presbyter, or the biographer of Saint Martin. Virginity was the specifically Christian virtue, and the essence of all virtues; in this conviction the meaning of the evangelical law was summed up.'[1]

In these words the learned writer has no doubt mainly in his view the excesses to which the Christian ascetics of the third century were carried, but the emphasis on sexual morality, which found such extravagant expression in that age, has remained, though in more reasonable measure, the normal temper of Christians in succeeding ages. Christian morality has ever been most sharply distinctive in its treatment of the problems of sex. It was the grossness of sexual life in the Graeco-Roman world that forced primitive Christianity into the embarrassing situation of an almost complete alienation from general society. Throughout Christian history it has been in the sphere of sexual relations that the influence of dualistic asceticism has been most extensive and most baleful. In the modern world it is still the Christian treatment of the problems of sex that provokes the most vehement challenge. Lord Morley's description of 'the revolution wrought by Voltaire' as 'the one great revolt in history which contained no element of asceticism' indicates the salient character of the fierce challenge to the Christian tradition which that revolution embodied.

'Voltaire's ascendency', writes Lord Morley, 'sprung from no appeal to those parts of human nature in which ascetic practice has its foundation. On the contrary, full exercise and play for every part was the key of all his teaching direct and indirect.

[1] v. Harnack, *History of Dogma*, iii. 128.

He had not Greek serenity and composure of spirit, but he had Greek exultation in every known form of intellectual activity and this audacious curiosity he made general.'[1]

The French Revolution was directed against the ascetic character of Christian morality as well as against the dogmatic demands of Christian faith. It was the first rather than the last which gave it such tremendous popular appeal, though at the time the fact was obscured by the enormous scandals of the established ecclesiastical system. The situation remains essentially unchanged.

We may take as a sufficient illustration the Feminist Movement which during recent years has succeeded in transforming the status, function, and social outlook of women within the civilized communities of the world. That movement, like most human movements, is mingled. While it does certainly give expression to elements of Christian morality which have been very generally ignored or inadequately recognized, yet its dramatic success is not explicable by this fact, but by its avowed and apparent revolt against the ascetic principle which inspired the traditional morality of Christendom. Thus the Feminist Movement in its more extreme developments is in temper and tendency largely opposed to Christianity. The facilities for divorce, which mark the marriage codes of some modern civilized communities, are in apparent discord with the Christian view of the marriage union. The wide circulation and increasing acceptance of theories hostile to the family involve an open breach with fundamental Christian assumptions. In fact, sex is the central issue

[1] v. Voltaire, pp. 34, 35 (Macmillan, 1891).

on which Christian morality and the modern world come into direct and avowed conflict.

In view of these facts it may well be thought that the argument of these lectures, viz. that Christian morality is natural, developing, and final, is, when the problems of sex are in question, audacious to the point of paradox. Nevertheless, I believe that the Christian solution of those problems can be shown still to 'hold the field', and that the vehement challenges of the modern world have not so far been accompanied by any adequate and superior solutions.

I propose, then, to inquire how far the new factors which have entered into the practical problem, and cannot be excluded from Christian recognition, do really affect the Christian tradition, and whether they can be said truly to conflict with its essential principles. Obviously it is of cardinal importance that these principles should be clearly apprehended, and carefully distinguished from whatever elements in the ethical tradition are merely temporary and conventional.

Let us note on the threshold of our inquiry that the teaching of Jesus was never more impressively original than when He dealt with sex life. His emphasis on purity, His insistence on monogamy as a Divine institution, His condemnation of divorce, and, in significant connexion therewith, His exaltation of childhood, and, along with these specific teachings, His version of human life as inexorably personal, essentially spiritual, in the fullest sense responsible and destined for eternity, could not but have the effect of lifting sex life, in all its forms, out of the merely physical and social connexions in which it was everywhere seen and ordered, and investing it with a novel and supreme sanctity and greatness. If it be said that in all this Jesus did but adopt, extend, and interpret the teaching of the later prophets of His people, the fact may be allowed, but it must, at the same time, be pointed out that in His hands the prophetic doctrine, rescued from nationalist limitations and set free from current perversions, was rooted in a larger and nobler conception of God.

Monogamy among the Jews was conditioned by a wide liberty of divorce. The limits of that liberty were much debated in the time of Jesus, the members of the school of Hillel advocating an extreme laxity in the matter, and those of the rival school of Shammai insisting that divorce was only permissible for the single cause of adultery. The Evangelists record that on one occasion Jesus was directly challenged on the subject, and returned an answer which scandalized His disciples at the time, and has perplexed the Church ever since. For it has been variously understood, according as Christians incline towards the laxity of Hillel or adhere to the severity of Shammai.

There has ever existed among Christians a disposition to read into the Words of Jesus a legal character which they do not properly possess. No doubt this tendency was facilitated by the obvious parallel between Moses, the historic founder of the Old Dispensation, and Jesus, the historic Founder of the New. Since the one had been a lawgiver, so, it was assumed, must be the other. But in this parallel the salient difference between the two dispensations was forgotten. The one was legal, the other spiritual. Therefore it was inevitable that Moses should enact laws, and not less

so that Jesus should enunciate principles. Obedience
to a written code was the essence of duty in the one case,
faith in a guiding Spirit in the other.

The common assumption that, in His treatment of
divorce, He departed from His normal habit, and en-
acted a law of perpetual obligation, cannot be justified,
for not only does it imply an improbable procedure
on His part, but the relevant record is marked by an
embarrassing ambiguity, and the subsequent action of
the Christian society is inconsistent with the existence
of such a law. There is in point of fact no *rule* with
respect to divorce which can properly claim to be, in
the full and final sense of the word, Christian. For the
great historic divisions of the Christian society are not
in agreement on the subject. Western Christianity has
moved in one direction: Eastern Christianity, holding
more closely to the Roman law, in another. Protestantism has taken a line of its own, and degenerated but
too frequently into a laxity which ignores the Christian
principle altogether. Thus ecclesiastical history delivers
a strangely confused and contradictory witness. The
Christian ideal of a lifelong union in marriage has been
upheld by the Church in circumstances of extreme
difficulty, for the Church has never possessed any adequate control over the conditions under which marriage
may be rightly contracted. Yet without such control
the effort to impose on average mankind the Christian
principle of indissolubility cannot but be futile. Nothing is more evident than that the effort has been
disastrously unsuccessful. The attempt to embody the
Christian ideal in secular codes of law, binding the high
morality of Christ on general societies of which the

majority of the members do not, in any effective sense, acknowledge His authority, has invariably and scandalously failed.

We may not, indeed, forget that the existence within society of a large number of persons who for themselves do acknowledge the Christian ideal of indissoluble marriage has maintained in the general mind an impressive protest against sexual licentiousness. The sweetness and beauty of Christian homes have told for good on human life, and slowly fashioned standards of conduct which have commanded acceptance far beyond the limits of definite Christian profession. It is certainly true to say that the level of sexual morality within Christendom has been definitely higher than in pre-Christian and non-Christian societies. But this fact has not been the direct result of a rigid law enforced by penalties, but rather the indirect consequence of the Christian ideal, consciously accepted and loyally pursued. Always the effective instrument has not been legal coercion, but personal example. Law has been surprisingly helpless. The corruptest societies of Christendom have been those in which divorce was altogether prohibited. It would be difficult to demonstrate that sexual morality is lower in those states of the American Republic which are notorious for the laxity of their divorce laws than in those wherein divorce is either severely conditioned or wholly disallowed. Prohibition of divorce, if it is to be effective, demands in the community a higher ethical standard than many of its members have reached. The identification of Church and State in Christendom has never been more than fictional. For this reason the marriage laws of Christendom have ever tended to assume the aspect of a humiliating accommodation to intractable facts. They reflect the strength of the oppugnant forces which yet they seek to restrain. Just because the marriage law cuts so deeply into personal life, the primary condition of its successful enforcement is its congruity with the reason and conscience of the community. A breach between the law and the public conscience is paralysing.

In an earlier lecture attention was directed to the divergence between the Jewish estimate of women in the first century and that which was implicit in the behaviour and teaching of Jesus. It was pointed out how deeply entrenched in Jewish minds was the assumption of female inferiority, and how tenaciously that assumption holds its own even in the civilized Judaism of the modern world. I maintained that this low view of women as such, though it was mitigated and in a measure disguised by the relatively high standard of family life which honourably distinguished the Jews from their pagan contemporaries, was neither cancelled nor even corrected; and that, while the discipline of the Jewish household was strong and lofty, the position of the Wife was so completely overshadowed by that of the Mother of the children as to exclude the notion of an equal partnership in the union of marriage. Jesus established that equality of the sexes which is now rapidly becoming the unchallengeable assumption of civilized thinking. He definitely condemned polygamy, which is perhaps the most flagrant violation of sex equality. Theoretically the Jews who were His contemporaries were polygamists. As disciples of Moses they could be nothing else. The study of the sacred literature confirmed them in a theoretical acceptance of polygamy; and the strong continuous influence of human depravity always secured a certain amount of poly- gamous practice. Herod the Great had no less than ten wives, and though this was regarded as unusual yet it was admittedly lawful. Indeed the rabbis, following their favourite method of giving precise shape to every- thing, laid it down that eighteen wives were permitted to a king, though to a private man not more than four or five.[1]

The polygamous theory among the Jews was no doubt generally disregarded, and practically the Jews of the time of Jesus were monogamists, but it would be a mistake to assume that the theory had no influence on Jewish opinion. The precedents of the patriarchs went far to neutralize the protests of the prophets. Even within Christendom, in spite of the teaching and example of Jesus, the prestige of the sacred text could carry eminent Christian teachers into condoning polygamy for reasons of State. We cannot doubt, therefore, that among the Jews a doctrine which was rooted in the Scripture tended to stimulate and strengthen what- ever factors in social life tended to lower the status of Jewish women. The revolting institution of the levirate marriage was so far authoritative among the contem- poraries of Jesus that the Sadducees did not scruple to base on it an argument against the doctrine of resurrec- tion. It was in practice obsolete, but in theory it held its place and exercised a certain influence for evil on Jewish thought. It emerges in the Bible like a piece of

[1] v. Schürer, *Jewish People in Time of Jesus Christ*, div. i, vol. i, p. 455, note.

the virgin rock which may be seen obtruding even in the busy thoroughfares of a modern Scandinavian city. All the evidences of culture and progress are around it, but it tells a story of far-distant days when the red granite stood out bleak and naked to the northern storms. The consecration in Israel of a whole national literature created many moral and social problems when the nation had outgrown its primitive conditions and looked back with perplexity on sacred precedents, which offended its conscience. Polygamy and the levirate marriage were instances of such sacred but unsatisfactory precedents. The influence of the prophets was hostile to polygamy. Indeed the later members of 'the goodly fellowship' were consistently monogamists. Partly, their relatively intense individualism rebelled against the primitive treatment of women as rather chattels than persons; partly, their lofty conception of the Divine character rendered them increasingly insistent that no conduct could be fitting in man which ran counter to the righteousness of his Creator. The prophets were also poets, and they invested the marriage relationship with the moral dignity which made it the favourite and most eloquently suggestive symbol of Israel's relation to Jehovah. And, when once they had established that train of religious associations in connexion with marriage, polygamy was in every devout Israelite's mind bound up with polytheism and stricken with the fatal character of apostasy.

Jehovah is represented as Israel's husband; the worship of other gods is a violation of the marriage covenant; devotion to Jehovah alone is as the chastity and faithfulness of a pure wife. The prophet Malachi emphasizes the duty of faithfulness to the marriage bond not only by adducing the Divine hatred of all treachery, but also by representing that Jehovah Himself is the witness to the marriage covenant. The prophetic teaching, then, had checked, and to a great extent corrected, the tendency of the law and the history to perpetuate, under sacred sanctions, morally obsolete types of marriage. It must be added that the circumstances of the nation in the period preceding the advent of Jesus had contributed to the same result by bringing the Jews into closer relation with the rest of mankind. The Greeks and Romans were monogamists, and the Jews of the Dispersion were, in spite of themselves, compelled to mitigate their provincialism in many respects. The sexual licence of the Graeco-Roman world was, indeed, truly repugnant to the best instincts of a race which treasured the pure teachings of the prophets and held the family in high regard, but in the particular matter of polygamy the Jews were probably assisted by the influence of their Gentile neighbours to escape in practice from their own vicious theory.

In grounding monogamy on the Creator's original intention, Jesus proclaimed it to be the truly natural form of sexual relation, and invested it with religious sanctions. The equality of the sexes was connected with their complementary character and correlated with an inevitable, because natural, subordination.

The coherence of the family was guaranteed by the permanence of the marriage union, and the root of all discipline was planted in the natural primacy of the father as head of the household. Permanence, equality, subordination, discipline—all these were integral to marriage as the natural union *par excellence*. At every point the naturalness of the Christian morality is established. The home is, in the phrase of St. Chrysostom, 'a little church', and citizenship finds its earliest expression in the 'give and take' of domestic life. That this version of the equality of the sexes fails to satisfy the extremer champions of Feminism is apparent and inevitable, but the discord reflects rather the unnatural character of the new doctrine than the inadequacy of the old. The Feminists appear to regard facile divorce as the evidence and guarantee of sexual equality. Nor is this surprising, for their conception of equality seems to involve the assumption that women should stand alongside men on every plane of social activity, that sex should have no place in the allocation of social functions, and that the equal competence of the two sexes for all purposes should be the postulate of legislation. In all this I apprehend that there is much confusion of thought, and not a little social risk. Equality is not inconsistent with difference; and, if it be the case that the two sexes are different in natural function and aptitude, it would seem plainly reasonable that the fact should find expression in social habit and political system. But we must be careful not to overstate the case on either side. Equality of status and divergence of function are plainly not incompatible. All claims must finally be grounded on competence, and competence can only be demonstrated by practice. How far women in the body politic should be entrusted with the same functions, social and political, as those which men have hitherto alone fulfilled, is a matter not of morality but of practical expediency. Opinion on the subject varies greatly both among men and women. Christianity would seem to be wholly indifferent. When, however, the essential issue of sexual morality is raised in connexion with those functions of supreme importance which can only be fulfilled by women, viz. the functions associated with the conception, birth, and nurture of children, it is apparent that the distinction between the equality of the sexes and the distinctiveness of their rôle in society becomes of primary importance.

Christian marriage is a union of free and equal persons, distinctive and complementary, designed primarily for the perpetuation of the race under conditions which shall guard and develop human quality, therefore a permanent union, carrying to the individuals therein united the powers and graces of a genuine fellowship, and also securing to their offspring a salutary and disciplined framework in which to grow up. Marriage is the natural union *par excellence*, the normal school of the social instincts, and the necessary basis for the civilized state.

Marriage normally implies the family, and its character as permanent and disciplined is determined by that fact. Childlessness indicates the failure of its primary purpose. The birth of children is not the only purpose of marriage, but it is clearly the first. The familiar Exhortation in the English Prayer Book cannot be bettered as a statement of the Christian view of marriage. It sets forth three 'causes for which Matrimony was ordained':

'First, It was ordained for the procreation of children, to be brought up in the fear and nurture of the Lord, and to the praise of his holy Name.

'Secondly, It was ordained for a remedy against sin, and to avoid fornication; that such persons as have not the gift of continency might marry, and keep themselves undefiled members of Christ's body.

'Thirdly, It was ordained for the mutual society, help, and comfort, that the one ought to have of the other, both in prosperity and adversity.'

These 'causes' reappear as motives, and probably all three are included in most normal marriages. There is the deep instinct which finds satisfaction in parenthood, the physical pressure of the sexual passion, and the desire of the sex for mental and moral fellowship with the other 'complementary' sex. It is, however, matter of common observation that many marriages are not thus complete. The motives vary almost infinitely, and sometimes the circumstances in which marriage is contracted imply a limitation of its content. Thus, in the case of persons who marry at a comparatively late age, it is apparent that the desire for 'mutual society, help, and comfort' must be the dominant, perhaps the sole, motive. Such exceptions cannot affect the general argument. The primary motive in normal marriage is the desire to have offspring, and thus to create a family. Something more is at stake than the continuance of the race, though in truth that interest is supreme. There is also the ethical interest of mankind. Parenthood brings to bear on personal character the most searching and salutary of all the influences which can shape it. Who has not noted with reverent wonder the deepening and sweetening of the man's character which follows the birth of his child? Is not the richest version of woman's nature expressed in motherhood? As the children grow from the pathetic helplessness of infancy, through childhood to adolescence, demanding at every turn large measures of self-surrendering affection, and linking husband and wife in an ever closer comradeship of parental service, they bring to the marriage bond new sanctity and new strength, making it able to withstand the separating forces of the world and to become an impregnable citadel of loyalty and love. Society itself rests on the family as on a foundation of rock, and the best school of citizenship is the home.

Now the view of marriage which enables this rich ethical life is plainly and distinctively Christian, none the less so because the natural unit of the family is coeval and coextensive with humanity itself, nor yet because the natural affections which find their normal expression within the family have not rarely inspired relationships among non-Christians almost Christian in their strength, beauty, and self-sacrificing grace.

Christianity marked a new epoch in the domestic life of civilized mankind, an epoch in which (to name but one illuminating illustration) it would be inconceivable that a man of eminent ability and noble character like Cicero could, without consciousness of fault or fear of censure from his contemporaries, for no better reason than some financial embarrassment, divorce his wife Terentia, with whom he had been united for more than thirty years, and marry his own ward, Publilia, a young and wealthy maid. How could family life be either sacred or secure when its continuance was thus evidently dependent on the caprice of the husband? It is important to remember that the source from which this higher conception of marriage has been derived is none other than the life and teaching of the Founder Himself.

Jesus made much of children, and the Christian society has not been unfaithful to His teaching and example. Paganism was distinguished by the callousness and cruelty which marked its treatment of childhood. Thus, from the first, Christian morality conflicted sharply with the prevailing habit of Graeco-Roman life. Infanticide and the exposition of infants were dark features of paganism which could plead the acceptance, not of the brutal and degraded sections of society merely, but also that of the educated and important.

'Infanticide,' observes Lecky, 'as is well known, was almost universally admitted among the Greeks, being sanctioned, and in some cases enjoined, upon what we should now call "the greatest happiness principle," by the ideal legislations of Plato and Aristotle, and by the actual legislations of Lycurgus and Solon.'[1]

Mr. Tarn has discussed the question of the fact, extent, and character of infanticide in ancient Greece, and his conclusions are unhesitating:

'Polybius says that Greeks in the middle of the second century were refusing to rear more than one, or at most two, children; and there is plenty of evidence to bear him out.

'The prevalence of infanticide in Greece has been strenuously asserted from the literary texts, and as strenuously denied; but for the late third and the second centuries the inscriptions are conclusive. . . . More than one daughter was practically never reared, bearing out Poseidippus's statement that "even a rich man always exposes a daughter". . . .

'The general conclusion from c. 230 onwards seems certain: the one child family was commonest, but there was a certain

[1] v. *History of European Morals*, ch. iv.

desire for two sons (to allow for a death in war); families of four
or five were very rare; more than one daughter was very seldom
reared; and infanticide on a considerable scale, particularly of
girls, is not in doubt.'[1]

The exposition of children may be regarded as practically identical in moral turpitude with infanticide,
and of exposition we may safely affirm that it was the
rule and not the exception of pagan life.

'The exposition of children', says Gibbon, 'was the prevailing
and stubborn vice of antiquity: it was sometimes prescribed,
often permitted, almost always practised with impunity.'[2]

Christian morality would make no terms with these
abominable practices, which offended grossly against
its fundamental assumptions.

In the earliest treatises on Christian morals which
have survived we note that abortion and child-murder
are specifically condemned. I will content myself with
a single reference to the *Doctrine of the Twelve Apostles*,
a manual probably not later than the end of the first
or the beginning of the second century:

'And the second commandment is this: Thou shalt not kill,
thou shalt not commit adultery, thou shalt not corrupt boys,
thou shalt not commit fornication, thou shalt not steal, thou
shalt not procure abortion, nor shalt thou kill the new-born
child, thou shalt not covet thy neighbour's goods.'[3]

In the interesting comparison between Christians and
pagans which is drawn in the Epistle to Diognetus it
is claimed for the former that 'they do not cast away
their offspring'.[4] St. Justin Martyr offered two reasons
for the avoidance of these fashionable pagan practices.

[1] v. *Hellenistic Civilization*, p. 92 f.   [2] v. *Decline and Fall*, c. 44.
[3] v. *Apostolic Fathers*, ed. Harmer, p. 215 f.   [4] Ibid., p. 506.

Many of the exposed children were trained for purposes of prostitution, and many perished, immersing those who exposed them in the guilt of homicide. The compassion of Christians went forth to these abandoned little ones, doomed by their parents to vice and death. The widows and virgins of the Church included among their regular works of piety the care of these outcast babes. Among the first recorded charitable institutions we find mention of children's homes or orphanages. When persecution ceased, and, with the conversion of Constantine, the perilous era of secular prosperity began, these institutions for destitute children attracted the lavish support of Christians, and they have retained their place in Christian concern until the present time. Lecky's summary of the facts is both true and just:

'It may be safely asserted that the publicity of the trade in exposed children became impossible under the influence of Christianity, and that the sense of the serious nature of the crime was very considerably increased. . . .

'This minute and scrupulous care for human life and human virtue in the humblest forms, in the slave, the gladiator, the savage, or the infant, was indeed wholly foreign to the genius of Paganism. It was produced by the Christian doctrine of the inestimable value of each immortal soul. It is the distinguishing and transcendant characteristic of every society into which the spirit of Christianity has passed.'[1]

From the ancient world, in which the ethical contrasts which we have dwelt upon at such length were arrestingly apparent, we pass to the world of to-day, and inquire how far the Christian morality which we have inherited from the past is able to justify itself in the

[1] v. op. cit., pp. 32, 34.

novel and perplexing situations of the present. Immediately we find ourselves confronted by some new factors of far-reaching consequence. The phenomena of sexual life are seen now by civilized men in a new framework of circumstance. Sexual morality has in our case to include considerations which lay outside the concern of former Christian teachers, and to take account of facts which were to them unknown. How far can Christian morality hold its ground?

The actual situation in which we now stand is effectively described by Professor Carr-Saunders in the Galton Lecture delivered before the Eugenics Society on 16 February 1935. He is directly concerned with the problems of population, but some of his observations are relevant to our present discussion. Thus he dwells at some length on what he describes as 'the alleged retreat from parenthood', and contrasts very strikingly the old and the new points of view from which the birth of children has been commonly regarded. He suggests that the real change has not been in the desire of married women to avoid the birth of children, but in the measure of their ability to satisfy their desire. What they have ever wished for they can now with little risk to themselves obtain. The grave question arises, therefore, whether in these circumstances there will be enough children born to replace the normal wastage of the population by death. Since, owing to the new scientific methods of contraception which are now easily accessible to women, parenthood has been effectively severed from marriage and transformed into an optional incident of married life, can we any longer depend on a sufficient birth-rate, or must the nations accept the melancholy fate of a gradual but assured extinction? The professor is himself disposed to take an optimistic view of the future, but such a view is not the necessary, nor perhaps the most probable outcome of his argument.

'Children were formerly the inevitable accompaniment of married companionship and home life. There was no question of any attitude to size of family; that settled itself. There was no thought of replacing the present generation; replacement as yet plays no part in those deliberations. To how many people does it ever occur to connect the size of their family with the future of their country? No such notion ever enters the head of the man in the street.

'Voluntary contributions have, as we all know, to be earnestly solicited; but for these essential contributions there is as yet no solicitation on behalf of society. It is therefore a mistake to speak of a retreat from parenthood if by that is meant a deliberate refusal to replace the present generation. Replacement is not and never has been a conscious matter. But with a system of voluntary parenthood it must become so if society is to survive. . . .

'Voluntary parenthood is the greatest innovation that the race has ever made. It may well be misused for a time; a few centuries are as nothing in the history of the race, and the next few generations may perhaps see a dramatic decline in numbers. . . .

'Whether we take long or short views, voluntary parenthood occupies the centre of the field.'[1]

'Voluntary parenthood' is an ambiguous description. In normal circumstances no marriage could be rightly contracted if it did not imply the deliberate desire of the two persons concerned to become parents. The

[1] v. *The Eugenics Review*, April 1935.

parenthood which is the natural consequence of marriage could not be properly regarded as other than voluntary. What is intended is a deliberate separation of sexual intercourse from conception, and the consequent control of parenthood. A new gloss is appended to the old text, 'They shall have children at their desire'. What has hitherto been in human experience natural and normal is henceforth to become optional and voluntary. Thanks to the new scientific devices described as 'contraceptives', it is now possible, or assumed to be possible, for married people to determine whether their union shall be childless, or, if not, what the size of the family shall be. Such parenthood as they decide to accept will be self-determined and self-delimited.

Putting on one side, for the sake of the argument, the important questions which are raised by the highly speculative character of the assumption that human nature is quite as amenable to manipulation as the notion of 'voluntary parenthood' would appear to imply, we cannot avoid the moral issue which the theory obviously raises. How far can 'voluntary parenthood' be brought into agreement with the Christian doctrine of marriage? How far can the use of contraceptives be included in the sexual morality of Christians? The 15th Resolution of the Lambeth Conference of 1930 is concerned with these issues. It runs thus:

'Where there is a clearly felt moral obligation to limit or avoid parenthood, the method must be decided on Christian principles. The primary and obvious method is complete abstinence from intercourse (as far as may be necessary) in a life of discipline and self-control lived in the power of the Holy Spirit. Nevertheless in those cases where there is such a clearly felt moral obligation to limit or avoid parenthood, and where there is a morally sound reason for avoiding complete abstinence, the Conference agrees that other methods may be used, provided that this is done in the light of the same Christian principles. The Conference records its strong condemnation of the use of any methods of conception-control from motives of selfishness, luxury, or mere convenience.'[1]

This resolution is so cautiously worded, and the sanction of the use of contraceptives by Christian people is so carefully conditioned, that it may well appear practically valueless. Its real significance lies, less in what it actually permits, than in the decisive breach with ecclesiastical tradition which it involves. This was clearly perceived by the large Committee of Bishops who considered the subject of Marriage and Sex, and was frankly stated in their *Report*:

'It must be recognised that there is in the Catholic Church a very strong tradition that the use of preventive methods is in all cases unlawful for a Christian. We acknowledge the weight of that testimony, but we are unable to accept that tradition as necessarily final. It must be admitted that it is not founded on any directions given in the New Testament. It has not behind it the authority of any Oecumenical Council of the Church. Moreover, it is significant that the Communion which most strongly condemns in principle all preventive methods, nevertheless in practice recognises that there are occasions when a rigid insistence on the principle is impossible. If our own Communion is to give guidance on this problem, it must speak frankly and openly, with a full appreciation of facts and conditions which were not present in the past, but which are due to modern civilization.'[2]

Such a 'full appreciation' of the new factors in the

[1] Carried by 193 votes to 67.   [2] v. *Report*, p. 90.

problem of sexual morality, as is here said to be requisite, will probably involve far more considerable change in the tradition of Christendom than the extremely modest resolution of the Lambeth Conference seems to contemplate. A 'moral obligation to limit or avoid parenthood' may, and perhaps must, grow from larger considerations than those which normally determine marital relations. Modern science and social experience have revealed much, and will assuredly reveal more, as to the conditions under which marriage may be wisely contracted, wholesomely maintained, and rightly cancelled. The new knowledge brings enhanced responsibility, and Christianity is true to itself when it insists that Christian parenthood, being fully responsible, must imply a frank recognition of all sound and relevant knowledge. The tradition must be, and assuredly will be, revised in the light of this waxing illumination. The public aspects of sexual conduct will be more clearly perceived, and the merely individual treatment of marriage will be increasingly discouraged and disallowed.

The birth of children will be controlled as never before when the interests of health in mother and infant have been intelligently considered, when the concern of the state in the physical and mental soundness of its citizens has been recognized, and when due weight has been allowed to the economic situation private and public. Irresponsible parenthood will no longer be suffered to shelter itself under religious pleas. The power of transmitting life, which of all man's natural endowments is the most important and the most mysterious, cannot lie outside that responsibility which Christianity interprets and emphasizes. The responsible use of this novel and potent method, which science has placed within human reach, cannot be regarded as inconsistent with Christian morality. It is easy to imagine situations in which its neglect would certainly be so. If it be right in certain circumstances to limit the birth of children (and so much would seem to be generally admitted), the question of morality turns on the methods actually employed, and the motives with which they are employed.

The ancient and still widely prevalent methods of abortion and infanticide have from the first been condemned by the Christian conscience. Both involve the destruction of life, and do violence to human self-respect. But contraceptives may be morally unobjectionable, if they be used for adequate reasons. The facility with which the new method may be misapplied ought not to lead to an indiscriminating prohibition, but to a scrupulous care in its use. That use, if it is to be compatible with Christian morality, must be limited by the ascetic principle which that morality embodies. It must serve, and not weaken, self-control; strengthen, and not endanger, the marriage bond; assist the due fulfilment of parenthood, not enable its repudiation; exalt family life, not destroy it.

Christian morality does but follow the law of its own development, when it includes within itself whatever truth can be learned from physical science and social experience. Its conflict is not with truth, however destructive of time-honoured precedents, but with the shallow sentiment and lax sexual habit of the modern world, which too frequently profane truth's name. Sexual life in the fashionable literature of our time is frankly brought down to its physical implications, and cut adrift from all those higher emotional and spiritual factors which have rescued it from crude animalism, and quickened it with all the highest potencies of culture. The pseudo-asceticism of dualism, as well within the Christian sphere as without, would ignore the physical aspects; and, by this violence to Nature, provoke the contradictory reactions of moral debasement and dehumanized severity. But this is not the true Christian way. The asceticism of discipline insists on holding the animal passions—and among them pre-eminently the sexual passion, which of all the physical appetites is the most important and the most insistent—under the control of the higher instincts of man's nature, and thus maintaining, at whatever cost of inner conflict, the essential franchise and true balance of manhood. Moral liberty, that is, the liberty proper to man as a moral agent, natural liberty (so have declared the greater teachers of every age and of every race), is attainable only by way of subjection to discipline. Inasmuch as man is a created being, the true law of his nature can only be his Creator's Will, in conformity to which alone he can gain the franchise which is his birthright. This is the underlying assumption of all genuine education. There is no short cut to liberty; nor may that prize be otherwise gained than by the 'narrow way' of obedience. 'No cross, no crown' is the formula of human enfranchisement, not the hectic joys which 'the plausible casuistry of the passions' proposes, not the vulgar bribes of mundane success, nor yet the more distant boons of secularized religion, but self-mastery through discipline and conflict.

Nor sang he only of unfading bowers,
  Where they a tearless, painless age fulfil,
In fields Elysian spending blissful hours,
  Remote from every ill:

But of pure gladness found in temperance high,
  In duty owned, and reverenced with awe,
Of man's true freedom, which may only lie
  In servitude to law;

And how 'twas given through virtue to aspire
  To golden seats in ever-calm abodes;
Of mortal men, admitted to the quire
  Of high immortal Gods.

IX

PROBLEMS OF RACE

FEW modern problems are more difficult of satisfactory solution than those which grow out of the
racial differences of mankind. Science bears potently
and in many ways on the phenomenon of race. The
pride of nationality, and the ambitions of empire, and
the ramifying interests of economic development are
all concerned in the practical questions which must be
answered. 'A vast pseudo-science of "racial biology"
has been erected which serves to justify political ambitions, economic ends, social grudges, class prejudices.'
The distinguished men of science who have collaborated
in the volume *We Europeans* have rendered a great,
and greatly needed, public service by demonstrating
how baseless are the racial doctrines which inspire
the barbarous anti-Semitism of Germany, and give a
fallacious appearance of scientific justification to the
fanatical nationalism which now disturbs the civilized
world. The final paragraph of the volume may be
quoted:

'The violent racialism to be found in Europe to-day is a
symptom of Europe's exaggerated nationalism: it is an attempt
to justify nationalism on a non-nationalist basis, to find a firm
basis in objective science for ideas and policies which are gener-
ated internally by a particular economic and political system,
and have real relevance only in reference to that system.
The cure for the racial mythology, with its accompanying
self-exaltation and persecution of others, which now besets
Europe, is a re-orientation of the nationalist ideal, and, in the
practical sphere, an abandonment of claims by nations to

absolute sovereign rights. Meanwhile, however, science and
the scientific spirit can do something by pointing out the
biological realities of the ethnic situation, and by refusing to
lend her sanction to the absurdities and the horrors perpetrated
in her name. Racialism is a myth, and a dangerous myth
at that. It is a cloak for selfish economic aims which in their
uncloaked nakedness would look ugly enough. And it is not
scientifically grounded. The essence of science is the appeal
to fact.'[1]

On the threshold of a discussion in which we must needs
speak much of 'race' and 'racialism' it is important that
the merely conventional character of these terms should
be understood, and this emphatic statement of scientific
doctrine kept in mind.

If Christian morality is to justify its claim to satisfy
the requirements of developing humanity, it must
include with respect to racial issues some guidance
which shall be able to command the assent of modernly
civilized men as sound, self-respecting, and sufficient.
At this stage, indeed, all solutions must be obscure,
provisional, and, so to speak, experimental, for knowledge is so far very inadequate, and experience is yielding
its guidance gradually, but at least the lines on which
racial problems may be solved ought to be visible, and
the principles of Christian morality shown to be practically sound. So much our argument seems to require,
and so much it is able to provide.

The racial problems, which confront the modern
citizen in the great industrial communities which com-
pose Western Christendom, are complicated by their
intimate connexion with economic and political interests

[1] v. *We Europeans*, p. 287.

which become ever more perplexing and ever more vital. No ethical scheme could suffice which left these matters outside its reference.

We may distinguish between two categories of the racial problem. On the one hand, there are the questions raised by the contact of civilized Europeans with un-civilized or semi-civilized peoples. On the other hand, there are the very different questions which require answer when the relations with other civilized peoples, different in colour and culture, are at issue. The first are, from the Christian point of view, comparatively simple. However difficult it may appear to secure an acceptance of the requirements of Christian morality in the actual procedure of civilized Europeans, there is no real doubt as to what those requirements are. The second are far more perplexing, and present the Chris-tian moralist with questions which he will not easily answer. Yet with respect to these also the issue is not left wholly in doubt.

Christianity affirms the spiritual equality of men as such, and proclaims a morality which is binding on all its professors without distinction of race. Born and cradled within the sphere of Jewish nationalism, the religion of Jesus is catholic in spirit and claim. From the first this catholic character was apparent. Con-fronted by the hereditary religious privilege of the Jew, the cultural exclusiveness of the Greek, and the hard arrogance of the Roman, the Christian missionaries preached a gospel of equal brotherhood. St. Paul's words to the Galatians did but formulate what was the experience of his converts.

'Ye are all sons of God, through faith, in Christ Jesus. For as many of you as were baptized into Christ did put on Christ. There can be neither Jew nor Greek, there can be neither bond nor free, there can be no male and female: for ye all are one man in Christ Jesus. And if ye are Christ's, then are ye Abraham's seed, heirs according to promise.'[1]

This complete equality was limited—the Apostolic Christians were content that it should be limited—to the spiritual sphere. Filled with the enthusiasm of their new discipleship, and looking forward with ardent faith to the triumph of their crucified Master, they had no interest in the relatively petty affairs which absorbed their pagan neighbours. 'The things which are seen are temporal', they said; 'the things that are not seen are eternal.' The same lofty detachment from merely mundane concerns which showed itself in martyrdom dictated their indifference to the gross oppressions of their normal situation. But plainly this temper could not survive the discovery that Christianity had a long future in front of it, and that Christians would have to bring into some tolerable congruity their spiritual beliefs and their secular procedures. All the normal problems of social life began to reappear within the area of Christian duty, and among them the problems of race. It does not appear, however, that the first generations of Christians had any acquaintance with the kind of racial problems which now perplex civilized men. The slaves of antiquity embodied a gross violation of elementary human rights, and so far challenged the Christian conscience, but they suggested rather harsh fortune than racial inferiority. 'They were almost without exception white men, and there was therefore

[1] Galatians iii. 26–8.

none of that racial contempt and disgust which was often felt for the black.'[1]   There was not among the ancients anything quite analogous to the attitude towards the negroes which was common among the slaveholders of America.   The painful picture of negro slavery in Jamaica in 1778 drawn by an English tutor could hardly have been paralleled in the Roman Empire:

'A Creole Gentle—I shou'd have said Savage—man told me, "that he believed the Negroes to be no more than overgrown Apes, and that a man could not hurt them, except he killed them".   Whether this person was, as he wished to appear or no, I positively believe the Island is cursed with those who abstain from killing an offending Negro upon the same principles that they do not choose to kill a Horse or an Ass, because they cost them so much money.'[2]

The Roman slave was a mere chattel without rights, and his lot might be truly woeful at the hands of a cruel and vicious owner, but he was not physically designate as an inferior type of humanity.   Neither racial feeling nor religious theory contributed to his social degradation.   He was the victim of misfortune, not a creature intrinsically semi-bestial.

The frequent wars filled the slave markets with captives who had been free men, and were in many cases superior to their purchasers in intelligence and education.   Such cultivated slaves were commonly employed in suitable occupations, and sometimes came to hold positions of considerable importance.   The great

---

[1] v. Bigg, *Origins of Christianity*, p. 5.
[2] v. *Diary of the Rev. William Jones, 1777–1821*, p. 25.   This very interesting diary includes a most painful picture of slavery painted from life.

households of the wealthy Roman capitalists demanded considerable variety of service.

'Not only the ordinary domestic helpers of all kinds', says Mr. Warde Fowler, 'but copyists, librarians, paedagogi as tutors for the children, and even doctors might all be found in such households in a servile condition, without reckoning the great numbers who seem to have been always available as escorts when the great man was travelling in Italy or in the provinces.'[1]

Manumission in the Roman Empire was easy and frequent. Freedmen were found everywhere holding positions of importance and social distinction, in the Emperor's household, in the law courts, in the civil service, in society, in literature and commerce. At least two even of the emperors, Pertinax and Diocletian, were of servile descent. The freedmen could not but cast back a certain dignity on their original status, which in their own persons they seemed to link with power and fashion. At least they tended to obscure in the general mind its essential degradation. There is nothing in antiquity equivalent to that doctrine of the blood taint ('the touch of the tar brush') which has envenomed African slavery in modern times. The racial prejudice is so strong that not even enfranchisement can exorcise it. A century has passed since De Tocqueville wrote his famous study, *Democracy in America*, and two generations part us from the final abolition of slavery in the United States, yet the language in which the brilliant Frenchman pictured the situation of the negroes, even in those States where they were legally free, is not yet obsolete:

'It is true, that in the North of the Union, marriages may be legally contracted between negroes and whites; but public opinion

[1] v. *Social Life in Rome in the Age of Cicero*, p. 216.

would stigmatize a man who should connect himself with a negress as infamous, and it would be difficult to meet with a single instance of such a union. The electoral franchise has been conferred upon the negroes in almost all the States in which slavery has been abolished; but if they come forward to vote, their lives are in danger. If oppressed, they may bring an action at law, but they will find none but whites amongst their judges; and although they may legally serve as jurors, prejudice repulses them from that office. The same schools do not receive the child of the black and of the European. In the theatres, gold cannot procure a seat for the servile race beside their former masters; in the hospitals they lie apart; and although they are allowed to invoke the same Divinity as the whites, it must be at a different altar, and in their own churches with their own clergy. The gates of Heaven are not closed against these unhappy beings; but their inferiority is continued to the very confines of the other world; when the negro is defunct, his bones are cast aside, and the distinction of condition prevails even in the equality of death. The negro is free, but he can share neither the rights, nor the pleasures, nor the labour, nor the afflictions, nor the tomb of him whose equal he has been declared to be; and he cannot meet him upon fair terms in life or in death.'[1]

There has certainly been some improvement. The Great War, in which large numbers of negroes served as American soldiers in France, has had a profound influence on the negro population. The new discontent with their social inequality cannot but have far-reaching consequences, both political and economic. Dr. Weatherford, in the notable volume *Race Relations: Adjustment of Whites and Negroes in the United States*, published in 1934, concludes his study on a note of cautious optimism:

'Perhaps one would sum up the situation by saying that great

[1] v. *Democracy in America*, translated by Henry Reeve, i. 427.

masses of American white people have not changed their attitudes from the attitudes held during slavery, but the leaders of the
whites have undoubtedly adopted much more liberal attitudes;
and since these leaders ultimately set patterns of thought, the
social prejudice will gradually disappear and the relation between the races will slowly but surely become more friendly.'[1]

This embittering racial prejudice, which has shown
itself to be too strong for law and political theory and
even religious principle, had no place in ancient slavery.
The Greek attitude towards those who were scornfully
described as 'barbarians' had little resemblance to the
European attitude towards the coloured races, for by a
Greek was understood rather the possessor of a specific
culture than the member of a specific race. Nor was
there anything among the ancients equivalent to the
pseudo-scientific racial doctrines which, in recent years,
have undoubtedly provided plausible excuses for many
abominable procedures. Mr. Oldham, in his well-
known and excellent book, *Christianity and the Race
Problem*, has directed attention to this feature of the
present situation:

'The policy of exploitation received a powerful reenforcement
in the nineteenth century in the Darwinian conception of organic
evolution. This exerted a profound influence on the mind of
the age. Progress appeared to be the result of a grim struggle.
Nature cared nothing for the individual but only for the type.
To yield to feelings of humanity and pity was to attempt to
reverse nature's inexorable law that the weak should give place
to the strong. The process by which weaker peoples were dis-
possessed by the stronger or made to subserve their purposes
was regarded as inevitable.'[2]

[1] v. *Race Relations*, p. 517.
[2] v. *Christianity and the Race Problem*, p. 94.

This pseudo-scientific doctrine of human progress by the destruction of the weaker types has coincided with the amazing increase of the European populations in the forcing-house of industrialism. This increase of the population is perhaps the characteristic of the modern world which differentiates it most sharply from the ancient. The entire population of the Roman Empire at its greatest extent is thought very probably not to have exceeded sixty-five millions. Professor Carr-Saunders describes the amazing increase of persons of unmixed European stock during recent years:

'It has been estimated that in 1929 there were in the world 642 million persons of unmixed European stock, of whom 478 millions were living in Europe. The remainder, 164 millions, were living outside Europe, and, with the exception of some 13 millions in Asia, they were situated overseas from Europe. Only four hundred years ago all Europeans, numbering probably less than 100 millions, were to be found in the continent after which they are called. Thus the overflow of Europeans into other continents falls within recent history. Indeed far the greater part of the exodus has taken place in the last hundred and fifty years, almost in our own day and under our own eyes; and the expansion of Europeans in numbers (they have multiplied more than six times in three hundred years), coupled with their extension in space, has been one of the outstanding features of modern world history.'[1]

Two consequences of this astonishing increase are apparent. First, the pressure of the population on their normal food supplies is compelling industry to expand rapidly, for only by industry can the waxing multitudes be fed. Every census shows the urbanization of the Western communities to be proceeding at an ever

[1] v. *We Europeans*, p. 241.

accelerating pace. The people can only be fed by the imported foodstuffs which the export of manufactures enables them to purchase, and, therefore, as their numbers grow, manufacturing industry must correspondingly expand.

Now the expansion of industry implies two things— the possession of abundant raw materials with which to feed the mills and factories, and open markets in which to sell the manufactured goods. But raw materials are largely found in countries inhabited by uncivilized and semi-civilized peoples. Accordingly, under the waxing impulse of economic need, the nations included within the sphere of modern industrialism have become aggressively imperialist, laying hands on the relatively undefended lands of Africa, Asia, and Australasia, and bringing their inhabitants under a continuing coercion. There has been a dominantly economic motive in the process of imperial expansion. Raw materials and markets have been the prizes of empire. Trade has followed the flag. Political pressure has been brought to bear on the native populations in order to compel them to serve the material interest of their conquerors. Therefore they must labour; and therefore they must provide markets. The one necessity may demoralize, and the other impoverish them. Nevertheless commercialized imperialism requires both.

But how shall this process of conquest and exploitation be brought into any tolerable harmony with Christian morality? The answer is not quite so apparent as might at first sight be imagined. Is a great part of the habitable earth to be earmarked for ever as the property of savages? Have the native inhabitants such a right to the vast territories which they occupy as will authorize them to withdraw those territories from the use of mankind as a whole, to keep unutilized the treasures of natural wealth which they contain, and to do this in spite of the economic distress which may be inflicted on the civilized communities of the world? Is there not an unexpressed condition under which nations, like individuals, possess property, namely, that they use it with reasonable regard to the general interest?

The arrival of Europeans, eager to grow quickly rich by exploiting the natural wealth of tropical countries, raises the whole series of problems which are compendiously summed up under the word 'Labour'. Under tropical conditions the only available labour is native labour, and, if mines are to be worked and crops grown at a profit, that labour must be cheap, sufficient, and regular. The kind of labour needed conflicts with native interests, as well physical as moral, and with native habits. Dr. Albert Schweitzer in his well-known book, *On the Edge of the Primeval Forest*, has discussed the practical question with characteristic insight and sympathy:

'People imagine in Europe', he writes, 'that as many labourers as are wanted can always be found among the savages, and secured for very small wages. The real fact is the very opposite. Labourers are nowhere more difficult to find than among primitive races, and nowhere are they paid so well in proportion to the work they do in return. This comes from their laziness, people say: but is the negro really so lazy? Must we go a little deeper into the problem?'

Dr. Schweitzer is persuaded that the accusation of laziness is not merited, for the negro is capable of sustained and devoted labour when he perceives the necessity for it; but he is always a casual labourer:

'The negro, then, is not idle, but he is a free man; hence he is always a casual worker, with whose labour no regular industry can be carried on. . . .

'There is, therefore, a serious conflict between the needs of trade and the fact that the child of nature is a free man. The wealth of the country cannot be exploited because the native has so slight an interest in the process. How train him to work? How compel him?'[1]

A twofold process of indirect coercion drives the native into industry. He wants money to pay his taxes, and he wants money to enable him to buy the many desirable things which the missionaries of trade are for ever pressing on his notice. Money can only be gained in the form of wages. He enters into contracts which withdraw him for considerable periods from his native village. Dr. Schweitzer speaks of conditions in the French Congo, but his words apply with little modification throughout Equatorial Africa:

'Many get homesick. Others cannot put up with the strange diet, for, as no fresh provisions are to be had, they must as a rule live chiefly on rice. Most of them fall victims to the taste for rum, and ulcers and diseases spread rapidly among them, living, as they do, a kind of barrack life in overcrowded huts. In spite of all precautions they mostly get through their pay as soon as the contract time is up, and return home as poor as they went away.

'The negro is worth something only so long as he is in his village and under the moral control of intercourse with his family and other relatives; away from these surroundings he easily goes to the bad, both morally and physically. Colonies

[1] v. *On the Edge of the Primeval Forest*, ch. vii.

of negro labourers away from their families are, in fact, centres of demoralization, and yet such colonies are required for trade and for the cultivation of the soil, both of which would be impossible without them.'[1]

How far can this treatment of the native races be brought into line with Christian morality? How far can the assumption that the natural resources of Africa must, with whatever cost to the native peoples, be developed, be rightly permitted to override the moral objections to the only known method of developing them? I remember sitting in the House of Lords during a discussion of the provisions made for protecting the rights of the natives in the gold-yielding districts of Kenya. The case for the natives was stated with admirable moderation and unquestionable authority, and it was received with many assurances of sympathy by the spokesman of the Government, but on both sides there was the assumption, as disconcerting as it was unquestioned, that in any case the gold must be extracted. As a nation we seem committed to a contingent humanitarianism, a Christian morality with limited liability. Christianity is suffered to affect national policy so far, and only so far, as it does not interfere with what are conceived to be national interests.

Next, urbanization not only indicates an immense increase in the population, but also a far greater complexity of social and economic system. The right organization of popular life in the congested industrial areas, which are by courtesy called towns, creates a

[1] v. *On the Edge of the Primeval Forest*, ch. vii, 'Social Problems in the Forest'.

series of formidable problems. All the questions connected with their civic quality become increasingly pressing. The mere massing together of these multitudes tells potently on individual health, character, and economic value. How shall a sound type of citizen be secured? How far does civic soundness depend on ancestry? how far on education? how far on economic system? how far on social order? A whole group of sciences has to be reckoned with—biology, physiology, embryology, psychology, sociology, economics. Their several deliverances must be correlated in any sound solution of the population problem which now presses on the public mind and conscience. We are concerned here only with the question of race. Must we in the interest of the community prohibit intermarriage between individuals of different races? If so, may we distinguish between the races, permitting intermarriage for these, and prohibiting it for those?

But how may such discrimination between races be harmonized with the Christian doctrine of racial equality? It may, perhaps, suffice to answer that Christianity is pre-eminently the religion of truth, and that, therefore, every relevant factor must be given due place in the Christian version of human duty. The equality which Christianity insists upon may not be understood to necessitate any procedure which is known to conflict with the well-being of mankind. We are only by degrees coming into possession of the truth. If experience demonstrate that the blending of, say, Africans and Europeans produces a composite type which is physically, mentally, and morally unsatisfactory, can it be reasonably maintained that the prohibition of intermarriage between Africans and Europeans conflicts with Christian morality? If such prohibition involve hardship, even severe hardship, to individuals, is it therefore inconsistent with Christian principle? To both these questions the negative answer appears to be required. Christian morality assumes the facts of Nature, which are only gradually coming into Christian knowledge. The moral code by which Christians are bound cannot be complete until every constituent element has been fully included in it, and knowledge of the facts of Nature, discovered by science and unfolded in experience, which is assuredly one such constituent element, will not have been thus fully included until science has spoken its last word and experience has reached its conclusion. In effect, the conditions of rightly ordered sexual life are being gradually learned, and racial congruity cannot be excluded from the description. To give it frank recognition involves no violation of that racial equality which Christianity affirms. To distinguish between racial stocks which may, and racial stocks which may not, be wisely permitted to blend is no more than to acknowledge the fact of racial distinctiveness. The language of St. Paul may fairly be thought to extend to the case of such deliberate recognition of natural difference: 'The God that made the world and all things therein . . . made of one every nation of men for to dwell on all the face of the earth, having determined their appointed seasons, and the bounds of their habitation.'[1]

The principle being thus frankly admitted, it would seem to follow that the consequences which flow

[1] v. Acts xvii. 24, 26.

properly from its application should also be allowed. If the intermarriage of widely disparate racial types be rightly prohibited, then it cannot be wrong to insist upon such measures of social segregation as the effective prevention of intermarriage may require. It would surely be morally indefensible to permit free social intercourse between adolescents who may not be suffered to marry if, as is so probable as to be practically certain, they should so desire. There is no affront to any Christian principle in a segregation, on the basis of race, which is both prudential from the point of view of society, and equitable from that of the individual. All turns on the security of the fundamental assumption that the facts of Nature are such as science affirms and experience discloses.

The same reasoning may, perhaps, extend to the case of divergent cultures. Can it be fairly contended that Christian morality is violated by the exclusion of Asiatics from a dominion controlled by Europeans on the specific ground that the culture which the Asiatics would introduce would be inconsistent with the ethical unity of the population, and that such a moral incoherence as would inevitably follow would conflict with the highest interest of the European community? I think that the moral legitimacy of the policy of racial exclusion in Australia would turn mainly on the proved competence of the Australians of European stocks to populate and develop the territory from which they sought to exclude the Asiatics. In the present state of the world, when large populations are hard pressed to find adequate food supplies, it could not be equitable, and *a fortiori* it could not be accordant with

Christian morality, that a European community should set a fence round large territories, which it was patently unable itself to occupy or develop, and which by its exclusive policy it could but keep out of effective use. How severe may be the pressure of population on food supplies is painfully apparent in Japan. The well-known American publicist, Mr. Lothrop Stoddard, in his recently published volume, *Clashing Tides of Colour*, quotes the following description from a French writer:

'In several prefectures, peasants are living on roots and herbs. There is wholesale selling of girls; in some districts there are many villages with no more girls of marriageable age. Before reaching that point, some peasants burn their houses in the secret hope of collecting insurance, but there have been so many fires that the insurance companies refuse to pay. . . . Families are dissolving. Husbands and wives are separating; children are abandoning their parents.'[1]

No policy which did not give fair consideration to such a situation of grim want as is here described could be reasonably thought to be reconcilable with Christian morality.

Christian morality, just because it is in principle theistic, and therefore natural, emphasizes whatever is genuinely humane. It stands for the rights of man as such. Therefore it can make no terms with methods of handling men which involve an outrage on personality. However savage, or backward, or untutored, men may be, yet, if their manhood must be admitted, they may not be treated as chattels and deprived of the essentially human franchises. It is at this point that the

[1] v. *Clashing Tides of Colour*, p. 260.

distinctive requirement of Christian morality becomes apparent.

Racial equality is not, from the Christian point of view, incompatible with differences of colour, culture, and competence, but it cannot possibly consist with anything that contradicts the basal factor of humanity. This was the essential vice of slavery, not its subordination of the individual to control, nor yet the severity of the discipline which it might imply, for these might be requisite in the interest of the individual, and serve to assist his advance, but in the violation of essential human rights which it had generally come to involve. Christian morality for adequate reason could allow the subordination and applaud the discipline, but it could never tolerate the outrage on human personality.

It is certain that the absolute inconsistency of slavery with the personal franchises which inhere in manhood was not soon perceived, nor easily admitted by the Christian society. But with the passage of time experience accumulated, and the truth became apparent. The pagan persecutor drew no distinction between freeman and slave when he sought to override the rights of conscience. In the amphitheatre, or in the mines, Christians, free and servile alike, gained the martyr's crown. The marriage of slaves was legally insecure, but it was often permitted. Many pagan owners tolerated out of kindness what all Christians owners conceded on principle. As Christians prevailed in society, the worst outrages on the slave's personal rights ceased, and the imperial law, under the twofold influence of the Stoic philosophy and the Christian religion, became increasingly humane. Moreover, the social situation within the Roman Empire made the abolition of slavery impracticable and almost inconceivable. Thus it happened that slavery rather petered out than was deliberately abolished. It passed by insensible degrees into the serfdom of feudal Europe, which lingered until modern times. Individual Christian missionaries among the Celts and Teutons condemned the slave trade and pressed on their converts the virtue of manumission, but the Church itself was too deeply implicated in the maintenance of slavery, as itself a large owner of slaves, frankly to condemn the institution. Some of the servile incidents were even insisted upon in the Church's canons. The incongruity of slavery and the morality which Christianity required was never wholly unperceived, but its frank recognition was hindered by the strength of custom and the pressure of interest. Economic causes rather than religious principle caused slavery to disappear from Christendom. When, at the close of the Middle Ages, slavery was deliberately revived by Christians, the atrocity was masked by literalism and casuistry. The black races were assumed to be the descendants of the accursed Ham, carrying the visible impress of their infamous derivation, and predestined by Divine sentence to perpetual bondage. Their enslavement by Christians was pictured as a providential provision for their conversion to Christianity. Such casuistry might suffice to silence the scruples of the pious, and to hoodwink the understanding of the simple; but, for the multitude of men, the obvious material gains of the new slavery sufficed. The time was propitious for the new departure. Just when the Spaniards were perplexed by the failure of native Indian labour in America, the Portuguese opened up a limitless supply of negro labour in Africa. The demand created in the New World by official oppression was met by the supply from the Old World through private cupidity. The Spanish taskmaster entered into an unholy comradeship with the Portuguese slave-dealer. In due time the paramount power in America and the empire of the seas passed to Great Britain, which thus gathered into its hands both slave-owning in one continent and slave-stealing in another.

The slave trade for a century took rank as a cardinal British interest, the very foundation of Britain's waxing empire. The record of our race received its blackest chapter. Again the old paradox appeared. Christians were strangely blind to the grossness of the contradiction between their practice and their principles. The old sophistries still confused their minds. No doubt the horrible facts were generally unknown, though they could hardly have been altogether unsuspected. The desire to evangelize the enslaved blacks led Christian men to go to strange lengths in condoning a situation which, whatever its evils, did at least provide an opportunity for their well-meant efforts. Even so their way was not easy. The door of opportunity was not readily opened, for the insight of the slave-owners was keener than the vision of the missionaries. Few controversies in the whole course of Christian history are more surprising or more humiliating than that which was raised between the American slave-owners and the Christian clergy as to the proper consequence of conversion. Did not baptism *ipso facto* cancel slavery?

Could the Christian doctrines of Divine Fatherhood, and of man's equal sonship in the Heavenly Home, be safely trusted to leave the economic fact of bondage unaffected? If slaves became Christians, would they be content to remain slaves? What about Christian marriage? Would Christian slaves continue to be treated as breeding animals on a stud-farm? And so forth. By slow degrees the Christian conscience was stirred, and the Christian understanding cleared, but the process was so gradual that Christianity only emerged victorious with a loss of credit and influence which has been heavy and permanent. Yet, and this is the fact which most concerns us here, the process was continuous, and led finally to a conclusion which is seen to express the true principles of Christianity.

The backwardness and helplessness of primitive peoples, which render them the facile victims of force and fraud, constitute an irresistible claim to consideration, protection, and sympathetic guidance. It is not unusual to hear them spoken of as 'child races', and the expression is well justified, for it indicates a parallel which is sound and illuminating. In the great and various family of mankind they are children, with children's disadvantages and with children's rights. As children they are properly regarded as the wards of the civilized peoples, who are bound to treat them as children ought to be treated, not harshly, not selfishly, but in the interest of their healthy development. The XXIInd Article of the Covenant of the League of Nations stands on record as a solemn affirmation of the Christian view of the right treatment of these 'child races'. In view of the actual history of the relations between civilized and uncivilized peoples, that Article must needs read like a stern censure. Thus it runs:

'To those colonies and territories which as a consequence of the late war have ceased to be under the sovereignty of the States which formerly governed them and which are inhabited by peoples not yet able to stand by themselves under the strenuous conditions of the modern world, there should be applied the principle that the well-being and development of such peoples form a sacred trust of civilization and that securities for the performance of this trust should be embodied in this Covenant.'

It needs not that I should point out that this 'principle' cannot be limited in its application to the 'mandated' territories. It has universal validity, and it expresses precisely what is the requirement of Christian morality with respect to the matter with which it deals. Would it be possible to find a weightier testimony to the argument of these lectures that Christian morality is able to command the endorsement of the civilized conscience, and by that fact to demonstrate its right to be regarded as in the true sense of the word natural? 'He hath shewed thee, O man, what is good; and what doth the Lord require of thee, but to do justly, and to love mercy, and to walk humbly with thy God?' The theology stands confessed in the morality which it requires and inspires.

The contact of civilized Europeans with the uncivilized peoples, whom they conquer and exploit for their own material advantage, has unquestionably brought in its train a long succession of evils which destroy the happiness, and even menace the survival, of their victims. No blacker chapters can be found in the record of humanity than those which tell the story of

greed, cruelty, and lust which the white race has contributed to the experience of mankind. 'If we reasoned
from what passes in the world,' observes De Tocqueville when he is considering the case of the aborigines
of America, whom the colonists destroyed, and the
negroes, whom they enslaved, 'we should almost say
that the European is to the other races of mankind,
what man is to the lower animals;—he makes them
subservient to his use; and when he cannot subdue, he
destroys them.'[1] In this woeful picture there is one
redeeming feature, which saves it from unrelieved
repulsiveness, I mean the heroism of the apostles of
Christianity. In that description I allow myself to
include, not only the missionaries who, with deliberate
purpose and self-dedication, have sought to Christianize
the people, but also that noble company of public
servants—governors, explorers, soldiers, and civil ad-
ministrators—who, consciously or unconsciously, have
fulfilled their distinctive duties in the Christian spirit.
These men have put to the proof the 'principle' which
the League of Nations affirms, and they have proved its
soundness. The Christian missionaries have come to
the people with the very purpose of assisting their 'well-
being and development', and have lived and died among
them with no other concern. They have made mistakes.
Their minds have been clouded by foolish misunderstandings, and they have not always seen their task in
true perspective; but in spite of all defects, and in the
teeth of much difficulty and prejudice, these men and
women were carried forward by the purest altruism,
illustrating in their daily lives the morality of Christ's

[1] v. *Democracy in America*, i. 394.

religion. Nor is it only in the scenes of their labour that their beneficent influence is to be traced. Here at home, where life tends to sink to lower levels of self-absorbing secularism, we feel their presence. Missions are, in spite of many faults, a standing protest against self-indulgence, cynicism, and vanity. Take away foreign missions from the recent history of Britain, and you would have robbed that history of its purest glory. No one can have any knowledge of religious society in this country without knowing how noble, unselfish, and courageous is the enthusiasm which carries to the end of the earth young men and women to whom life in Britain is rich in promise. They go forth under no illusions, for the records of their predecessors are before them, and those records are eloquent of privation and death. They consecrate with their graves the desperate wastes and pestilential swamps of Africa, the bleak solitudes of Polynesia, the ice-bound plains where the Esquimaux wander, the plague-haunted purlieus of Oriental cities. Those graves perish quickly, the rank vegetation of the tropics or the all-obliterating snow shrouds them from sight; but the tradition of heroism does not perish. It flows ever through the nation, swollen by a thousand contributions of personal service, a stream of holy and gracious influences, fertilizing character, and beautifying life.

X

THE STATE

CHRISTIAN morality cannot exclude from its reference the civic obligations which attach to the individual, and which he cannot reasonably ignore nor rightly repudiate. Being in principle religious, and for that reason truly natural, Christian morality can never be merely conventional, endorsing the obligations which social custom or public law may prescribe.

The Theist, and *a fortiori* the Christian, can never yield an unqualified submission to any secular authority, whether of the general opinion crystallized in prevailing social customs, or of the State. Individual responsibility may not be simplified into unconditioned civic obedience. It involves the difficult and often invidious duty of bringing every demand of external authority under the criticism of the private conscience, and limiting obedience to such demands as the private conscience can endorse. Among the ancients who, excepting Hebrews and Zoroastrians, were polytheists, individual responsibility was submerged in a rigid conformity to external authority. The tribe, the nation, the State 'called the tune' of religion for the individual. Conformity to the public requirements was the alpha and omega of his religious duty. Church and State were indivisibly one, and a divided allegiance was unthinkable. Philosophers, like Socrates and his great disciple Plato, might see through and beyond the reigning assumption, but, for the mass of men, the notion of religion as a matter of personal conviction, and as the dynamic of a congruous morality, of which the broad requirements were divinely disclosed in the private conscience, was unknown. Christianity effected a revolution. The speculations of the higher Greek philosophy became the assumptions of a religion which won the acceptance of common men. Duty was for Christians something super-mundane, the

Stern Daughter of the Voice of God.

The external, impersonal yoke of custom and law was broken, and men moved in the large franchise of their divine sonship. 'Where the Spirit of the Lord is, there is liberty' runs the terse and luminous summary of St. Paul. The noble doctrine of the Hebrew Prophets, gathered up in the saying, 'The spirit of man is the candle of the Lord', was in Christianity affirmed, interpreted, and applied. It is surely significant that the first public utterance of the leaders of the Christian society, when they were confronted by the Sanhedrin's prohibition, was the rebellious declaration, 'We must obey God rather than men'. Henceforward there could be no question for any Christian of a single allegiance. Always he had to make his count with two claimants to his obedience. His earthly citizenship would ever coexist with another and a higher. Jesus Himself had clearly envisaged this inevitable duality. His contemporaries in Palestine were much exercised in mind on this very point of their civic duty. How could they be loyal to their Jewish faith and at the same time dutiful subjects of the Roman Caesar? The question was proposed to Jesus, and His answer has ever been regarded as a luminous declaration of fundamental principle.

'They send unto him certain of the Pharisees and of the Herodians, that they might catch him in talk. And when they were come, they say unto him, Master, we know that thou art true, and carest not for any one; for thou regardest not the person of men, but of a truth teachest the way of God: Is it lawful to give tribute unto Caesar, or not? Shall we give, or shall we not give? But he, knowing their hypocrisy, said unto them, Why tempt ye me? bring me a penny, that I may see it. And they brought it. And he saith unto them, Whose is this image and superscription? And they said unto him, Caesar's. And Jesus said unto them, Render unto Caesar the things that are Caesar's, and unto God the things that are God's. And they marvelled greatly at him.'[1]

May we not say that, in His answer to the Pharisees and Herodians, Jesus disallowed, in advance of Christian history, the two famous and persistent errors, which are described oddly enough as Erastianism and Ultramontanism. Both these names had a curious origin. The German physician whose Graecized name Erastus gave title to the exaggerated theory of State authority in religion afterwards advocated by Thomas Hobbes in the *Leviathan*, appears to have held so high an estimate of the Church's spiritual character that he could not tolerate the prevailing use of coercion in the interest of religion. If excommunication, as was then universally the case, involved secular penalties, then Erastus maintained that excommunication must be the business, not of the Church, but of the State. He would certainly have abhorred the view that the State could prescribe to the Church its faith and worship. 'Ultramontane' is a word which alters its sense with the locality of the speaker. In Italy it meant the dwellers to

[1] v. St. Mark xii. 13–17.

the north of the Alps, and in France the dwellers to the south. The latter sense has prevailed. In the Tridentine and post-Tridentine controversies as to the extent of the papal power the Italian canonists held the most exalted view of the Pope's authority, and the French canonists the least. 'Gallicanism' took its place in history as a minimizing heresy. The Ultramontane is the exact opposite of the Erastian.

In the Middle Ages the papal supremacy had been so exaggerated as to leave no independent authority to the State. A thorough-going Ultramontane was the medieval pontiff, Boniface VIII, who is said to have declared himself, as St. Peter's successor, both Caesar and Pope.

'During the Jubilee he had displayed himself alternately in the splendid habiliments of the Pope and those of the Emperor, with the crown on his head, the sceptre in his hand, and the Imperial sandals on his feet; he had two swords borne before him, and thus openly assumed the full temporal as well as spiritual supremacy over mankind.'[1]

Against this exorbitant figure, the supreme embodiment of 'Ultramontanism', we may set the typical Erastian, Henry VIII, who styled himself 'the Supreme Head of the Church of England', and, in Bishop Stubbs's phrase, claimed to be 'the pope, the whole pope, and something more than the pope'. I may observe that the profane title, 'Supreme Head', was laid aside by Elizabeth, for whom, since she was a woman, it was particularly inapt, and has never been resumed by any British sovereign. Nor has Protestantism lacked its Ultramontanes. The spirit and style of

---

[1] v. Milman, *Latin Christianity*, vii. 104.

the medieval popes found vigorous expression in Calvin and his Scottish disciples, Knox and Melville. In our own age the Secularist and the Clericalist perpetuate the old antagonism of the Erastian and the Ultramontane.

Since, then, the Christian is always a citizen who acknowledges in the State no more than a limited right to order his life, and since he himself must needs be the only authority competent to decide where the limit of his civic obligation shall be fixed, it is obvious that the more highly developed the State comes to be, the more exalted its theory, and the larger the range of its direct action, the greater will become the probability that the Christian will find himself unable conscientiously to satisfy its demands, and will thus be driven, albeit with reluctance and, so to say, in spite of himself, into the odious category of disloyal citizens. Nor is this all. The Christian is not merely an individual guiding his civic behaviour by the light of his own illuminated conscience, an unattached disciple of an unseen Master, a professed subject of 'another King, one Jesus', and, as such, exposed to the not unnatural suspicions of the State to which he confessedly owes allegiance, but he is of necessity also a member of an organized visible society, the Church, which wields over him an authority, indisputable, and, within certain limits, of which he is himself the ultimate judge, supreme, a society, moreover, which is charged with a social mission of its own, which claims a supernational character, and has secular interests inseparable from its functions.

The area of potential discord between membership of the organized State and membership of the organized

Church will vary with the extent of the authority over its members claimed by the rivals. Christianity, it has been said, is unique among religions in 'its claim to penetrate and control the whole of life'; and, although the practical admission of this claim need not necessarily be made by the Church, as such, but may grow from the deliberate and independent action of individual Christians, yet it is apparent that, when social reform is in question, ecclesiastical action will be normally the method actually adopted. Moreover, in this secularist modern epoch, the absorption of Christians in the social applications of their religion predisposes them to welcome in the State the advent of a power plainly superior to the Church in effectiveness. In the vulgar phrase, the State 'can deliver the goods'. A new Erastianism is emerging in Christendom born, not of individual timidity and ambition, nor yet of the low-toned policies of hierarchical self-interest, but of a short-sighted and impatient, but not essentially ungenerous, desire to Christianize society as quickly as possible.

The Church is confessedly not wholly comparable with the State, and although it be the case that, since Church and State must exist within the confines of time and place, there is a close resemblance between them, and a large extent of common ground in which they cannot but co-operate or conflict with one another, still the essential difference between Church and State remains, and cannot rightly be forgotten, or in practice ignored. How deep does the difference go? How far can a working agreement be secured by a segregation of the rivals? Can the self-respecting Christian bisect his life, allotting so much to the control of the secular forces, and so much to that of the religious principles? Can he not, after the manner of those modern thinkers who succeed in combining a blank agnosticism in the laboratory with an ardent devotion in the sanctuary, sever his spiritual from his mundane obligations, living a double life, here frankly Christian, and there as frankly non-Christian? The attempt has been often made, but has never long succeeded. The State may become 'Totalitarian', claiming a control over the entire life of its citizens, and admitting no rival allegiance at any point. The Church may become secularized, conditioning its activities by its temporal interest, conforming its witness with meticulous assiduity to the requirements of the State, and lending to the changing phases of social fashion the protean consecration of its facile and futile countenance. Against the first, the martyrs utter an unconquerable protest: against the last, the unfailing succession of reformers is in irrepressible revolt. But the problem of harmonizing the rival claims, and effectively unifying human life, which has haunted Christian thinking from the first, remains still unsolved, as perplexing, as persistent, as painful as ever.

At this point we may fitly consider the question, which cannot fail to present itself to every student of the New Testament who seeks to bring its moral teaching to bear on the life of society, and who desires to find in that teaching a sufficient directory of secular conduct—How far does personal morality apply to politics? Can the Christian citizen be reasonably required to govern his civic action by the principles and precepts of the Gospel? In an earlier lecture I pointed out the essential unreasonableness of the literalism which would transform the Sermon on the Mount into a legal code to be literally and authoritatively applied to Christian life in all circumstances. It is not how the precepts of the Gospel are to be understood, and given their due place in the construction of Christian morality that concerns us now, but what is the sphere within which Christian morality ought to govern human action? Does Christian morality rightly control the relations of classes and nations as well as those of individuals? Can it mark out the lines of sound economic system? Can it be reasonably applied to the policies of sovereign States? Can it suffice for the government of that complicated *mélange* of past tradition and present fashion which we call civilized society? Is there, in short, a real distinction to be drawn between personal and public morality? The famous Archbishop of York, Dr. Magee, immersed himself in considerable and rather acrimonious controversy by insisting on the essential distinction between the moral obligations of the Christian State and those of the individual Christian. His argument was, perhaps, weakened by his tacit assumption that the precepts of the Sermon on the Mount may rightly be regarded as rules, and not statements of ultimate principle, an assumption which his argument did not really require, and which, as we have seen, is unsound in itself.

He had no difficulty in showing that 'a Christian State carrying out in all its relations literally the precepts of the Sermon on the Mount could not exist for a week'; but as much could be said with equal truth of a Christian individual. Regarded as a manual of conduct to be precisely followed, the Sermon on the Mount could have no practical value. Apart from a few eccentrics and sectaries the Church has never so regarded it. But more reasonably understood, the Sermon provides the most complete version of essential Christian morality which the Church possesses. Are the temper which the Beatitudes disclose, and the principles of action which the precepts properly imply, relevant to the policies and procedures of Christian statesmen? Archbishop Magee had no hesitation in returning a negative answer. The State, he argues, had to take into reckoning factors and forces which had no reference to individual conduct:

'It was to him perfectly clear that a State could not continue to exist on the condition of carrying out all Christian precepts for the individual, and their Lord said so. He said, "My kingdom is not of this world." It was, therefore, a huge mistake to attempt to turn His kingdom into a kingdom of this world, or to turn the kingdoms of the world into His kingdom. Again, he thought they could not speak of the State as if it was an individual and apply all the maxims of individual ethics absolutely to it. The State was not an individual. It was a trustee for a great many individuals. It had to preserve the rights, the lives, and the properties of those who were entrusted to its charge, and they could not make a greater mistake than to suppose that the relations of a State to other States, or to its own subjects, were simply those of one individual to another. But still more he held that any attempt on the part of the State to turn the laws of the Church into laws of the State would only lead to absurd and legal consequences. The great law of the Church of Christ was self-sacrifice, and the motive power of that law was love. The principle of the State was justice, and the motive power of the State was force, and that was the essential difference between the two.'[1]

The Archbishop was far from thinking that Chris-

[1] v. *Life of Archbishop Magee*, ii. 276.

tianity had no bearing on the State's action, or should
not govern the Christian's conduct in business and
politics, as well as in his private life. Only he maintained
that the influence of Christianity was always indirect
and conditioned. He held that the Church was required
so to fulfil its divine mission as to leaven human life
on every plane with Christian influences, and thus to
bring human society into an ever closer agreement with
the mind of Christ. It cannot be reasonably denied that
the action of the State must be determined with reference to considerations which are not relevant to private
behaviour; nor is it doubtful that the objects of the
State are not the same as those of the individual. Much
may be rightly required of the Christian citizen in the
interest of the State which in any other interest would
be morally unlawful. Take for a sufficient example the
case of military service which, for obvious reasons, has
become the subject of eager and persistent debate in
Christian circles.

Nothing could at first view conflict more sharply with
Christian morality than military service, and it is matter
of fact that the Christian conscience has from the first
been much exercised with respect to it. Nevertheless
the deliberate judgement and the almost invariable
practice of the Christian society have decided that, in
the familiar words of the 37th Anglican Article, 'It is
lawful for Christian men, at the commandment of the
Magistrate, to wear weapons, and to serve in the wars'.
It is regrettable that the familiar English version of the
Article omits a word which appears in the Latin, and
which is obviously of great importance. 'Christianis
licet ex mandato magistratus arma portare et justa bella

administrare'. That word *justa* is given its full weight in Bishop Burnet's famous 'Exposition':

'But though wars, that are in their own nature only defensive, are lawful, and a part of the protection that princes owe their people; yet unjust wars, designed for making conquests, for the enlargement of empire, and the raising the glory of princes, are certainly public robberies, and the highest acts of injustice and violence possible; in which men sacrifice to their pride or humour the peace of the world, and the lives of all those that die in the quarrel, whose blood God will require at their hands. Such princes become accountable to God, in the highest degree imaginable, for all the rapine and bloodshed that is occasioned by their pride and injustice.

'When it is visible that a war is unjust, certainly no man of conscience can serve in it, unless it be in the defensive part; for though no man can owe that to his prince to go and murder other persons at his command, yet he may owe it to his country to assist towards its preservation, from being overrun even by those whom his prince has provoked by making war on them unjustly. For even in such a war, though it is unlawful to serve in the attacks that are made on others, it is still lawful for the people of every nation to defend themselves against foreigners.'

Burnet had in mind the protracted wars which the pride and ambition of Louis XIV had occasioned, and he was a thorough-going partisan of his patron, William III, the French king's principal opponent. He would be at no loss for a decision as to the justice of any war in which these sovereigns were engaged. He assumed the legitimacy of the established practice which treated peace and war as matters for the sole determination of the ruling prince. He did not contemplate the responsibility which must needs attach to the individual citizen in a democratic state. The important point in his exposition of the Article is his clear recognition of the contingent character of the Christian's obligation to 'serve in the wars'. He does not say who is to determine that crucial issue of 'justice', but plainly it could not be one of the belligerents, for no man, and no nation, may be accepted as judge in his own case. If we believed the declarations of the Governments concerned, all wars have been just, because all have been, directly or indirectly, defensive. Where, however, personal duty is concerned, the case is sufficiently clear. None but the individual citizen himself can finally determine whether the war in which his service is demanded by the State is a just war, and if it should fall out that his private conscience disapproves of the view which his Government takes, there appears no avoidance of the unpleasant consequences which may follow.

Ought we to set aside the traditional Christian doctrine about war as part of the accumulating mass of outgrown and obsolescent morality, and to recognize that, in the circumstances of the modern world, Christian morality can no longer include military service among legitimate human employments?

There is undoubtedly a strong, perhaps an increasing, tendency in this direction throughout the ecclesiastical world. Canon Raven's book, *Is War Obsolete?* is a remarkable illustration of the trouble of Christian consciences on the subject of war. The author writes with passionate earnestness and a sustained altitude of ethical feeling which is extremely impressive: he realizes intensely, and describes with moving pathos, the horror and tragedy which he witnessed in France; he plainly regards with scornful repugnance the conventional pleas by which war is defended. But he is too clear and candid a thinker to endorse the pacifist attitude. He 'can conceive of circumstances under which physical force is legitimate and necessary'; and, he adds, 'such an admission involves consequences which cannot honestly be avoided'.[1] He can see no alternative to force in dealing with uncivilized fanatical peoples:

'Many of us who would assert without hesitation that war between Christian and cultured men is as out-of-date as duelling cannot so promptly denounce it when used against those to whom it seems the only effective instrument. It is the situation in Palestine or on the North-West frontier that is the serious obstacle to a policy of total and immediate disarmament. For here we are dealing with peoples whose whole training, tradition, and religion glorifies the warrior, whose power to kill is at present restrained by the use of superior military force, and from whom we are pledged to defend men and women who would otherwise be their victims.'[2]

The same reasoning would surely cover the case of civilized peoples who are not less bellicose than the hill-tribes of north-western India or the Moslems of Palestine. It is difficult to imagine a League of Nations which could maintain the peace of the world if it abjured the use of war as an ultimate sanction. Canon Raven does not face this question, and, indeed, it would not be unfair to say that he is sometimes betrayed by his facile rhetoric into perilous exaggeration, and that he does not seem to think out the full implications of his statements. His assumption that 'the only folk who can discuss war are the people who saw it at close quarters' is precarious, to say the least. There is also truth in the familiar proverb that 'the onlooker sees

[1] v. p. 151.   [2] v. p. 152.

most of the game'. The actual combatants were commonly so situated that they could not see the campaign as a whole, nor understand the ultimate interests at stake in the war itself. Neither the trench nor the stricken field is really favourable to a just estimate of policy or to a clear insight into essential principles. The rightness of military service cannot really turn on the measure of the misery and havoc which modern war inflicts. Indeed a concentration of the mind on the incidental horrors of warfare may confuse the judgement by disturbing the imagination. If we would judge truly the moral quality of human action, we must ignore its physical or material consequences. 'What is a man profited, if he gain the whole world, and lose or forfeit his own self?' asks the supreme moral Teacher of mankind. Prudential considerations can dictate a course of action or inaction which may coincide with the requirement of morality, or may not. In either case it is not itself moral. The popular saying, 'Honesty is the best policy', may be, and probably is, confirmed by experience; but if honesty be prompted by the belief that it is the best policy, it is emptied of moral content. The vast cost and limitless horror of modern scientific warfare may well induce men to seek peace and ensue it, but, as the motive is in that case merely prudential, the peaceful policy which it dictates need not be essentially superior in moral quality to the war which, in different circumstances, would express the same selfish concern.

Fiat justitia, ruat coelum is the rule of genuinely moral action. The parade and dramatic emphasizing of the infinite horrors of modern scientific war may and probably does multiply pacifists, but it leaves the essential problem unsolved, and rather obstructs than facilitates the discovery of its true solution. The moral question of the rightfulness of using force in the interest of righteousness is as truly raised when a criminal is sent to jail or a bad boy birched, as when nations resist aggression with all the fell and formidable forces of scientific warfare. The pacifist may be the unconscious victim of his own disturbed imagination rather than the obedient servant of reasonably ordered thought or a rightly guided conscience. The problem, of which war is at present the only solution known to human experience, must be solved if civilization is to continue or, indeed, if humanity itself is to survive.

The essential problem is, how to restrain the lawlessness of States, and to vindicate in the sphere of international policy the authority of the moral law. Christian morality does certainly demand the solution of that problem, and, as certainly, it has hitherto failed to provide any sufficient alternative to the only known solution, viz. war. Mere acquiescence in oppression would be indistinguishable from a guilty co-operation with the oppressor.

, So long, indeed, as Christianity was an obscure and persecuted sect, the only form of warfare possible to Christians was that passive resistance which the long succession of Christian martyrs illustrated. But with the victory of Christianity came the risks and responsibilities of political power. Christianity could not avoid or ignore its new and formidable responsibilities. The Christian ruler had to determine his attitude towards aggression, and to interpret his duty in relation both to his own nation and to other nations than his own. Within Christendom, and, when Christendom had been broken

into fragments, within the sovereign States which replaced it, Christianity established or, to speak exactly,
assisted in establishing, the reign of law, and organized
a righteously regulated coercion in the interest of social
order and justice. Thus the excesses of individual
wickedness were brought under control, and the law
court replaced private violence.

But when the same problem is presented, not as a
domestic issue between individual citizens, but as a
political dispute between States, what solution is available? It is no doubt true that, if men were reasonable
and rightly informed and wisely governed and frater-
nally minded, that is, in short, if they were quite other
than they actually are, they would not resort to violence
for the settlement of international disputes, but perceiving that their own permanent interest could only be
injured by strife, would accept with alacrity arbitration,
or the verdict of some competent international tribunal
as an alternative to the doubtful and dreadful arbitra-
ment of war. But, being what they actually are—passionate, ignorant, prejudiced, greedy, and cruel—what
method is there apart from war for restraining ambition, protecting the weak, and asserting for justice
some authority among men? Humanitarian enthusiasts
too easily forget that mankind develops at a very uneven
pace, that all phases of moral development coexist
among men, and that the most advanced communities
are in some sense at the mercy of the most backward.
Certainly not the least formidable obstacle to the abolition of war to-day arises from this cause. There is no
general agreement even among civilized men as to the
intrinsic turpitude and folly of war. In English-speaking

communities, indeed, there is a widely spread opinion
that war is equally irrational and immoral, a stain on
civilization, and a relic of barbarism which ought to be
discarded, but is it certain, or even probable, that that
opinion prevails in any other part of civilized mankind?
Is it not apparent that in many nations, by no means
uncivilized, war is regarded as a normal and not necessarily malefic factor in human life? In these circumstances, then, can Christianity, the religion of truth and
of personal responsibility, be likely to prohibit military
service, as such, to its professors?

Necessitas non habet legem. There are situations in
which normal disciplines must needs be cancelled, and
to which accepted principles of conduct do not properly
apply. There is a famous incident related in the Book
of Maccabees which conveys a moral of which Christian
history provides many illustrations. When the army
of Antiochus came upon the Jews on the Sabbath day,
the Jews allowed themselves to be massacred rather than
that they should by fighting break the Sabbath law.

'They said, We will not come forth, neither will we do the
word of the king, to profane the sabbath day. And they [i.e.
the enemy] hasted to give them battle. And they answered them
not, neither cast they a stone at them, nor stopped up the secret
places, saying, Let us die all in our innocency: heaven and earth
witness over us, that ye put us to death without trial. And they
rose up against them in battle on the sabbath, and they died,
they and their wives and their children, and their cattle, to the
number of a thousand souls.'

This scrupulous legalism was condemned by the Jewish
leader:

'And Mattathias and his friends knew it, and they mourned

over them exceedingly. And one said to another, If we all do as
our brethren have done, and fight not against the Gentiles for
our lives and our ordinances, they will now quickly destroy us
from off the earth. And they took counsel on that day, saying,
Whosoever shall come against us to battle on the sabbath day,
let us fight against him, and we shall in no wise all die, as our
brethren died in the secret places.'[1]

Had Mattathias been, not a Jew, but a Christian, and
had the issue been not ceremonial, the observance of
the Sabbath law, but moral, the explicit denial of Christ's
authority, would he have given any other advice to
his co-religionists than history records that he gave
them?

We see, then, that, while the pacifist who condemns
war as such, and disallows military service in all circumstances, is seriously misrepresenting the requirement of
Christian morality, those are guilty of an even graver
misrepresentation who would allow the Christian
citizen to exempt himself from the delicate and difficult
obligation of sitting in judgement on his country's
claim, and determining whether in any given case he
ought to obey its call. It may be conceded that in most
cases the character of a war is apparent in advance, and
that, since democratic government reflects very fully
and fairly the feeling, if not the reason, of the nation,
most citizens in voting for war have already declared
their verdict and decided the issue of their duty, still
it is important to insist that Christian morality requires
that the individual conscience shall be brought to bear
on the question of personal duty, and that if the war
cannot be waged without the approval of the citizen's

[1] v. 1 Maccabees ii. 34 f.

own conscience, he is not, as a Christian man, free to render military service therein.

When, thus, the part of the individual conscience is affirmed, and the Christian citizen is constituted the warder of justice to the full extent of his civic influence, it is apparent that Christianity will tell potently, though indirectly, against war. How few are the wars recorded on the pages of history which could sustain the criticism of the conscience which had been developed and guided in the school of Christ! The conscience of civilized men is growing ever more restive under the dolorous necessity of war, and this restiveness is itself a consequence of the deepening repugnance with which Christian citizens acquiesce in so flagrant a violation of their professed principles. It is significant that the League of Nations has its main, perhaps its only, support in the Christianized sections of European society. The ideal of international fellowship which the Christian Church upholds is commending itself increasingly to men of goodwill in all countries; and if the abolition of war is destined to be finally achieved, it will be because Christian morality has made good its claim to the acceptance of civilized mankind.

It has been objected that patriotism has no place in the scheme of Christian virtue, and that Christianity may even have an enfeebling effect on those stronger elements of human nature which are indispensable to healthy citizenship. Such plausibility as this objection possesses derives from a twofold misconception. On the one hand it misconceives Christianity; on the other hand it misconceives patriotism. In both cases the misconception is easily intelligible. Take the case of

Christianity. It is an easily explicable error to attribute
to the religion an appearance of moral lopsidedness which
was in fact due to the circumstances in which it was
first preached. Since the converts of the apostles were
drawn mainly from the humblest ranks of society, the
moral qualities which were mostly insisted upon were
those which matched the actual circumstances in which
they would have to live. Accordingly the category of
Christian heroism included types which the ancient
world did not greatly honour, and excluded those which
it held in highest regard. The new importance attached
to the woman and the child, the new dignity of service
however lowly, the new franchise of the spirit which
ignored social status, above all, the new sovereignty of
the human conscience, reversed the established values
of antiquity and created new ideals of greatness. How
real this revolution was may be seen in the language
of St. Paul. Himself, if we may use familiar modern
terms, a scholar and a gentleman, a man of affairs and
belonging to the propertied class, one who combined
the fastidious dignity of a cultured Pharisee with the
easy habit of a Roman citizen, St. Paul was amazed at
the paradox which the Christian religion exhibited:

'Behold your calling, brethren,' he writes to the Corinthians,
'how that not many wise after the flesh, not many mighty, not
many noble, are called: but God chose the foolish things of the
world, that he might put to shame them that are wise; and God
chose the weak things of the world, that he might put to shame
the things that are strong; and the base things of the world, and
the things that are despised, did God choose, yea and the things
that are not, that he might bring to nought the things that are:
that no flesh should glory before God.'[1]

[1] 1 Corinthians i. 26–9.

The New Testament belongs to that first age, in which Christianity perforce expressed itself mainly in the humblest members of a despotically governed society. It is not therefore surprising that the morality which it inculcates has, in the eyes of free, self-governing citizens of modern democratic States, a certain inadequacy, as if it over-emphasized one set of obligations and ignored another. But this impression is removed when the New Testament is read, as it surely ought to be read, in the light of Christian history, when the fact and the method of moral development are rightly considered, and when the principles of the original teaching are seen in their latest and most authoritative application. Martyrs are not moral weaklings, yet it is precisely martyrs who have been the most honoured heroes of Christianity. Nor is it without significance that Christianity has become the religion of the most virile races of mankind, and that democracy and all the civic virtues which it demands and honours have flourished within Christendom.

Misconception of Christianity has gone along with misconception of patriotism. Too often patriotism has been identified with a self-centred, vainglorious nationalism, with which in truth it has no necessary connexion. It is certainly true that Christian morality can make no terms with nationalism, but it does not exclude genuine patriotism. The principle of neighbourly love, which Christianity insists upon as of primary importance, involves also a more extensive reference. Love of country and love of the human race are implicit in love of neighbour, but they claim recognition in a natural order. The narrower duty leads on to the wider, which only so can be attained. Cosmopolitanism cut adrift from patriotism is the vaguest and least exacting of creeds: and patriotism which does not spring from love of one's neighbour is the sorriest cant. Bishop Butler writes admirably of the necessary relation between these widening phases of social affection:

'Persons more practical have, instead of mankind, put our country; and made the principle of virtue, of human virtue, to consist in the entire uniform love of our country; and this is what we call a public spirit; which in men of public stations is the character of a patriot. But this is speaking to the upper part of the world. Kingdoms and governments are large; and the sphere of action of far the greatest part of mankind is much narrower than the government they live under: or however, common men do not consider their actions as affecting the whole community of which they are members. There plainly is wanting a less general and nearer object of benevolence for the bulk of men, than that of their country. Therefore the Scripture, not being a book of theory and speculation, but a plain rule of life for mankind, has with the utmost possible propriety put the principle of virtue upon the love of our neighbour; which is that part of the universe, that part of mankind, that part of our country, which comes under our immediate notice, acquaintance, and influence, and with which we have to do.'[1]

This natural order of moral development is very repulsive to the kindling imagination and eager activity of social reformers. Yet its disregard gives the key to the paradox, which revolutions never fail to exhibit, of the combination in the same individuals of callous cruelty and humanitarian ardour. Private oppression of the most barbarous kind may, and commonly does, coexist

[1] Butler, Sermon xii, 'Upon the Love of our Neighbour', v. *Works*, i. 155, ed. Bernard.

with a generous concern for the wrongs of classes and peoples and humanity itself. Revolutionaries would seem to set their altruistic zeal in one direction against their contempt for human rights in another. Christian morality discloses its fidelity to Nature in no respect more impressively than in its emphatic rejection of the revolutionary method. Avoiding the snare of a cheap and generous sentimentalism, and uniting in its version of social duty an altruism which takes concern for all human necessities and a rational egotism which ignores no natural requirement, Christianity appoints a man's own claims to be his measure of other men's needs, thus transforming the very organ of selfishness into the herald of charity, and finally reforming society by first transforming its constituent members. The sum and the method of Christian morality is thus formulated in the Sermon on the Mount: 'All things therefore whatsoever ye would that men should do unto you, even so do ye also unto them: for this is the law and the prophets.'

In a negative form the Golden Rule may be found in the teachings of other masters, but its positive form appears to be due to Jesus Himself. Thus He brought together into a working harmony the two sets of natural instincts which must be given frank expression in any morality which shall do justice to human nature—the self-regarding and the social. From the one He averts an easy degradation into mere egotism. From the other He averts its facile exaggeration into an unreal and impracticable altruism. Self-respect and service of others blend in Christian morality.

Patriotism, or love of one's native country, is a generous sentiment, the very principle of a sympathetic

and understanding regard for the same sentiment in
foreigners. Herein it is the precise contradiction of that
hard and arrogant nationalism which rides roughshod
over the feelings of others and takes no heed for their
natural aspirations. Patriotism pictures humanity as a
composite of many distinctive national types, enriched
with the various achievements of history. Nationalism
dreams of a subject world, an empire of its own wherein
all men serve its interests and minister to its magnificence. Patriotism seeks association and interchange
of specific qualities, pursuing the ideal of an ultimate
fellowship from which shall be excluded no portion of
mankind. Nationalism, pushing ever more widely its
frontiers over the earth, regards all men as the potential
agents of its own selfish triumph.

Nationalism, political or racial or economic, is re-
vealing itself ever more clearly as a principal root of
war, and the main condition of its continuance. So
great are its evils that not even the immense calamities
which it inflicts on mankind can finally deter men from
resisting its tyranny. In a very acute analysis of the present international situation, a well-informed American
publicist has fastened on economic nationalism as the
main obstacle to peace:

'The price of peace in the contemporary world must then be
clear to all who undertake to analyze the present danger of war.
That price is, moreover, the assurance of economic security to
the peoples of all the great powers. For it is only upon the
basis of such security that it is possible to establish a community
of interest in the prevention of conflict. . . .

'Today the challenge of economic nationalism can only be met
by war or by some form of international agreement which will
assure to all peoples, on reasonable terms, access to the essential

raw materials and minerals of industry. For, failing such assured access, many peoples will find themselves condemned to intolerable hardship and turn to war as the more attractive alternative.'[1]

If this view of the international situation be well founded, and nationalism is both the principle of war and the pledge of its recurrence, it is apparent that Christian morality in condemning nationalism accords with the apparent interest of mankind.

[1] v. *The Price of Peace*, by Frank H. Symonds, Litt.D., and Brooks Emery, Ph.D., pp. 342, 343.

XI

INDUSTRIALISM

INDUSTRIALISM is the latest phase of civilized economic organization, for even the Communist system which is being established in Russia appears to be conforming, as it were by an inner necessity, to the industrialist model. Ruthless violence to individuals may finally succeed in forcing collectivist agriculture on the Russian peasants, but the substitution of groups for individuals leaves the main characteristics of industrialism unaltered, and even exaggerates some of the worst. Historically, industrialism has developed within Christendom, and has intertwined itself very closely with organized Christianity. It is extending under Christian auspices throughout the world. The merchant and the missionary march hand in hand. Industrialism penetrates Asia and Africa and is not unnaturally assumed by Asiatics and Africans to be the distinguishing feature of Christian civilization. It is no marvel, therefore, that there should be a general assumption in men's minds that there is some proper connexion between Christianity and industrialism, and that Christian civilization must of necessity take this form; and therefore that the enormous mischiefs of industrialism may fairly be carried to the credit, that is, the discredit, of the Christian religion.

Christianity, we should keep ever in mind, has no essential association with any specific type of economic organization, though it cannot but affect for good whatever type is associated with it, and tend to strengthen in human society whatever morally sound elements it may encounter therein. Christianity introduces an assimilating influence within the economic system, and thereby brings it by insensible degrees within the lines of Christian morality.

It would appear that man's capacity for moral awareness is severely limited. Keen sensitiveness to the abominable wickedness of the slave trade in Africa could coexist in the same Christian minds with a comfortable acquiescence in the oppression of women and children in the mines and factories of England. Use and wont have a deadening effect on the conscience as well as on the intelligence. We do not easily perceive the moral paradoxes involved in procedures which are accustomed, established, and expected. In fact there is an inevitable parasitism about historic Christianity. Nothing less would appear to be required by its proper task of Christianizing society. The primary purpose of ecclesiastical organization is to bring the Christian religion to bear effectively on human life, and therefore men must be approached where they are actually living and in the circumstances which determine their secular procedures. Only so shall they be brought within the range of Christian influence. This practical necessity explains what has often attracted the notice of historical students, and moved the scornful comments of hostile critics, viz. the close modelling of ecclesiastical on contemporary civil arrangements. The articulated hierarchy of the Catholic Church was obviously designed to provide a parallel to the hierarchy of the civil government. Over against the imperial functionary was ever placed an ecclesiastical officer whose authority extended over the same area, and who, with certain inevitable reserves, acknowledged in the emperor a like supremacy.

The same parasitism is observable in the sphere of economics. It is severely normal that, in the modern world, industrial methods and tempers should be closely paralleled in the field of ecclesiastical activity, and that 'good business men' should tend to displace saints and martyrs in the regard of the churches.

Christianity was originally introduced into a world economically ordered on the foundation of slavery. That foundation determined the form of the super-structure. Commerce proceeded within the Empire on a great scale, but its character and distribution were largely determined by the supply of slaves and the distinctive requirements of slave labour. Production was allocated according to the natural capacities of specific districts. There was competition between pro-ducers and retailers, and the rewards of success went to the most efficient, but there was nothing in the ancient world quite equivalent to the fierce and many-sided rivalry which marks modern industry. Free labourers did exist, but tended to disappear. Within the restricted area of their employment the combinations of workmen, so familiar to the present age, were not un-known, but nowhere wielded any comparable political influence. Society was mainly agricultural, and labour was mainly servile. This was the economic framework within which Christianity had to take root and develop. The Church made no attempt to alter it, but by bringing into it a new spirit did in fact affect it very potently. The influence of Christianity was felt in raising the general tone of society, discouraging the harsher features of slavery, enlarging the horizons of human thought, and silently but surely destroying the assumptions on which ancient society rested. The transition from the imperial economy based on slavery to the medieval based on serfdom was effected gradually, and, so to say, unconsciously. Feudalism had an independent origin, but it developed in a society which professed and called itself Christian. Thus medieval Christendom took shape as it were by a natural process. Europe was baptized in its infancy. The cost of so frank an identification of church and society was heavy. Morally and intellectually Christian standards were lowered by an acute secularization, but the creation of Christendom, a social order consciously Christian, was a salutary achievement of far-reaching and permanent consequence. The economic system was brought into some confessed relation, not wholly ineffective, with Christian morality. For this society the term Christendom was not entirely inappropriate, though it rather confessed the ideal than described the reality.

The roots of industrialism are planted deeply in the soil of medieval life. The cities of Italy, Flanders, and Germany, in which commerce flourished and the aggressive, independent, enterprising spirit of commerce shaped men's minds, were so many centres of revolt against the reigning conditions of medieval thought and life. Christendom was in great measure destroyed from within long before its framework, political and ecclesiastical, was broken up. Industrialism was not Christian in origin, though it developed within Christian society: nor are its spirit and tendency in any special measure congruous with Christianity, though they seem to prevail in Christian civilization. Industrialism has created a new social and economic framework into which the Christian religion has perforce to fit. History is again repeating itself. The same capacity of almost limitless acquiescence, which enabled the religion of freedom to tolerate slavery, and the religion of equality to tolerate feudalism, is being exhibited in the modern world in the case of industrialism. The religion which interprets, develops, and protects human individuality acquiesces in an economic system which so dwarfs and depresses individuality as to threaten its total destruction. The paradox is persistent and perplexing, but its significance is not entirely hidden.

History provides the key to the enigma which it presents. In every case acquiescence is seen to be the weapon by which the Christian religion conquers the hostile forces in its secular environment, and slowly but surely introduces its own transforming spirit. Slavery disappears, but it enriches Christian morality with that conception of service as something inherently great which was burnt into the Christian mind by the long association of servile status and spiritual achievement. Feudalism disappears, but it bequeaths to Christian morality that sensitive loyalty and high chivalry which were shaped by the long discipline of feudal subordination. Christianity ever stoops to conquer. Industrialism will but renew the lesson which slavery and feudalism have already taught. But we must consider the case of industrialism more closely, for it differs in some important particulars from both slavery and feudalism. There is no radical falseness of ultimate assumption to be reckoned with. Industry is obviously good in itself.

St. Paul gives expression to the verdict of the general conscience when he formulates the rule—'If any will not work, neither let him eat'.[1] The interchange of commodities in the mutual interest of those who exchange them, which is the essential content of commerce, is an inevitable inference from the social character of man. Wages and profits have an incontestable title to be regarded as morally legitimate.

Since men are unquestionably unequal, and the extent of their risks and labours varies indefinitely, equity itself authorizes a large inequality of recompense. Property, and the unequal distribution of it, would seem to be morally defensible. The accumulation of capital from the product of industry, and its investment in commercial undertakings, cannot be said to lack moral justification. Interest on capital cannot be morally distinguished from wages and profits, being indeed a form of the latter. The division of labour, which finds such extreme expression in the factory system, is in itself as morally unobjectionable as it is practically advantageous. All the subsidiary features of industrialism—banking, advertisement, and speculation—can be justified to reason and conscience. They are indispensable to the conduct and expansion of industry. Unlike slavery, which embodies a false principle, and feudalism, which implies a false conception of society, industrialism does not necessarily do violence to any moral truth, nor run counter to right reason. Its mischiefs, which are confessedly very great, flow from certain monstrous exaggerations which, in the circumstances of the modern world, have marked its develop-

[1] v. 2 Thessalonians iii. 10.

ment. The unprecedented size of modern communities,
and the new facilities of communication between them,
have so deranged perspectives and so complicated procedures as to obscure or contradict the very principles
of legitimate industry.

Christian morality accords easily with commerce in
its less complicated aspects, for it emphasizes precisely
those virtues which are most requisite for commercial success. Conscientiousness, personal responsibility,
truthfulness in speech, thoroughness in work, a high
standard of integrity, dependableness in agreements—
these are the constituents of the commercial character
at its best. What was observed in the case of the early
Quakers, and goes far to explain both their remarkable
success in business and their great unpopularity with
their contemporaries, was their fraternal co-operation,
their superior rectitude, and their practical efficiency.
They did better work and they charged fairer prices
than their rivals and critics. Add that, like the ancient
Christians and the modern Jews, they formed a closely
linked association, free from local attachments, which
assisted its members with early and trustworthy information as to markets, and thus facilitated their trading
interests, and we can be at no loss to understand either
their exceptional success in business or the odium in
which it immersed them.

It has been maintained, not without reason, that the
distinctive features of Reformed Christianity—its exaltation of the individual, its substitution of the infallible
Bible for the infallible Church, its Calvinist theology,
and its puritanic hostility to the arts—tended to give
marked stimulus to commerce throughout the sphere

of the Reformation. The severe and logical system of Calvin could not but strengthen the individuality of those who accepted it, and, in the case of insincere professors, might too easily encourage a divorce between creed and conduct which would be as serviceable in business as it was ruinous in religion. The excessive deference to the Old Testament carried its inferior morality into Protestant habit, and established, even in sincerely religious minds, that association of divine favour and mundane prosperity, which marked the religion of ancient Israel, and expressed what in morals is the cardinal heresy, that 'the end justifies the means'. The iconoclasm which wrecked the medieval churches, and banned the arts from Puritan concern, encouraged, and almost compelled, a concentration of the mind on the practical affairs of life, which secured success in business at the price of a certain moral lopsidedness. It is not therefore extravagant to trace a connexion between the monstrous Mammon-cult of modern America and the Calvinist creed and Puritan habit of the early settlers. The genuine religious devotion which coexisted with creed and habit, and went far to redeem them, has now largely disappeared; but habits long survive the convictions which originally they expressed, and, when thus severed from their original ideas, may take exorbitant and malefic forms. Something must, perhaps, be attributed to the fact that, among Protestants, preaching became everywhere the principal, almost the only, duty of the Christian minister. Sacraments and liturgies fell into the background; the sermon replaced both in the habit of the people. It seemed as if the prophet had finally vanquished the priest in the age-long conflict.

Now sermons have this ineradicable defect as moral instruments, that, in the preacher always, in his hearers often, they stimulate the perilous tendency to separate theory from practice, giving amplest expression to the one, and not securing any adequate attention to the other. Pecksniff, ever uttering the unctuous platitudes of morality, and never facing obvious personal duty, is a familiar figure in Christian society at all times. Rhetorical artistry and emotional appeals may sweep congregations into ecstasies of religious fervour, but they neither quicken the conscience nor govern the will. Bishop Butler's grave words have the authority of continuing experience, and they give the key to the distressing enigma which confronts every Christian preacher, viz. the moral impotence of Christian preaching:

'But going over the theory of virtue in one's thoughts, talking well, and drawing fine pictures of it; this is so far from necessarily or certainly conducing to form a habit of it, in him who thus employs himself, that it may harden the mind in a contrary course, and render it gradually more insensible, i.e. form a habit of insensibility, to all moral considerations.'[1]

In view of the affinity between important elements of Christian morality and the qualities most requisite for commercial success, it is not surprising that in America it is not uncommon to hear business described as a distinctive sphere of Christian service, and to emphasize the large benefits which it bestows on the community. It is not, however, wholly irrational to suspect that the very largeness of the benefits, that is the benefactions, which flow from modern industrialism, have more to

[1] v. *The Analogy*, part i, ch. v.

do with the shaping of the theory than any Christian principle. In any case, a little reflection will make it apparent that, as matters now stand in America and in industrialized society everywhere, this method of presenting the claim of Christianity to discipline, direct, and consecrate all properly human activities is beset with very formidable risks.

The step from emphasizing potential services to condoning actual procedures is a short one, and there are cogent reasons why preachers should take it. 'A man's foes shall be they of his own household.' Christian ministers, hard pressed to raise funds for maintaining the great machinery for religious and philanthropic work which has been built up by the zeal and sacrifice of their predecessors, are ill placed for pressing the inexorable demands of the moral law on the wealthy individuals whose financial assistance they hope to receive. The Christian imagination may be kindled while the Christian conscience is dulled. So much that is religiously desirable and impressive can only be secured by great expenditures of money. From time to time I receive from America a rather sumptuous and beautifully illustrated periodical called *The Cathedral Age*. It describes by pen and photograph the great churches of Europe which are very old, and the great churches of America which are very new. It dwells on the prevailing tendency in the ecclesiastical world of America to spend immense sums of money in building cathedrals and cathedral-like churches. It is suggested that this edifying megalomania of the American churches provides something like a demonstration of the soundness of American religion. The considering and observant student of American society will find it difficult to accept this view. He will be unable to banish from mind the accumulating evidences of moral failure which are provided by social statistics and unparalleled scandals, and he will reflect that the magnificence and costliness of its buildings was not included by the Divine Founder of Christianity in the proofs of genuine discipleship.

Far be it from me to suggest that this paradox of ecclesiastical pomp linked with moral failure is peculiar to America, though there it is perhaps more notably apparent than elsewhere. The spectacle is coeval and conterminous with Christianity itself. I shall never forget the impression made on my mind when, on visiting the United States for the first time, I received from an American, in answer to my inquiry as to the place held by the Christian churches in American society, the brusque declaration, 'Churches, Sir, they are only the kept mistresses of the Trusts.' I have no doubt that this statement was as unfair as it was uncharitable, yet I cannot exorcize from my mind the suspicion that it enshrines such a measure of truth as may well cause searching of hearts among Christian folk on both sides of the Atlantic. My own observations during a fairly long ministry lead me to think that the financial obsessions of the Christian churches must take rank as among the major hindrances to their spiritual influence.

Industrialism, as it exists in the world to-day, has developed far beyond the simple stages in which the connexion between Christian morality and commercial success was apparent. Industry is now cosmopolitan in range and mechanical in method; and neither characteristic is easily consistent with the rigorous personal claims of morality. Moreover, the civilized world as we know it is so truly the creature of industrialism that it is hard to see how it can continue under any other system. The vast populations which depend on industry, organized on a world-wide basis and proceeding by methods ever more mechanical, both for the necessaries of life and for all the elements of civilized living, cannot abandon the industrial economy which they now possess without finding an economic alternative which shall be demonstrably superior. Thus the ethical problem is presented in an economic framework which leaves little freedom to the Christian moralist. *Necessitas non habet legem.*

Even though industrialism be in itself morally defensible, would it not cease to remain so if it could be shown that the inevitable result of its methods on those whom it affects is physically, mentally, and morally injurious? This is precisely what is alleged to be the case with the extreme subdivision of labour involved in 'standardization'. The greatly increased rapidity of output makes possible such a lessening of the costs of production that standardized commodities can be brought within the purchasing power of multitudes of poor people who would otherwise be unable to enjoy them. Thus an apparent public advantage can be claimed. But—and this is the point now before us—this advantage is gained at the price of the permanent debasement of the workers. Is it morally legitimate to pay that price? De Tocqueville commented in 1831 on the extreme division of labour which he observed in

America. The lapse of a century has but added emphasis to his words:

'When a workman is unceasingly and exclusively engaged in the fabrication of one thing, he ultimately does his work with singular dexterity; but at the same time he loses the general faculty of applying his mind to the direction of the work. He every day becomes more adroit and less industrious: so that it may be said of him, that in proportion as the workman improves the man is degraded. What can be expected of a man who has spent twenty years of his life in making heads for pins? and to what can that mighty human intelligence, which has so often stirred the world, be applied in him, except it be to investigate the best method of making pins' heads? When a workman has spent a considerable portion of his existence in this manner, his thoughts are for ever set upon the object of his daily toil; his body has contracted certain fixed habits, which it can never shake off: in a word, he no longer belongs to himself, but to the calling which he has chosen. It is in vain that laws and manners have been at the pains to level all barriers round such a man, and to open to him on every side a thousand different paths to fortune; a theory of manufactures more powerful than manners or laws binds him to a craft, and frequently to a spot, which he cannot leave: it assigns to him a certain place in society, beyond which he cannot go: in the midst of universal movement, it has rendered him stationary.'[1]

De Tocqueville wrote when the process of standardizing industry was in its infancy. In the course of the century, which has elapsed since he drew his vivid picture of its disastrous influence on the workman, democracy has attained to maturity of political power. Popular life has been in many of its aspects transformed, but the standardizing tendency has continued with ever waxing vigour, and the resentment which it provokes in

[1] v. *Democracy in America*, ii. 190.

its victims is all the fiercer because they are by comparison with their predecessors educated and politically powerful. No measure of advance is felt to compensate for the degradation of the individual workman inherent in the standardizing process itself.

Nor is it only the workman who is personally worsened by the distinctive method of modern industrialism. His employer also is morally injured by the excessive control over other men's lives which he must needs acquire, and the vast wealth which he may be able to gain. In fact the employer and the workman are in the same condemnation. Nor is even this the whole extent of the mischief. The community itself is affected unwholesomely by the ramifying influence which wealth enshrines. This power may be vested, often is vested, in individuals who may be among the least respected or respectable of their generation. It is hard to say whether the virtues or the vices of multi-millionaires are the more to be dreaded. Ambition to exercise the vast power latent in wealth may lead the wealthy man to make himself master of the press, or to impose his own preferences, which may be far from sound, on municipalities, colleges, and even churches. Thus the very springs of political life may be corrupted, and the balance of education, and even of religion, may be dangerously disturbed. Nor is even this all. The mere existence of so much wealth vested in private individuals fires the imagination of the public, sets before the young a false measure of success, and silently inducts the multitude to the sordid worship of Mammon. Vulgar profusion paraded before the masses moves both cupidity and resentment. Even the great benefactions

which seem to redeem private wealth, by proving its
serviceableness to the general good, are not unshadowed
by formidable mischiefs, none the less formidable because they are undesigned and unperceived.

In saying this I am not forgetful of some noble exceptions to the general rule. We have all known instances
of wealthy benefactors, whose generosity has been so
conditioned by wisdom and modesty that few or none
of the disadvantages which have been indicated can
fairly be said to attach to it. These are exceptions to
the general rule, and that is not doubtful. A spirit of
dependence is fostered in the community, and the very
magnitude of the gifts of the wealthy tends to discourage
the modest benefactions of the relatively poor. Universities and churches pay a heavy price for the patronage
of the millionaires to whom they owe their sumptuous
buildings, their well-stocked libraries, and the lavish
endowments of their pulpits and professors' chairs.

There is, however, another side to the picture. In
dwelling on the exorbitant developments of industrialism, which have been terribly emphasized by the world-
wide economic dislocation caused by the Great War,
we must be on our guard against belittling, or even
denying, the vast benefits which it has brought to man.
Civilization, in the large sense which the word carries
to modern Europeans, would be unthinkable without
the material resources which only industrialism could
provide. The immense wealth which mechanized industry creates has been the indispensable condition of
social advance. Civilized society, as it now exists in
Christendom, is marked by grave scandals, but it is
beyond all precedent possessed of order, leisure, and

the means of rational enjoyment. Much turns on the point of view from which industrialism is regarded. Consider its positive achievement in maintaining the vast populations of Christendom in a state, so far as the great majority are concerned, of comparative comfort, and you can hardly avoid the conclusion that industrialism is the most beneficent economic order known to human experience. Direct your study to the hideous incidents which appear to be inseparable from modern industrial life—monotonous and even brutalizing labour, the destruction of the family under the influence of congested slums, the injury to mind and body inflicted by the unavoidable conditions of urban life, the desperate resentments flaming out in savage crime, the servility of spirit bred by abject dependence, and, along with these, the abounding wealth, sensuality, and arrogance of plutocratic society—and you are moved to an irrepressible repugnance by a system which can inflict on humanity such cruel and degrading mischiefs.

The more sombre view tends now to prevail, not merely because the far-reaching dislocation of society by the Great War has forced the worst aspects of industrialism into an arresting prominence, but also because the imagination of the people is widely disturbed by the knowledge of former social oppressions which have become the theme of an extensive, able, and sometimes brilliant literature. Lord Bryce has commented on this modern phenomenon:

'The resentment of the wage-earners at the appropriation by employers of what seems an inordinately large part of the product of labour, and the vehemence of this resentment against the present generation of the wealthier class, which has shown

far more sympathy with the aspirations of the worker than the
two preceding generations had done, is an instance to verify
the old saying, "The fathers have eaten sour grapes, and the
children's teeth are set on edge." Injustice always brings punishment in its train, but the spirit of revenge often grows with time,
and is stronger in the descendants of those who have suffered
than it was in the sufferers themselves; while the penalties fall
not on those who did the wrong, but on their more innocent
successors who are trying to atone for the past.'[1]

At no previous phase of human history has the mind
of man been more steadily directed towards the removal
of social inequalities and the improvement of the conditions of popular life. Democracy has been the political
expression of industrialism, and provides the corrective
of its worst excesses; for though democracy has formidable risks and disadvantages of its own, it has ever this
supreme merit that it cannot ignore the wrongs and
hardships of the people.

The rapid mechanizing of industry, which has dis-
placed human labour on a great scale, and will continue
to do so on a greater, has created a situation of much
perplexity and potential risk, but it cannot be more than
a passing phase of secular history. We cannot doubt
that the inherent resources of the human mind, not
undirected by the Divine Wisdom from which they are
ultimately drawn, will be adequate to the solution of the
latest, as of all the earlier, problems implicit in the
process of human development.

Christian morality, subjected again to the pressure of
circumstances, which, as we showed in a previous
lecture, has been one of the main shaping influences

[1] v. *Modern Democracies*, ii. 637.

brought to bear on it in history, will discover fresh applications of its essential principles, and thus garner from its most recent, as from all its earlier, experiences larger perceptions of the content and character of human duty. Christianity has fulfilled, and still fulfils, its proper mission of leavening human society with its own truth, and thus silently transforming it into something higher. No doubt the old price has had to be, and will have to be, paid. Christianity, in leavening the industrial order with its own justice and humaneness, cannot escape a certain depravation. It has become perilously commercialized and infected with the secular cult of mundane success. 'Filthy lucre' has drawn to itself a measure of Christian regard which is equally intelligible and degrading. The emancipation of Christianity from industrialism will be a costly process, entailing disillusionment, humiliation, and impoverishment, but it will bring a further enrichment of Christian morality, and recommission Christianity for its age-long crusade.

It will not have escaped notice that, in ascribing to experience this shaping influence on Christian morality, I tacitly disclaim that directness of political and economic leadership which is now often claimed for the Christian Church. I am unable to perceive that Jesus ever commissioned His disciples as such to enter thus authoritatively into the world's affairs, and I am quite sure that Christian history demonstrates their incapacity for doing so. It is not, in my belief, justifiable to use language which, if it have any serious meaning, implies that Christians as such are specially responsible for the social and economic ills of society, and that, if only Christians did their duty, these ills would disappear. We may all admit that, if Christians were free from the faults and limitations of human nature, and if they understood rightly the requirements of their profession in all the complicated situations of modern civilized life, and if they loyally satisfied those requirements, the world would be, to the full extent of their personal influence, greatly benefited, but, since none of these conditions are, or can be, satisfied, there is little advantage in assuming the contrary.

Religion gains nothing, nor is society helped, by an exaggeration, albeit well intentioned and plausible, of religion's true rôle in human history. Christianity has but half learned the sobering lesson of its own failures; Mr. Christopher Dawson writes wisely on this point:

'There is no longer any danger of Christians attempting to force their beliefs on others at the point of the sword or of their trying to make men religious by act of Parliament. The danger today is rather that well-meaning people are apt to reduce Christianity to the level of secular idealism by identifying it with whatever social or political course is most popular at the moment, whether it be National Socialism in Germany or humanitarian socialism in England. In a sense it is quite true to say that all our troubles are due to the neglect of Christian teaching and that Christianity is the remedy for our social as well as our individual evils. But it is not like a patent medicine that is warranted to cure all diseases. It offers no short cuts to economic prosperity or social stability. A century ago there was a tendency to treat Christianity as a kind of social sedative that kept the lower classes obedient and industrious, and the consequence of this was the Marxian denunciation of religion as the opium of the poor. And if today we treat Christianity as a social tonic that will cure economic depression and social unrest and make everybody happy, we shall only ensure future disillusionment and reaction. It is impossible to create a Christian social order *ab extra* by the application of a few ready-made principles or by introducing legislative reforms. And even if it were possible, it would be of little profit to get the world to accept Christian economic principles, when it does not accept Christian intellectual and moral principles. The well-meaning people who talk about the possibility or the necessity of a Christian revolution do not consider where the Christians are to come from who are to carry it out.'[1]

Christians as such have no private and plenary illuminations as to the solution of the obscure and puzzling problems which confront the statesman and the economist. No royal road lies open to them in their religion. They too are left to the painful and repulsive necessity of learning and unlearning, and thus, with effort and sacrifice, reaching some modest measure of sound knowledge. It is vain to deny this necessity; it is dangerous to forget it. Reason and modesty unite to require that Christians, not less than other citizens, should remember the extreme complexity of modern economics, the difficulty of tracing accurately the lines of causation in social problems, the largely impersonal character of the prevailing factors in politics, and, in short, the folly of magnifying unduly the importance of individual action in human affairs. Morality has little to do with the greater physical calamities of mankind—famine, earthquake, flood, pestilence, and plagues of insects. Nor are the tides of economic movement so plainly subject to individual wills as to authorize the assumption that with respect to them individual responsibility may reasonably be affirmed.

---

[1] v. *Religion and the Modern State*, p. 121.

History abounds in illustrations of economic changes brought about by quite impersonal causes. Every new invention applied to industry may involve, and generally has involved, extreme hardship to numerous workers who are thrown out of employment. One of the major causes of unemployment at the present time is the rapid displacement of human labour by machinery. How can such unemployment be reasonably, as it is very generally, described as the consequence of Christian selfishness and disloyalty to acknowledged principles? When we seriously consider what is the bearing of Christian morality on economic questions, we must be careful to set those questions in true perspective. No moral issue is necessarily raised by economic confusion or human suffering. These may result from any one of a thousand impersonal causes. The discovery of new mineral deposits, or of new trade routes, or of new uses for which the soil is suitable, may redistribute the population, reduce flourishing commercial communities to stagnation and decay, alter the habits of multitudes, and in a hundred ways affect for good or for ill the fortunes of mankind. It was not irreligion or immorality that caused the prosperity of the Italian and Dutch republics to decline, but mainly the alteration of the world's trade routes. The ruin of the Lancashire textile industry, which now appears to be rapidly approaching, will have no connexion with morality, but will be wholly explicable by the fact that new competitors have entered the markets of the world who can produce the requisite commodities far more cheaply than workers in Lancashire. And so *ad infinitum*.

The inveterate and seemingly incorrigible habit of religious men to discern moral factors where none exist, to infer fault from misfortune,

> He must be wicked to deserve such woe,

diverts attention from the true causes of human calamity, creates a volume of irrelevant suspicion, and is responsible for much confusion and many scandals. However unwelcome and even repulsive the fact may be, it is the fact that human liberty is very narrowly limited, so narrowly that often man appears the helpless victim of his circumstances. Indeed, when full allowance has been made for the influence of non-moral factors in the development of civilization, it is not surprising that many students should yield to the temptation to think that there are, in fact, none other. This disastrous error, for such I must needs hold it to be, gains an additional plausibility from the irrational exaggeration of the moral factor which has so often marked the language of religious men.

To sum up. Industrialism is but one phase in the continuing evolution of human society. There are now many indications that it is nearing an end, for its latest developments have been so exorbitant and demoralizing that neither the conscience nor the reason of civilized men appears able to tolerate them. The mighty fabric of industrial society seems to be giving way in its foundations. Like the great image of Nebuchadnezzar's dream its magnificence is endangered from below, and its final destruction will derive from thence.

'Thou sawest till that a stone was cut out without hands, which smote the image upon his feet that were of iron and clay, and brake them in pieces. Then was the iron, the clay, the brass, the silver, and the gold, broken in pieces together, and became like the chaff of the summer threshing-floors; and the wind carried them away, that no place was found for them.'[1]

Industrialism is visibly disintegrating, but the nature of the phase which will replace it is as yet undisclosed. That industrialism will pass is certain, but what will be the manner of its passing, whether with extreme violence and suffering as in Russia, or by slow stages and, so to speak, naturally, as we like to think may happen in Great Britain, we cannot yet discern. For even in Russia the permanent effect of the fearful events which have filled the years of revolution is still doubtful, and in Great Britain there may be intractable and explosive forces, which we but half perceive, which may immerse that country also in the violences commonly associated with revolutions. Christian morality is indifferent to the precise form which the political and economic changes, which are evidently impending, may assume; but it must ever be inviolably true to Nature. Its acceptance of the systems, political, social, economic, which the indomitable and enterprising human spirit creates in the course of history for the service of mankind, is never unconditioned. Like St. Thomas of Canterbury confronting his masterful sovereign, Henry II, it thrusts into every project of agreement the indispensable and exasperating clause, *salvo ordine meo*.

Christian morality holds a brief for the fundamental franchises of humanity, and cannot possibly make terms with any system which does violence to the rights of man. Accordingly, wherever Christian morality

[1] v. Daniel ii. 34, 35.

determines human action, there is introduced into society a force which is intractable, persistent, and ultimately, in the measure of its acceptance, transforming.

Christian morality must either prevail in society or be rigorously prohibited. The State is shut up to the dilemma, either it must surrender or it must persecute. It is no accident that the conflict between the modern State and the Christian Church discloses itself in connexion with the private conscience and the family; for these form the very citadel of Christian morality. And these are precisely the cardinal human interests which industrialism, as we know it now, most evidently imperils.

XII

FINALITY

W E have maintained that Christian morality has shown itself to be uniquely assimilative, and for that reason uniquely capable of development. It garners whatsoever is morally sound in the societies into which it is introduced, and makes the most of its gains. Thus it ever carries forward into new historic situations the wisdom gathered from the old, and, while ever retaining its hold on the past, is ever able to sustain the demand of the future. It can associate itself with the forward movement of mankind, and give that movement its own colour and direction. Yet in this double process of assimilation and development Christian morality never loses, though it sometimes endangers and obscures, its individuality, or fails to preserve its identity with its original and vital principles. For it is anchored fast to its historic Source. In its Founder it possesses an unalterable norm of truth, alike theological and moral. His teaching and example embody the ideas which must determine Christian faith and conduct through all the changes and chances of Time. Above the bewildering scene of ecclesiastical history, so full of mutation, so shadowed by paradox, stands the legend which gives the key to its interpretation and proclaims the secret of the Finality which Christian morality alone possesses —'Jesus Christ is the same yesterday and to-day, yea and for ever'.

'I am sure', writes Professor Halliday, 'that an unbiased study of contemporary ethics and religion will throw into greater and greater relief the life of Jesus as depicted in the three first gospels as being the essential revolutionary event in the religious life of mankind.'[1]

In this lecture we are concerned with Christian morality as in some true sense final. This finality may indeed be said to be implicit in the fact that Christian morality is natural, expressing the requirement of the human conscience not merely at some particular stage of human development, but at every stage. Natural morality can never become obsolete, for obsoleteness would prove that it is not genuinely natural. Morality that is merely traditional becomes archaic, artificial, unreal, and finally repugnant to the developing moral sense of mankind. It is discarded together with the religion with which it is historically associated, and apart from which it has no sufficient *raison d'être*.

When we seek the explanation of this unique power which Christian morality possesses, we can but find it in the uniqueness of the Founder of Christianity. I do not hesitate to use the word 'uniqueness' in spite of the objection which Dr. Dibelius has expressed:

'Science', he says, 'knows only of processes that have hitherto remained without analogy; but to these the word "unique" in the sense of "unique in its kind" is inapplicable.'[2]

To say, as Dr. Dibelius is prepared to say, that the life of Jesus has 'hitherto remained without analogy' is equivalent to saying that, so far as human experience has gone, Jesus is unique. He could only cease to be so if another, superior to Him, should emerge on the scene of history. In Him His disciples acknowledged

[1] v. *The Pagan Background of Early Christianity*, p. 322.
[2] v. *Gospel Criticism and Christology*, p. 101.

the moral ideal itself to be recognizably embodied. His
character, as disclosed in the surviving records of His
life on earth, illustrated for them personal morality in
its completest expression. His precepts, ever elucidated
by His recorded example, were by them accepted as
expressing the ultimate principles of morality. On this
point of the final and plenary authority of the Founder's
teaching and example there has never been any difference among Christian folk. What precisely was the
bearing of His revelation of human duty on the actual
situations in which His servants found themselves
has been variously understood. They have been ignorant, superstitious, reluctant, timorous, unfaithful. But
demonstrably there has been advance, slow, intermittent, embarrassed, but none the less genuine, advance.
It is true to say that Christ's demand is more clearly
perceived as His followers learn, and unlearn, in the
hard school of history. But, it has been objected, we,
who must needs read the Synoptic Gospels in the new
light of modern critical scholarship, do not possess a
measure of knowledge about Jesus adequate to justify
the exalted estimate of His character which has prevailed in Christendom. Critically examined the Gospels
tell us extremely little about Him, so little that we really
do not possess sufficient materials for a verdict on His
character. This appears to be the position maintained
by Mr. Claude Montefiore in a recent article, entitled
'What a Jew thinks about Jesus', which appeared in the
Hibbert Journal for July 1935. The critical conclusion
as to the historical value of the Synoptic Gospels which
this article assumes would by many scholars be rejected,
and by few Christians allowed. After setting on one

side the belief that 'Jesus was God in the guise of a man', a belief which lies outside our present concern, he proceeds:

'But supposing the records of a *man's* life only began a month before he died, could one reasonably say of such a life that it revealed the noblest and most beautiful character which has ever been known? Perhaps the answer is: "No, but if the records extend for eighteen months or two years, then one can." For me, to speak frankly, this question of the length of the ministry constitutes a very real difficulty. From the sparse record in Mark, cautiously and sparingly supplemented by Matthew and Luke, I infer a fine, a very fine, character, unlike the teachers of his age, a sort of eighth-century prophet born out of season, a combination of Amos and Hosea. Jesus is for me *one* of the greatest and most original of our Jewish prophets and teachers, but I should hesitate to say that he was *more* original than any one of them. Nor, in spite of a noble death, can I discover, in the number, or in the character, of the incidents of his ministry enough material to make me regard that brief career as the noblest, though it was in all probability the most important and influential, life which had ever been lived by man.'

'*In all probability the most important and influential life which has ever been lived by man,*'—that verdict of a candid and erudite Jewish scholar is richly suggestive. It cannot but raise the question, What was the nature of that unique importance? And what was the quality of that unique influence? What was the legacy which He bequeathed to mankind? What was there in His life that justifies Professor Halliday's description of it as 'the essential revolutionary event in the religious life of mankind'? You will not have forgotten the words of John Stuart Mill which I quoted in an earlier lecture. What was there in the words and acts of Jesus as set

forth in the Gospels which led that man of large mind
and detached outlook to think that 'not even now would
it be easy to find a better translation of the rule of virtue
from the abstract into the concrete than to endeavour
so to live that Christ would approve our lives'? Such
confessions might be multiplied almost indefinitely.
Their full significance is only apparent when they are
seen to be congruous with the estimate of Jesus which
His own followers were led by personal experience to
form, and which has been affirmed by all sorts and
conditions of men in all varieties of circumstance in every
succeeding age. It is precisely here, in the moral impression which He made, and continues to make, that
the originality of Jesus becomes apparent. None of the
Hebrew Prophets, not even the great Isaiah, still less
Amos and Hosea, whom Mr. Montefiore names, left
any similar personal impression on the generation that
came after them. From the first the marvel of the
Master's posthumous influence was felt by His disciples.
'Whom not having seen ye love' is a luminous phrase
which St. Peter uses when addressing the converts of
Asia Minor. Mr. Montefiore, in the course of the article
to which I have referred, quotes from the note-book
of a famous Master of Balliol, Dr. Benjamin Jowett, a
strange passage, strange when uttered by a Christian
minister:

'Is it possible to feel a personal attachment to Christ such as
is prescribed by Thomas à Kempis? I think that it is impossible
and contrary to human nature that we should be able to concentrate our thoughts on a person scarcely known to us, who
lived 1800 years ago.'

Dr. Jowett's astonishment at a spectacle which has

been witnessed on earth from the very beginning of Christian history is easily intelligible, although, perhaps, it is surprising that it should have led him to an explanation which is really equivalent to a denial of the fact. St. Peter, who had seen Jesus and known Him well, whose love was fed by a thousand personal recollections, and who could never lose from memory the form, the face, the voice, the manner of his Master, found to his amazement that an affection not less ardent than his own burned in the hearts of multitudes who had never known Jesus by sight nor heard Him speak. They were brought into great trouble by reason of their discipleship, the Government oppressed and persecuted them for their Christian profession, their pagan neighbours disliked, suspected, and injured them in resentment against their Christian habits, yet still their personal affection for their unseen Master sustained them. He writes to them as to persecuted folk, and his words have the note of wonder:

'Wherein ye greatly rejoice, though now for a little while, if need be, ye have been put to grief in manifold temptations, that the proof of your faith, being more precious than gold that perisheth though it is proved by fire, might be found unto praise and glory and honour at the revelation of Jesus Christ: *Whom not having seen ye love*; on whom, though now ye see him not, yet believing, ye rejoice greatly with joy unspeakable and full of glory: receiving the end of your faith, even the salvation of your souls.'[1]

We are not concerned with the faith of the Apostle, nor with the Messianic hopes of his converts, but the fact of Christ's personal influence, thus posthumously

[1] v. 1 Peter i. 6–8.

exercised, bears directly on our argument. For what was spoken about the Christians in the first century has been spoken about them in every century since, and certainly never more confidently than in our own.

The history of religion provides no parallel to the personal influence of Jesus.

In speaking of Jesus I do not forget the limitations which a Gifford Lecturer must needs acknowledge. I do not postulate any theory about Him, but I claim the right to include in my argument the facts which history records, and among them this fact of His unique, persistent, and unfailing personal influence. There is no equivalent to it in other religions, for in none other is the historic Founder recognized as the norm of personal morality. Jesus Himself lived normally: it was the accusation of His foes, and the wonder of His friends, that He did so. 'The Son of man is come eating and drinking; and ye say, Behold, a gluttonous man, and a winebibber, a friend of publicans and sinners!'[1]

So living He was able to embody for all time a moral ideal which normal men would be able to recognize, embrace, and pursue. The founder of Buddhism was no model for normal men: the founder of Mohammedanism was no model for any man. The problem of their modern disciples is to explain away, rather than explain, their personal record. Jesus alone is able to offer Himself as the sufficient illustration of His own doctrine. Christianity is unique in attaching vital importance to the personal character of the Founder. In every other case the religion is separable from its founder, having its title to men's acceptance in the

[1] St. Luke vii. 34.

truths which it expresses, but in Christianity everything turns on the competence of the Founder to satisfy His own theory. The moral teacher who calls his disciples to accept his example as the law of their conduct can only command their obedience so long as they own his moral supremacy. Failure in him draws doubt and unbelief in them. That there was no failure is the recorded verdict of Christ's contemporaries; and that verdict has not been successfully challenged since.

If it be urged, as indeed it may fairly be urged, that no human testimony could suffice to prove the moral faultlessness of any man, yet it may be pointed out that, even so, human testimony can certainly demonstrate moral fault, and that in the case of Jesus alone such hostile testimony is entirely absent. The tradition of his 'sinlessness', originating undoubtedly with those who had been in close and long-continued intercourse with Him, has never been questioned within the Church, and outside the Church has commanded such a measure of acceptance as places Jesus on a level which none other attains. He is admittedly the best man known to human experience. The type of character which He illustrated supremely has never failed since His time to be represented on earth, more or less faithfully, within the sphere of His influence. The Christian character has been exhibited in every variety of circumstance and on every plane of culture. It is demonstrably capable of illustration in some true measure by 'all sorts and conditions of men'. The Christian character, we repeat, is recognizable in every variety of natural temperament, of personal ability, of racial type, of secular circumstance. There is no Buddhist character or

Mohammedan character or Jewish character which can be placed in the same potentially universal category as the Christian. It is unthinkable that mankind, in all the rich variety of its types and cultures, should be Buddhist or Mohammedan or Jewish, but it is not only thinkable, but even probable that, if religion survive at all among mankind, that is to say, if mankind retain its distinctive feature, it will finally be Christian. Buddhism requires the Asiatic temperament, and Mohammedanism cannot be reconciled with the higher culture, and Judaism is incorrigibly nationalist, but Christianity is frankly human, and matches the need of humanity always and everywhere.

The great American preacher of the nineteenth century, Phillips Brooks, in the lectures on *The Influence of Jesus* which his biographer regarded as 'one of his most important contributions to the development of theological science', has drawn a luminous contrast between the Sphinx and the Sistine Madonna as 'the two expressions in art of the two religions—the religion of the East and of the West'.

'Fatalism and Providence they seem to mean. Both have tried to express a union of humanity with something which is its superior; but one has joined it only to the superior strength of the animal, while the other has filled it with the superior spirituality of a divine nature. One unites wisdom and power, and claims man's homage for that conjunction. The other combines wisdom and love, and says, "Worship this". The Sphinx has life in its human face written into a riddle, a puzzle, a mocking bewilderment. The Virgin's face is full of a mystery we cannot fathom, but it unfolds to us a thousand of the mysteries of life. It does not mock, but blesses us. The Sphinx oppresses us with colossal size. The Virgin is not a distortion or exaggeration, but a glorification of humanity. The Egyptian monster is alone amid its sands, to be worshipped, not loved. The Christian woman has her child clasped in her arms, enters into the societies and sympathies of men, and claims no worship except love. . . . The picture is Christian, because it is so truly human.'[1]

The historic function of the New Testament has been the preservation of the norm of Christian morality provided by the Founder's life and teaching. From the first the Church perceived the crucial importance of keeping this norm vividly clear to its members. This explains the truly amazing procedure which invested the New Testament with the same canonical authority as had from time immemorial belonged to the Old Testament. This explains the prominence assigned to the biographies of the Founder within the canonical writings, and the place of honour given to the Gospels in the public liturgy. In the undivided Church of the Roman Empire the reading of the Scriptures by lay folk was officially encouraged, and it only ceased to be general when the ability to read had become the distinction of the clergy. The New Testament in the Church has ever functioned as a corrective and reforming force, challenging current Christianity, and forcing Christians to realize the extent of their departure from the norm of morality which it sets forth. Thus the Church has been compelled to carry with it through history the rebuke of its own treasons, and the programme of its own recovery. Corruption is at all times accompanied by protest, and development is never wholly unchastened by principle. In the Middle Ages, when the Christian

[1] v. *The Influence of Jesus*, p. 74.

hierarchy was immersed in a secularity which seemed
to threaten spiritual asphyxiation, and the moral level
of Christian habit seemed to have fallen back to paganism, there were never wholly wanting men who, with
the New Testament in their hands and the Mind of
Christ in their hearts, raised their voices in protest
against the implicit repudiation of Christian morality.
Protestantism in the sphere of morals has preceded
Protestantism in the sphere of doctrine, and survived it.   In the long run the example of St. Francis
is more widely influential than the reasoning of St.
Thomas.

The authority of Jesus is final because it is limited
to the sphere of personal morality. He is not the
Universal Teacher bringing all knowledge within the
reach of His disciples, but He is the Ideal Man, in
whom all men can see the true version of their own
manhood. In Him men can learn how to think about
God as the Author of their life: how to interpret their
own nature on which His image is indelibly stamped:
how to regard their fellow men, with whom they are
inextricably bound in a covenant of mutual service.
Jesus did not, so far as we can discover, transcend the
narrow limits of His time in all those particulars which
have no true relation to personal morality. He appears
to have shared the prevailing notions of His age and
race with respect to all secular knowledge. He has no
place among the philosophical thinkers, or among the
literary men, or among the artists, or among the masters
of science, or among the political leaders, or among the
economists, or even among the social reformers of
mankind. All these types of human distinction are

intelligible, and readily honoured. But Jesus belonged to
none of them. The indifference of His contemporaries
to all He taught and all He was perplexes the historian,
and shocks the moralist. He passed His brief career in
Palestine unnoticed by the great world, and His death,
which has thrilled the generations since, was by His
contemporaries ignored. Yet He so lived and so taught
and so died that, wherever the knowledge of Him
comes, men bend in homage before His moral supremacy, and recognize the true Interpreter of their own
manhood. Apart from the knowledge of Jesus, following
loyally the inner light which is in every man the witness
of his Divine original, men may embrace the moral
ideal which He proclaimed and embodied. It is precisely
by the universality of its appeal that Christian morality
demonstrates its genuinely natural character. But Jesus
is morally unique. He alone satisfies the general conscience, authenticates the sainthoods of history, and
unifies the moral witness of the race.

'I, if I be lifted up from the earth, will draw all men
unto myself', is the luminous declaration which the
Fourth Evangelist attributes to Jesus, and which,
whether authentic or not, declares impressively the rôle
which He has filled, and over an ever-widening area
continues to fill, in the moral life of mankind. Here,
then, in the life and teaching of Jesus, is the test of
Christian morality, the guarantee that its development
shall not do violence to its essential principles, the
assurance that in all the changes and chances of Time
it shall preserve a recognizable identity, that is, shall
remain true to type. A memorable passage in St. Paul's
1st Epistle to the Corinthians may serve to state, and at

the same time to interpret, the Finality which belongs
to Christian morality:

'Other foundation can no man lay than that which is laid,
which is Jesus Christ. But if any man buildeth on the foundation gold, silver, costly stones, wood, hay, stubble; each man's
work shall be made manifest: for the day shall declare it, because
it is revealed in fire; and the fire itself shall prove each man's
work of what sort it is.'[1]

The discovery of moral quality, which the Apostle
pictured as the sentence of the Divine Judge in His day
of final vindication, is made apparent slowly in the
accumulating experience of mankind, and declared in
what we are accustomed to call the Verdict of History.
The years teach much which the days never knew, and it
has been said wisely that Truth is the daughter of Time.

When we try to form a clear notion of the morality
which found expression in the life of Jesus, we are
impressed by at least three features which give it
distinctiveness, and may be fairly called its prevailing
characteristics. These are personal goodness, social
service, and self-sacrifice. These characteristics arrested
the notice of His disciples, and were paramount in the
accounts they gave of Him. They have been recognized
throughout Christian history as the essential constituents of the specifically Christian morality, and they
are integral to the moral ideal which civilized men are
everywhere coming to acknowledge. They are the
supreme expression of theistic ethics.

The Saint, the Reformer, the Martyr—these belong
to mankind and have found their inspiration from all
religions, but in Christianity alone can men find the

[1] 1 Corinthians iii. 11–13.

prototype and perfected expression of all in an historic person. If, moreover, we turn from the character of Jesus to His recorded teaching, we are arrested by its unique independence of time and place, its adequacy for all men in all circumstances, its essential finality. The words of Jesus cut through all the veils of convention, all the fictions of self-conceit, all the mazes of casuistry, and confront men with the ultimate moral aspect of their own behaviour. Inevitably He is the Judge of Men, by Whose standard men must perforce measure conduct, and Whose verdict is without appeal. In Him the Divine and Final Judgement, echoed from within by the individual conscience, is pronounced:

'For the word of God is living, and active, and sharper than any two-edged sword, and piercing even to the dividing of soul and spirit, of both joints and marrow, and quick to discern the thoughts and intents of the heart. And there is no creature that is not manifest in his sight: but all things are naked and laid open before the eyes of him with whom we have to do.'[1]

Let me recall the argument of these lectures. It is based on the assumption that, since man is developing from the lowest phase of human life to the highest, the truth about his nature will be most fully disclosed in the latest phase of his development. When, therefore, we seek to know the meaning and content of that religious faculty, which is certainly an original constituent of every nature which can be described as fully human, we must inquire what forms religion has taken among civilized men, and whether there be any specific type which civilized religion tends to adopt. Moreover, since the quality of religion (of which theology is the

[1] v. Hebrews iv. 12, 13.

rational formulation) is disclosed by the morality which it requires and enables, we may hope to discover the theology, which is best entitled to be described as natural, by first ascertaining whether there be any morality which commends itself to men everywhere as they become civilized; and then, having discovered such a morality, by inquiring what is the theology with which it has been historically associated and with which it is properly connected. This theology, thus uttering itself in civilized morality, is properly described as natural theology, not the crude imaginings of undeveloped primitive men which may be doubtfully inferred by our anthropologists from the procedure of savages ancient and modern. Behind theology, providing the postulates on which it finally rests, stands philosophy, and the argument which moves from morality to religion cannot halt until it has moved from religion to philosophy.

I have maintained that Christian morality is the only version of religious morality which can command the acceptance of modernly civilized man, and I have engaged you in a consideration of its historic constituents, and of its bearing on some dominant and difficult questions of our time. I have invited you to conclude that Christian morality is natural, developing, and final, and I have suggested that such a morality points the way to a Theology which may properly be described as natural, and which, as being natural, is the prescribed subject of the Gifford Lectures. I shall certainly be reminded that my primary postulate, that man is naturally religious, and that morality has its roots in religion, has been definitely challenged, and is now being repudiated in Russia. There the attempt is being made with the utmost determination, and with the whole energy of a despotic government, to abolish religion altogether, to destroy the Christian tradition in all its expressions, and to reconstruct morality on the foundation of Marxian atheism. Here is a description of the Russian situation by a singularly clear-sighted and well-informed observer, Mr. Chamberlin. I quote from his recently published volume, *Russia's Iron Age*:

'New Russia, this younger generation that has now grown up entirely under Soviet influence, is developing very largely without three of the oldest and most deeply-rooted human institutions: religion, the family, and private property. In regard to the family and to private property, some compromise tendencies are already visible. The extreme sexual promiscuity which was both fashionable and general among the Young Communists and the "emancipated" Soviet younger generation a decade ago is now officially frowned on. Excessive loose living, like excessive drinking, is a recognized ground for expulsion from the Communist Party or from the Union of Communist Youth. There was a time when the typical Young Communist, rather amusingly and paradoxically, considered Western dancing immoral, while he looked on any kind of stable marriage with a good deal of contempt. Now the attitude is changing on both these subjects: Young Communist leaders extol the advantage of permanent marital relations,—provided, of course, that they are based on mutual love and comradely mutuality of interests,— and the fox trot and similar jazz dances are beginning to emerge from their former underground and surreptitious state as dance halls are being opened.

'While large fields of activity are barred for ever to private ownership under the Soviet system, there is a marked and increasing tendency to insist on the principle of unequal pay for unequal work. The importance of giving the individual more material stimulus by awarding higher pay and bonuses for more

capable work is becoming more and more firmly embedded in
Soviet psychology. . . .

'Only in the case of religion does Soviet antipathy to this
"opium for the people" remain uncompromising and unabated.
Here the great riddle of the future is whether Communism
itself will assume the functions of a popular religion or whether
the tendency to seek for some non-materialistic interpretation
of life will ultimately, in some form, reassert itself.'[1]

This is the picture of a society in unstable equilibrium.
It describes an experiment which is in process of failing.
Soviet Russia has broken with the old tradition, but
it has not established the new substitute. If in such
cardinal matters as property and the family the atheistic
rulers of Russia are finding themselves compelled to
revert to the standards of the past, standards which were
largely shaped by Christianity, it is not extravagant to
think that in the greater concern of religion they may
have finally to admit defeat. Another observer, whose
attitude towards the Soviet experiment is marked by
sympathy and optimism, thinks that the atheism which
is now dominant cannot finally prevail. 'I cannot help
thinking that future generations of Russian people will *re-
discover* Jesus, whose historicity is now denied and whose
gospel is now rapidly being obscured in the memory
of the present generation.' Dr. Julius Hecker proceeds:

'The young Soviet people have demands and interests which
to-day are not satisfied, so they reject both the existing religious
teachings and the anti-religious propaganda. There is need for
a message which synthetically would enrich the social message
of Communism with emotional and ethical values. This message
in content and form will be nothing like any of the old institutions of religion. It will be upon a much higher intellectual

[1] v. *Russia's Iron Age*, p. 249.

level, much more aesthetic in form and sentiment. It will greatly differ from the present crude presentation of atheist propaganda. We may be sure the future lies not in the *negation* of the past but in the *affirmation* of the new life for which the proletarian revolution has prepared the way, and the coming Communist classless society should be the most favourable environment for the development of a spiritual culture never before dreamed of by prophets, sages or poets.'[1]

Dr. Julius Hecker's speculation as to the form which the return to religion will take need not concern us. It is obviously coloured by the extremely unfavourable opinion of the Russian Church which he expresses in his book. But his testimony to the instability of the present situation gains in impressiveness from his evident endorsement of the Communist ideal. He also, like Mr. Chamberlin, describes a society in unstable equilibrium. The spiritual faculty in Russian human nature, repudiated and with violence suppressed, is in his belief unconquerable, and must finally assert itself.

There is yet another objection, and even more formidable. The new non-religious alternative to Christian morality, which the Russian atheists are so strenuously exerting themselves to establish, is yet unproved. So far as experience has made a judgement on its quality possible, the judgement is unfavourable, or at least hesitating. It yet remains a question, whether it is not so deeply repugnant to some indestructible factors of human nature as to be finally impracticable. The experiment proceeds, but with lessening confidence, and with multiplying indications of friction. Failure seems more probable than success.

[1] v. *Religion and Communism*, p. 273.

But it is objected that Christian morality is not necessarily bound to the religion with which historically it has been connected; that in fact Christianity is no more than the temporary scaffolding, which may be safely removed when the building, for whose erection it was rightly held to be indispensable, has been completed; that the modern world is turning away from the religion while retaining its hold on the morality; that this acceptance is contingent and temporary, for science has replaced religion as the teacher of the race; that the civilized morality of the future will develop in ever more conscious indifference to religious and theological considerations; and that, in short, morality has for modernly civilized men outgrown the motives and sanctions of Christianity.

It is apparent that there is much truth in these contentions. Christian morality has developed, is developing, and will develop. It will not have attained completeness until experience has ceased to revise, correct, and supplement tradition. Science teaches with authority within its own sphere, and Christian morality, just because it is Christian, cannot ignore or resist its teaching. But history, in recording the development of Christian morality, has disclosed the singular character of that development, as always ultimately determined by certain vital ideas or principles which were confessedly paramount in the life and teaching of Jesus, and which have in the sphere of personal character perpetuated His influence. This original determining factor has guaranteed identity through the mutations of Time, and tends to assert itself more effectively as mankind is carried on the stream of evolving process out of aboriginal savagery to the height of modern civilization. This factor, the specifically Christian factor, gives distinctive character to the civilization of Christendom.

Christian morality is religious morality. It assumes that 'the spirit of man is the candle of the Lord', and, being thus indestructibly theistic, it provokes against itself the resolute hostility of all who repudiate religion. It is the very assumption of the Gifford Trust that religion belongs to the essence of human nature, and that it is capable of being expressed in a natural theology.

Only because natural theology is rooted in ultimate truth could Lord Gifford say of it that it is a 'strictly natural science, the greatest of all possible sciences, that of Infinite Being'. Atheism may serve the study of natural theology by evoking the arguments by which its truth and meaning are established, but in itself atheism is the negation of the only supposition on which Gifford Lectures can be worth while.

Science cannot explain, and certainly cannot disallow, the witness of the human spirit. Agnostic it may, perhaps must, be. Atheistic it cannot be. Admittedly it is only on the theistic assumption that Christian morality is intelligible. It is only as the purest expression of theism that Christian morality can be defended as natural, or accepted as final. The Christian character, which perpetuates the personal morality of Jesus, does not provoke against itself any genuinely scientific protest. It holds the field. If it be said, and it may truly be said, that modern civilized society is filled with individuals who, while making no formal profession of Christianity, and even specifically rejecting the Christian theology, do yet exhibit very notably a personal morality which is recognizably Christian, we must answer that their conduct may have its explanations elsewhere than in their opinions. They are the heirs of a social tradition which from time immemorial has been saturated with Christian influences, they breathe an atmosphere which is richly charged with Christian ideas and ideals, they are in their personal habit far more subject to inbred Christian instincts than to theories which they have formed for themselves. In any case, the essentially Christian behaviour of individual unbelievers proves as little as the essentially atheistic behaviour of individual Christians. The question is too large to be answered by individual examples on the one side or the other. Is the Christian factor in civilized morality essential? Could civilized morality survive the abolition of Christianity? Secularism as a formulated theory antagonistic to religion is a modern phenomenon in Christendom. Individual secularists have never been lacking; and there have been times when the level of spirituality has fallen so low in society that secularism rather than Christianity might fairly be thought to be the reigning belief. Were those times conspicuous for a high standard of personal morality? Secularism in modern Europe has hardly yet had time and opportunity for disclosing its moral quality. But experience is accumulating, and suggests that the moral aspect of a dechristianized civilization may be disconcerting.

The thoughtful student of secularized Christendom will not fail to notice the reappearance of the characteristically pagan phenomena of unbridled self-indulgence, of suicide, and sexual perversion, nor will he miss the significance of the new contempt of liberty, political and social, the new emphasizing of racial divergences, and the new cynicism which colours international politics. New yet very old, for all have been persistent in human life, and only slowly and partially have been driven out of human acceptance in Christendom. It would seem that Christianity and Civilization, which grew together in Europe, must share a common ruin. Much attention has been directed recently to the grotesque revival of crude primitive paganism in some parts of Germany and Russia. It would appear that the revolt against Christian morality is confessing its retrogression from civilized standards by this reversion to pre-Christian paganism. The spread of occultism, spiritualism, and all manner of puerile superstitions, which has marked modern society since the War, insults the reason of civilized men not less apparently than the oppression of minorities, racial, religious, and political, insults the civilized conscience. It is no matter for astonishment, then, that the masters of science, even in the exultation of their multiplying victories over Nature, are beginning to speak with hesitation and fear as to the cumulative effect of their achievements. For it is becoming apparent that there is something in man which must finally determine his capacity to use with intelligence and self-control the mighty instruments of power and pleasure which science places in his hands, and that science, the donor of this wealth of potencies, is quite unable to discipline and direct that vital and enigmatic force.

In his well-known book, *Roman Society from Nero to Marcus Aurelius*, the late Sir Samuel Dill, writing in 1905, gives expression to a faith in the essential spirituality of man which eminent men of science are now often willing to confess. The situation of the civilized world to-day makes that faith at once more indispensable and more scientifically legitimate:

'The dream of an earthly paradise enriched with every sensuous gratification by a science working in bondage to mere utility may have serious results for the spiritual future of humanity. It may need a bitter experience to dispel the gross illusion; yet men may once more come to believe with Plutarch that, as it were, at the back of every soul there is an opening to the divine world from which yet may come, as of old, the touch of an unseen hand.'[1]

The balance of human nature, thus apparently endangered, can be restored only by bringing into recognition and exercise that moral factor which has been ignored or neglected or denied outright. Religion, which for civilized mankind must finally mean Christianity, gives primacy to the spiritual element in man, and embodies the principles of all rightful human action in the life and teaching of Jesus. In the acceptance of those principles, first in the sphere of personal behaviour, then in the widening extent of social conduct, finally in the world-wide fellowship of the human race, lies the hope of the world, and there will be found the crowning vindication of man's theistic Faith.

[1] v. op. cit., book iii, p. 440.

APPENDIX

THE RUSSIAN MYSTERY[1]

I

THE Russian Revolution is outgrowing the extreme violences which marked its earliest phases, and it is becoming possible to get a connected view of the events which have transformed society throughout the vast populations of Soviet Russia. A considerable literature has been produced of varied outlook and unequal merit. The victims of the Bolsheviks, such of them as have succeeded in escaping from the country, and are maintaining a precarious existence as emigrés mainly in Paris and Switzerland, have given to the world many narratives of their woeful experiences; the sympathizers with social change have eagerly hailed the events in Russia as a triumph for their own ideals, and exerted themselves to deny, belittle, or explain away the incidental outrages; non-Russians, as well those who have long resided in Russia as those whose acquaintance with the country is recent and limited, have described what they have seen and heard, and now the veteran social students who, disdaining their titles, prefer to describe themselves simply as Sidney and Beatrice Webb, have provided a careful, elaborate, and well-documented survey of the system which to-day, eighteen years after the downfall of Tsardom, exists in Russia. For this task they possess many notable qualifications, but they lack two which might be fairly thought to be indispensable, viz. a sympathetic understanding of human nature, and a personal knowledge of the Russian people. The able reviewer of their book in *The Times* (25 November 1935) dwells with good reason on the gravity of these defects, and holds that they destroy the claim of a work marked by many merits to be accepted 'as the

---

[1] *Soviet Communism: A New Civilisation?* by Sidney and Beatrice Webb, 2 vols., Longmans, Green & Co., 1935; *Russia's Iron Age*, by William Henry Chamberlin, Duckworth, 1935.

authentic record, at any rate for this generation, of the meaning of Soviet Communism'. 'It is a made book, constructed from documents and monographs', but destitute 'of a spirit of historical understanding'.

II. *The Achievement of the Bolsheviks*

When Lenin had succeeded in capturing the Russian State, he set himself to a truly gigantic enterprise.

'No government outside the U.S.S.R. has ever frankly taken as its task the complete recasting of the economic and social life of the entire community, including the physical health, the personal habits, the occupations and, above all, the ideas of all the millions for whom it acts—in short, the making of a new civilization.' (p. 107.)

The work was unquestionably facilitated by the uniform type of the Russian population, by the low level of its culture, even by the geographical conditions of its life. In that vast expanse of level country, social organization was rudimentary, and political combination extremely difficult. Against a well-organized central power, armed with modern weapons and directed by a master mind, effective resistance was almost impossible. Lenin brought to his task a clear intelligence, a long training in revolutionary psychology, a dogmatic economic faith, a cold and ruthless fanaticism, and an iron will. When he was removed by death, his name became the symbol of the Russian Revolution, and drew to itself the almost religious devotion of the peasantry. Stalin, his like-minded successor, in pushing forward the great work was able to avail himself of this popular sentiment. The dechristianized masses of Russia appear to be compensating themselves for the absence of their icons by a new cultus of Lenin. When, after the failure of the White Armies, the Western Powers realized that the Bolsheviks were too firmly entrenched in power to be dislodged by invasions from without, the great venture of Soviet Communism was able to proceed at a quickened pace. Its progress was marked by terrible outrages, by far-resounding scandals, by bitter religious persecution, and by an amount of human misery which has probably never before been equalled in human experience. But the experiment proceeded, and took definite shape. A new type of social order has been created, and is arousing the fearful or hopeful curiosity of social students in every Western nation. The substantial volumes before us provide the English reader with the most complete account of the situation in Soviet Russia which has yet appeared.

With practised skill and characteristic thoroughness the Webbs have handled the voluminous reports of the Soviet authorities. They have accumulated the official statistics which (always assuming their trustworthiness) disclose results equally amazing in extent and unprecedented in character. The Bolsheviks have, it is suggested, in a few years exceeded the achievements of centuries. A vast machinery of social and economic organization has been created, and now covers the whole extent of the Soviet dominion, stretching from the Arctic sea to the Caspian, and from the frontier of Poland to the Pacific ocean, and including a population of 170,000,000. It leaves no part of the citizen's life, from the cradle to the grave, unregulated. With rigorous decisiveness the Communist Government marks out for its subjects the lines on which they are to think, the employments in which they are to exert their energies, and the manner in which they may spend their leisure. In little more than a decade, we are assured, the most backward of agricultural communities has been transformed into the most advanced; the least developed of industrial states has become the most completely organized; the most poorly equipped of modern nations has become the most richly endowed in all that can make a people educated, healthy, and happy; the most religious of populations has been led into a general and even enthusiastic acceptance of atheism. Nor is this the entire story of Communist miracle-working. While the positive results have been so great, its negative results have been scarcely less considerable. The new civilization, we are told, has none of the drawbacks of the old. Soviet Russia has no unemployment, no prostitution, no social inequality, no economic strife. All the shadows which darken Western Civilization have vanished, and all the old obstinate problems have found solution. Before the happy inhabitants of the Soviet Union there has opened a vista of ever extending social well-being. It is an amazing picture. What is to be said about it? What should hold us back from eagerly following where Lenin points the way? I think that three considerations may well induce a certain scepticism, and compel a certain hesitation, even in those who, by temperament and training, are most disposed to regard Soviet Communism with sympathy and even with admiration. First, the cost of the great experiment has been excessive. Next, its method has implied a treatment of human nature so violent as to be ultimately intolerable. Thirdly, the whole scheme of government described by the Webbs has not yet been adequately tested. It has the aspect of delusive completeness which is the hall-mark of theoretical projects. The statistics are more impressive than convincing. Knowing the difficulty which is experienced even in this country, with its long record of social order, in making sure that legal requirements are effectively translated into practice, we cannot avoid a suspicion that the highly articulated provisions for education, health, recreation, &c., are, over great part of Soviet Russia, practically inoperative. In any case, the time has not yet arrived for passing a verdict.

III. *The Cost of the Experiment*

Before we can estimate justly the actual achievements of the Bolsheviks, we must consider the methods by which they succeeded in doing what they did. They had great advantages. Their seizure of the Government gave them at a stroke possession of overwhelming force. The resisting power of their victims was extremely small; and they allowed no moral scruples to limit their action. In these circumstances we need not be greatly surprised to find that they have succeeded in effecting drastic and rapid changes in Russian society. The obstacles which normally confront the social reformer in free communities did not confront the Bolsheviks. There was no public opinion to be propitiated. No 'vested interests' of property and tradition had to be satisfied. No legal and constitutional stages had to be traversed. Law and constitution had perished with the Tsardom in the great ruin. There was no sentiment of loyalty to the fallen autocrat, no affection for the local landlords, no popular devotion to the Church, nothing but the land-hunger of the peasants and their hatred for the ruling class. Apart from the innate conservatism of the people, which disinclined them to accept any requirements which involved some departure from immemorial custom, there was no serious opposition to be reckoned with. Moreover, while thus they wielded an almost irresistible power, they were able in doing so to utilize the scientific knowledge and the garnered economic experience of the West. Almost everything in the Bolshevist system has been borrowed—belief in the machine, disbelief in religion, zeal for education, standardization of industry, the Communist party, the methods of terrorism, even the horrifying procedures of the Tcheka and the Ogpu. With the minds of savages the disciples of Lenin have brought the latest science to bear on a population immersed in the ignorance and superstition of the Middle Ages. They have not scrupled to revive the long obsolete methods of ecclesiastical bigotry in the interest of Marxian atheism. Their amazing success is but the logical consequence of their resources, their circumstances, and their eclectic methods. For the first time in human experience mankind has been subjected to non-ethical barbarism equipped with the powers of modern science. It is difficult to set limits to the possibilities of a despotism which can be so described.

An unpleasant feature of the Webbs' book is the almost complete absence of moral feeling. The authors adopt a severely impersonal, unemotional attitude even when they have to describe the methods by which the Bolsheviks forced their system of Communistic atheism on the Russian populations. They allow themselves to use, without comment and without hesitation, the cold-blooded term borrowed from property-law, which the Bolsheviks employ in order to describe their most atrocious acts. The landlords, capitalists, professional men, above all the 'kulaks', are said to have been 'liquidated', when what is really meant is that they have been robbed, treated with savage cruelty, and in multitudes done to death in circumstances of aggravated atrocity. This impersonal attitude is, of course, the familiar characteristic of revolutionaries. Burke exposed and denounced it in the French. His language is equally relevant to the Russians. For the Bolsheviks the individual has no rights, and the family no sanctity, but they preach with vehemence the claims of 'the proletariate', and are eloquent on the franchise of humanity. The case of the 'kulaks' is specially illuminating, and must be more carefully considered. In the scene of misery and bloodshed, crowded with every conceivable outrage which the greed and power of tyranny can inflict on its victims, the case of the 'kulaks' has a woeful primacy.

IV. *The Liquidation of the Kulaks*

The Webbs write of the 'kulaks' with a marked absence of sympathy, and quote from the late Dr. Dillon a very hostile description. But Mr. Chamberlin gives a different impression. After pointing out that 'the Soviets have given the term "kulak" a different meaning from what it possessed before the Revolution', he proceeds:

'In Tsarist days the "kulak", or "fist", was a thorough-going exploiter, a man who perhaps had half the village in his "fist" through money loaned at usurious rates of interest. With their usual capacity for fastening opprobrious epithets on their opponents, the Communists began to apply the term "kulak" to every peasant who rose conspicuously above the low average living standard of the village, regardless of whether or not he was a money-lender. So, while the pre-war kulaks were a small number of village Shylocks, *the Soviet kulaks constituted 4 or 5 per cent. of the whole peasant population* and included all the peasant families that owned mills or other little enterprises, or possessed much in excess of the average amount of cattle and machinery.

'One would search the voluminous collections of Soviet decrees in vain for a precise definition of what constitutes a kulak. It was to the advantage of the Communists to keep the term loose and elastic. As the struggle over collectivization became more intense, *any peasant who spoke out strongly against the new system was likely to be denounced as a kulak if he possessed any property*; if he was too hopelessly poor to make the epithet plausible, he could be disposed of as a "kulak agent".[1] (Italics mine.)

When we remember that the peasantry, upon whom Stalin imposed by violent coercion a change of agricultural system so drastic that the Webbs describe it as a 'second agrarian revolution', numbered about 120 millions, we can form some conception of the magnitude of the tragedy which the harmless sounding term 'liquidation' may cover. Literally millions of the more thrifty and intelligent peasants were stripped of their possessions, driven in circumstances of extreme cruelty to labour as slaves in the timber camps, and on the vast projects which the Soviet Government organized, or suffered to perish of hunger in famine-ruined districts from which most of the available wheat had been seized for exportation to foreign countries. When we are asked to admire the economic triumphs of Soviet Communism, we must remember that an important factor in gaining them has been the utilizing of slave labour on a scale and with a ruthlessness unparalleled in human history. But the Webbs are so dazzled by the magnitude of the result, that they have no eyes to see or hearts to sympathize with the boundless miseries which led to it.

The destruction of the kulaks has undoubtedly secured the triumph of collectivization, but in the process it has withdrawn from the peasantry its most enterprising and intelligent members, and inflicted a moral impoverishment on the Russian people which, while rendering them helpless against the despotism of the Soviets, has immersed them in a lasting degradation of character. Mr. Chamberlin, who speaks with a personal knowledge of the facts to which the Webbs can make no pretence, has described the tragedy of the kulaks, and the sinister policy

---

[1] v. *Russia's Iron Age*, pp. 79, 80.

by which the Soviet Government utilized famine as a method
to coerce the peasants:

'The "liquidation of the kulaks as a class" in regions where collectivization was fairly complete was announced by Stalin as a policy and
was legally authorized and carried into effect in the winter of 1929–30.
Under this system the kulak families were driven from their homes,
with few possessions except the clothes on their backs, and were
either deported in freight cars to the northern forests and other places
of forced labour or obliged to live in dugouts and shanties on the
outskirts of the village. The measure was often executed with great
brutality, men, women, and children being driven out in the bitter
cold of the Russian winter; and its toll of death, especially among
young children and old men, was very great. It was quite in the
spirit of the Iron Age; it showed that the Communist leaders would
spare no weapon of ruthlessness in breaking the recalcitrant peasantry
to their will. . . .

'The most convincing argument to the average peasant was the
fate of his kulak neighbours. This was a plain enough intimation
that if he persisted in his individual farming and had any degree of
prosperity he would also be eligible for "liquidation". Moreover, any
peasant who talked loudly against the government measures at a
public meeting was likely to be regarded as a kulak and treated
accordingly. . . . Famine was quite deliberately employed as an
instrument of national policy, as the last means of breaking the
resistance of the peasantry to the new system where they are divorced
from personal ownership of the land and obliged to work on the
conditions which the state may dictate to them and deliver up whatever the state may demand from them.'[1]

Even the Webbs admit that 'the sum of human suffering
involved is beyond all calculation' (p. 567).

V. *A New Civilization*

In the 'Epilogue' which the authors have appended to their
great work they discuss the question suggested by the note of
interrogation on the title-page. Have the Bolsheviks succeeded
in laying the foundations of a new civilization destined to replace
the traditional civilization of Christendom? The Bolsheviks

[1] v. *Russia's Iron Age*, ch. iv, ' The Ordeal of the Peasantry'.

themselves claim nothing less, and certainly, if the social order which they have established should remain unchanged, and should succeed in winning general acceptance, it would be impossible to dispute their claim. If, however, there are already apparent indications that 'Soviet Communism' is by no means self-consistent or stable, that much of its organization is provisional, that changes have already been effected, and that further changes are clearly on the way, that, with the dying down of revolutionary fervour and the restoration of normal conditions, Russian society tends to resume many familiar features of the older society which has been discarded, we need not be too ready to accept the suggestion that in Russia an alternative has been discovered for the immemorial civilization of Christendom.

Before we can usefully consider the subject, we must understand what we really mean by civilization. The famous word has been used in many senses. The sense which Sidney and Beatrice Webb accept may be deduced from the following passage:

'For our present purpose there is no need to discuss all known or possible civilizations. It will suffice to start from the common division of the three thousand years' history of Europe since the days of Homer into the three successive civilizations that are covered respectively by the story of Greece and Rome; by the widespread adoption of Christianity and feudalism; and by the modern world from 1492 down to our own day. Everyone is familiar with the characteristics of contemporary civilization of this specifically European kind, which has undoubtedly resulted in great progress and has been carried by white settlers, traders or travellers all over the world. It will suffice to emphasize its four main features. First in date stands the Christian religion, with the code of conduct that it inculcates. Then, increasingly after the fifteenth century, comes the so-called capitalist system of the private ownership of property, notably in the means of production, to be utilized, under the direction of the owners, upon the incentive of the making of profit either by the employment of workers at wages or by trading in goods; or latterly, by the manipulation of money and credit by the financiers. Further we notice, continuously during the past two centuries, even if apparently momentarily arrested, a widespread trend towards government on the system of parliamentary democracy. Finally we have to note during the past hundred years, as peculiar to this particular civilization, an unprecedented increase, through knowledge, of man's command over Nature, along with an increasing application of science, under the influence of humane feeling, to the amelioration of the lot of some sections of the poor. Such being the starting-point, the question that is asked is whether what is developing in the U.S.S.R. since 1917 is so markedly different from the manner of life in the England or the France or the United States of the past three or four centuries as to justify calling it a new civilization.' (p. 1121.)

In this passage there is some confusion of thought. To speak of '*the widespread adoption of Christianity and feudalism*' is to link together, as if they were essentially united, two phenomena which are not in *pari materia*. Christianity is no more bound to feudalism than to the older order, social and economical, which feudalism replaced, or to that later order by which feudalism has been replaced. It consists with all, and colours all. Civilization may be imperial, feudal, democratic, industrial, socialist, even communist, but its identity through these various political, social, and economic systems will depend on the views men take of human nature and destiny, on the principles of social intercourse which they accept, and on the conceptions of personal obligation which shape their conduct. These are the invisible substructures on which civilizations are builded; these determine their character, and these determine also their strength and stability. Since of all the forces which generate motives, shape ideals, and discipline character the most potent are religions, they more than anything else give distinctiveness to the civilizations with which they are historically connected. Christianity, moreover, being of all religions the most ethical, and in its influence the most penetrating, possesses beyond any other the power of stamping a congruous character on the society which acknowledges its authority. Christian civilization is unique, and, like the religion which it reflects, potentially

universal. Is it really the case that in Russia, in the twentieth
century of the Christian era, a superior alternative has emerged,
destined to replace it in the acceptance of mankind?

VI. *Russian Christianity*

Russia has lain outside Europe, from which it has ever been
severed by racial type, by a dull and dolorous history, by a
singularly difficult language, by an alien culture, by a quasi-
Oriental political system, and by a form of Christianity which is
semi-barbarous and to Western Christians only half-intelligible.
The conversion of the Russians was late and partial. Slavonic
Christianity stood towards Constantinople as Teutonic Christianity stood towards Rome, and in both cases the daughter
churches reflected and exaggerated the idiosyncrasies of their
parents. The Russian Church reproduced in an accentuated
form the worst features of Byzantinism—its Erastian servility,
its morbid asceticism, its meticulous dogmatic zeal, its ethical
weakness. The conversion of the Russian people hardly went
below the surface. Primitive paganism lived on under Christian
disguises. The hierarchy was rather a civil police than a spiritual
force. It waxed powerful and wealthy in the service of the Tsars,
but it neither rebuked the proud nor raised the poor. Official
Russian Christianity came near to justifying the terrible phrase
of the Gospel—'salt which had lost its savour'. Accordingly, it
had but feeble roots in Russian life; and, when it was suddenly
required to meet the full force of a hostile State armed with
irresistible power and inspired by an aggressive atheism, the
ecclesiastical system collapsed with a facility and completeness
which amazed the Western World. Nowhere else had Christianity seemed to be so firmly rooted, or the established Church held
in higher regard. Sympathetic English visitors to Russia, on
the eve of the War, brought back enthusiastic descriptions of
Russian religion—the majestic ceremonial in the churches, the
simple piety of the ascetics, the touching simplicity of the
pilgrims, the deep devotion of the peasantry. The façade was

imposing, but the building behind it was honeycombed, and ready to fall, destined, at the stroke of Revolution, to

> drop like the tower sublime
> Of yesterday, which royally did wear
> His crown of weeds, but could not even sustain
> Some casual shout that broke the silent air,
> Or the unimaginable touch of Time.

The collapse of Medieval Christianity in the sixteenth century offers some parallel to the ruin of religion in Russia, but the latter differs in the circumstance that the assailant, before whose attack it fell, was not, as at the Reformation, itself religious, but frankly, vehemently, destructively atheistic. There seems to have been strangely little resisting power in Russian Christianity.

'When the Bolsheviks came into power in 1917, they made this defiant and dogmatic atheism the basis of their action. There is evidence that it did not lack extensive popular support. Up and down the country there ensued, in the villages as well as in the factories, a great deal of what we can only describe as spontaneous mass conversions to atheism; very much as there had been, a thousand years before, mass conversions to Christianity.' (p. 1006.)

There seems little reason for doubting that the atheistic policy of the Soviets is obtaining a large measure of success. The Church of Russia had been so closely linked to the Tsardom, and had rested so long and so contentedly on the patronage of the State, that when suddenly the Tsardom disappeared, and the State became openly hostile, it was for the time being reduced to practical impotence. The most recent reports from Russia are not encouraging. Religion, deprived of official recognition, driven with insult out of every sphere of public life, denied and ridiculed at every turn, insulted and calumniated in press and newspaper, yet restrained from self-defence, only suffered to exist under conditions which go far to paralyse its effective witness, is apparently fading out of Russian life. The Moscow correspondent of the *Observer* gave a melancholy picture of the situation on Christmas Day. 'Approximately thirty-five' churches out of the many hundreds, which once were the distinctive glory of 'Holy Moscow', were open for service, and 'most of the worshippers were old men and women'. There are still in Russia many devout Christians who maintain a brave front against the prevailing apostasy, but their number steadily dwindles.

'While it is impossible to estimate the actual number of believers who have stubbornly held out against the persistent anti-religious campaign, it is undeniable that their numbers have decreased greatly. The Bolsheviks believe that religion is doomed in Russia. Emelyan Yaroslavski, head of the Godless League, in a recent issue of the League's magazine, declared that there are between thirty and forty million persons in Russia who have severed relations with religion, and this appears to be a reasonable calculation.'[1]

VII. *The Future of Soviet Communism*

Nevertheless, in spite of so much that now seems to compel another opinion, I do not believe that Soviet Communism will persist, or that Christianity in Russia will be extirpated. The more I consider the picture drawn by Sidney and Beatrice Webb, the more doubtful I become as to the survival power of the system which it represents. The Soviet system contains some elements of weakness which are destined, if I am not mistaken, to bring it to failure in the not very distant future.

The Webbs, in their final verdict, though they profess belief in the final triumph of the 'new civilization' which they imagine the Bolsheviks to be creating, yet plainly contemplate the probability of 'modifications'. In point of fact the Soviet system is changing rapidly, and every change tends to bring back some discarded element of the older civilization which it claims to have replaced. In an admirably written review of the Webbs' book, that acute and balanced publicist Mr. J. A. Spender has stated both the fact and the character of the changing process so effectively that I avail myself of his words, and endorse them:

[1] v. *Observer*, 29 December 1935.

'As I see it, the most hopeful fact about Soviet Russia is that it is constantly changing. It changes so fast that nothing is more difficult than to get consistent accounts of any actual phase even from sympathetic observers. The Russian system is commonly called Marxian, but Marx, in fact, had little or nothing to do with it. The Revolution was not of the type that he predicted—the uprising of an industrial proletariat against its capitalist masters—but the capture of the post-war chaos in Russia by a little group of professional revolutionaries. When that was accomplished Marx could tell them nothing about what to do next. In all his voluminous writings he had neglected to supply what the writers call "the blue-print of reconstruction". So his disciples had to improvise and experiment, and after eighteen years they have produced something for which a name has yet to be found. With its differential wages, salaries, and favours, it certainly is not Communism. Nor with its numerous grades and castes—its bureaucracy, its privileged Communist party, its Generals and Admirals, its tolerated bourgeois, its untouchable "deprived" class—can it in any intelligible sense be called "class-less". Nor with so many opportunities for gaining more or less can it even be said that the profit-motive is abolished. The ghost of Marx is evoked at each stage, and there seem still to be fearful controversies as to whether this or that concession to human weakness can be squared with his gospel; but the ghost grows thinner and paler, and we may hope that the sincere devotion to the ideal of the common good which animates the young Communists will take on mercy and charity. Russia is a great country with more wealth at its disposal than any similar area in the western world. We need not stint our praise of what it has accomplished or be slow to mend our practice in anything it can teach us, but the idea that it has made any great discovery in political institutions or the art of government is, I believe, baseless.'[1]

The heart of the Soviet system is the Communist party. This is the most characteristic feature of the elaborate machinery of fictitious representation. The abundant opportunities for the limitless discussion, in which Russians and, indeed, all semi-civilized people, delight, are conditioned by an arrangement for providing leaders and determining policies. Lenin had no regard for liberty. 'It is true', he observed with characteristic cynicism,

[1] v. *Observer*, 8 December, 1935.

'that liberty is precious—so precious that it must be rationed.' (p. 1036.) The Webbs quote Stalin as follows:

'In the Soviet Union, in the land where the dictatorship of the proletariat is in force, no important political or organizational problem is ever decided by our soviets and other mass organizations, without directives from our Party. In this sense, we may say that the dictatorship of the proletariat is, substantially, the dictatorship of the Party as the force which effectively guides the proletariat.' (p. 370.)

The Communist party is charged with the education of the people, the direction of their assemblies, and the effective leadership of the State.

'It is on this point that the actual constitution of the Soviet Union . . . differs most substantially from any other known to political science. In the U.S.S.R. the function of affording to the population the necessary guidance of public affairs is assumed by a voluntary but highly organized and strictly disciplined Vocation of Leadership, which calls itself the Communist Party.' (p. 1130.)

'It is an absolute condition of membership that the candidates must be free from any vestige of belief in supernaturalism, and that they must continue to adhere to "Marxism", as from time to time authoritatively determined.' (p. 1131).

I should not be surprised if the Communist party will not finally be seen to be the 'Achilles heel' of the Soviet State. In constitution and method it is modelled on the famous Society of Jesus. In the cause of Marxian atheism the Communists display a fervour of missionary zeal, a self-devotion in service, and an undeviating submission to authority, which can only be paralleled in the record of the early Jesuits. Their extraordinary success recalls that of the Jesuits during the first century of their history. Will their later history be similar? The Jesuits at first carried all before them. They rolled back the Protestant hosts at the very moment when the Reformation seemed to be on the threshold of complete victory. With startling rapidity they re-established the authority of the Papacy in Poland, Hungary, Bohemia, central Germany, and France. Sweden and England were within an ace of being included in their conquests. Like the Communists they set themselves to get control over education, wormed themselves into courts and parliaments, and left no part of the national system outside their manipulating efforts. They had their hand round the life of the people at every point. Their disciples were cleverly introduced into every position of influence. The whole process of government was subtly coloured by their designs. The very completeness of their success was their undoing. Their ablest pupils resented the subservience in which they found themselves immersed. The reaction of wounded self-respect carried far. There came a time when the peoples turned on their masters. While the seventeenth century was filled with their political triumphs, the eighteenth witnessed their expulsion from every European State, and their formal suppression by the Pope. With the nineteenth century they have recovered a measure of their authority, but it is 'the shadow of a shade'. The modern world has outgrown them, and finds their once irresistible tactics obsolete and unimportant. Will it be otherwise with the Communists? They have one disadvantage which may expedite their downfall. They are committed to the questionable economic doctrines and the arid atheism of Marx.

The Communist party is maintained in its atheistic orthodoxy by frequent and drastic 'purges'. A large proportion of the members are degraded or expelled. There must be hundreds of thousands of these purge-victims in Russia. Will their influence tend to perpetuate the power of their former masters?

In the concluding paragraph of their great work the Webbs declare their belief that in Russia a new civilization is being created, and that it will finally prevail everywhere.

'At this point we hear an interested reader asking "Will it spread?" Will this new civilization, with its abandonment of the incentive of profit-making, its extinction of unemployment, its planned production for community consumption, and the consequent liquidation of the landlord and the capitalist, spread to other countries? Our own reply is, "Yes, it will." But how, when, where, with what modifications, and whether through violent revolution or by peaceful penetration, or even by conscious imitation, are questions we cannot answer.'

I must needs think that the 'modifications' will have to be so considerable as to destroy identity if a system, which does such violence to human nature, as that now established in Russia is to gain the lasting acceptance of genuinely civilized men.

INDEX

Abrahams, I., 88 f., 106, 107, 113.
Accommodation, 176, 178.
Acts of the Apostles, 39.
  apostolic sermons in, 236.
Africa, problem of native labour
  in, 232 f.
Agricola, 126.
Alexander the Great, 72.
Alexander VI, Pope, 11.
Alfred, 171.
Ambrose, St., 128, 141, 143.
America, United States of, 127,
  202.
  and slavery, 226.
  religion in, 279.
Animals, treatment of, 163 f.
Anti-semitism, 222.
Antoninus Pius, 117.
Apocalyptic literature, 75.
Apologists, the, 117, 121.
Apostles, Doctrine of the Twelve,
  212.
'Apostolic Fathers', the, 59.
Aquinas, St. Thomas, 305.
Aristides, Apology of, 117, 120.
Aristotle, 97, 128, 153.
Asceticism, 93 f., 133, 135, 162,
  189 f., 196.
Asiatics, exclusion of, 237.
Atheism in Russia, 329.
Augustine, St., 97, 165.
Augustus, 142.
Australia, and treatment of Asi-
  atics, 237.

Baptism and slavery, 241, 242.
'Barnabas, Epistle of', 59.
Benefactors, 285.
Bevan, Dr. E., 18, 123.
Bezae, Codex, 108.
Bigg, Prof., 226.
Birmingham, Bishop of, 37.
Bolshevism, 158, 320 f.
Boniface VIII, Pope, 249.
Britain and foreign missions, 245.
  and industrialism, 293.

Britain and the slave trade, 241.
Brooks, Phillips, 303.
Browning, R., 130.
Bryce, Lord, 144, 155, 286.
Buddhism, 20, 97, 301.
Burial service, the English, 183.
Burke, 323.
Burkitt, Prof., 36, 45, 46, 55, 58.
Burnet, Bishop, 256.
Butler, Bishop, 2, 3, 14, 25, 177,
  178, 267, 279.

Caird, Principal, 21.
Callista, 132.
Calvin, 250, 278.
Calvinism   and   industrialism,
  277 f.
Carlyle, 'Jupiter', 11.
Carr-Saunders, Prof., 214, 230.
Casuistry and slavery, 240.
  Rabbinic, 70 f.
Cathedral Age, The, 280.
Cato, 140, 163, 164.
Chalmers, 171.
Chamberlin, W. H., 159, 310,
  312, 323.
Character, persistence of Chris-
  tian, 302.
Charles, Dr., 75 f.
Child races, 242.
Children, attitude of Jesus to, 113.
  exposition of, 212.
Christendom   and   classical   cul-
  ture, 184.
  development of science in, 184.
Christianity   and   birth   control,
  214.
  and civilization, 151, 316.
  and commerce, 277.
  and economics, 273.
  and industrialism, 231, 271 f.
  and military service, 255 f.
  and nationalism, 269.
  and patriotism, 264 f.
  and personal morality, 120.
  and philosophy, 138 f.

12/6n   Mb.